ABOUT THE EDITOR

Bill Fawcett is the author and editor of nearly a dozen books on mistakes made in history, including *You Did What?, It Seemed Like a Good Idea . . . , How to Lose a Battle,* and *You Said What?* He is also the author and editor of three historical mystery series and two oral histories of the U.S. Navy SEALs. He lives in Illinois.

HOW TO LOSE A WAR AT SEA

Also by Bill Fawcett

Doomed to Repeat

How to Lose the Civil War

How to Lose WWII

How to Lose a War

It Looked Good on Paper

Oval Office Oddities

You Said What?

How to Lose a Battle

You Did What?

It Seemed Like a Good Idea . . .

The Teams

Hunters and Shooters

HOW TO LOSE A WAR AT SEA

FOOLISH PLANS AND GREAT NAVAL BLUNDERS

EDITED BY
BILL FAWCETT

WILLIAM MORROW
An Imprint of HarperCollins*Publishers*

HarperCollins books may be purchased for educational, business, or sales promotional use. For information please e-mail the Special Markets Department at SPsales@harpercollins.com.

FIRST EDITION

Library of Congress Cataloging-in-Publication Data has been applied for.

ISBN 978-0-06-206909-2

13 14 15 16 17 OV/RRD 10 9 8 7 6 5 4 3 2 1

In memory of the men of the USS Shark,
the first U.S. submarine lost with all hands in World War II,
on February 11, 1942

CONTENTS

They that go down to the sea in ships,
that do business in great waters;
these see the works of the Lord,
and his wonders in the deep.

—Psalm 107

AMERICA'S GREATEST NAVAL VICTORY?

Battle of the Chesapeake, September 1781

BY WILLIAM TERDOSLAVICH

The winds and the waves are always on the side of the ablest navigators.

—Edward Gibbon, 1737–1794

In the summer of 1781, the battered remnants of Lord Charles Cornwallis's army staggered into Virginia more dead than alive. They had just spent much of the year chasing Nathanael Greene's small force of Continentals up from the Carolinas. The Americans won no battles under Greene's command, which ironically made him the deadliest opponent the British ever faced. Every time Greene lost, he retreated faster than Cornwallis could pursue, through semiwild country that afforded little in the way of supply or shelter. Greene managed to keep his ragged force fed and moving, while Cornwallis's redcoats became tattered from long marches on short rations.

Upon reaching Virginia, Cornwallis received orders from his superior, General Henry Clinton in New York. They were very clear: Use your forces to establish a naval base somewhere along the shores of Chesapeake Bay and await the arrival of reinforcements. The Royal Navy will save the day!

Cornwallis abandoned his position at Newport, Virginia, moving his forces to a place called Yorktown, where the York River empties into Chesapeake Bay. He had nothing to fear. Every American army Cornwallis had ever faced had run away, allowing him to bag Georgia, South Carolina, and North Carolina for the Crown. Other subordinates had suffered defeat in smaller battles against the Americans, but the British did not see their position as a losing one. With fresh troops from New York, Cornwallis could march up to the top of the Chesapeake and cut off the land route between the northern and southern colonies.

Do this and Great Britain wins. There will be no United States.

They had only to hold some ground for a naval base and wait for help. The British navy was the finest in the world. Nothing could stop it. Help was a sure thing.

The Naval Balance of Power

A warship of the eighteenth century was a very different creature from the ones we know today. This was an age when ships were made of wood and driven by sails mounted on two or three masts, when guns fired solid iron balls aimed at the enemy's hull or chained shot at his rigging.

The seventy-four-gun ship of the line was the basic measure of naval strength. Mounting an array of 24-pound and 36-pound guns on two decks, this vessel was designed to dish out punishment—and take it—while sailing in a straight line with its sister ships, parallel to the enemy, exchanging fire.

The other ship that fleets of the day relied on was the frigate, a smaller, faster vessel mounting anywhere from twenty-four to thirty-eight 18-pound guns on a single deck. Frigates would typically sail ahead of a fleet, looking to make contact with the enemy, then get out of the way for the larger ships of the line to duke it out.

The American Revolution was a war between the Crown and the rebels until 1778, when France, Spain, and the Netherlands all joined the fight. Great Britain then found itself fighting a world war. Its fleet of 150 ships of the line had to protect the home country, Gibraltar, the Americas, and possessions in the Caribbean and India. More than fifteen years of penny-pinching left the fleet ill-equipped and in poor condition to contest naval supremacy with two near-peer rivals, Spain and France, which brought to war fleets with 60 and 80 ships of the line, respectively, for a combined fleet of 140.

The British found themselves in a bad strategic position. After assigning ships to protect the home country and various overseas possessions, they had nothing left to blockade the French ports and keep their warships bottled up. Time and again, the French had no trouble dispatching warships to help their American ally, vexing the British to no end.

How to Make Trouble

In 1778, the French managed to dispatch twelve ships of the line and five frigates under Admiral Charles Henri d'Estaing, looking for trouble in American waters. After unsuccessfully probing New York, the fleet made its way to Newport, Rhode Island, where the British had stationed a 5,000-man garrison, surrounded by not-so-friendly colonists. British admiral Richard Howe shadowed d'Estaing all the way there. Gale-force winds robbed both fleets of the chance to fight it out. Lacking a safe harbor, d'Estaing retreated back to France. So long as the Royal Navy ruled American waters, the French could not land an army. British troops could be shifted by the Royal Navy anywhere they were needed and supported anywhere they held a port.

Mariot Arbuthnot replaced Howe as British admiral for the American station. Confusion was reborn, and it came down to signal flags. The Royal Navy had a semistandard way for admirals to issue orders to the fleet by flying colored flags for standard orders, with the meaning of the flag changing depending on whether it was flown from the mizzenmast instead of the mainmast or foremast. Howe had written up a signal book that clarified the mess by relying on three-digit codes for standard orders, and he wrote the book in such a way that the menu of orders constituted a doctrine for naval battle. Arbuthnot combined aspects of Howe's system with the navy's semistandard practice.

This change confused the captains, a problem caused by the Royal Navy's Fighting Instructions, which advocated the practice of forming the fleet in "line-ahead" to exchange shots with the enemy line. This mandatory tactic often resulted in inconclusive battles. The French did not mind this, as their navalists believed it was more important to have a fleet handy than to destroy the enemy's ships. The French navy could always fight another day, or, short of that, maintain a strategic stalemate facing off against the British. Once you destroy the enemy fleet, the sea is yours by default. You have total freedom of action to move anything (goods, troops, etc.) anywhere. But this was not a sure thing when the British and French fleets faced stalemate in American waters. Any advantage would be temporary, depending on a fleet being in the right place at the right time with no enemy present.

Lieutenant General Henry Clinton, who now commanded the British Army in America, abandoned Newport in 1779, recalling the 5,000-man garrison there to strengthen New York. Admiral

George Rodney, an able strategist in his own right, called this the worst mistake of the war. Narragansett Harbor was the best anchorage on the east coast, as New York was compromised by the bars at Sandy Hook, which could be cleared only at high tide. The French did not forgo the opportunity to fill a British vacancy, sending Admiral Charles-Henri-Louis d'Arsac de Ternay with seven ships of the line to take Newport and land another 5,000 men under the command of General de Rochambeau. It was July 1780, and America's French allies were finally in the war with ground troops. The British lost no time blockading Newport, thus bottling up de Ternay's squadron. But Clinton would not march up from New York to retake Newport, fearing Washington would slip into the city while the British were away.

The revolution would reach its nadir in 1780. Washington was nearly arrested and handed over to the British by the traitor Benedict Arnold at the fortress of West Point. If successful, Arnold would have given the redcoats both Washington and control of the Hudson River. The French second division could not sail for the southern colonies, being temporarily blockaded at Brest by the Royal Navy. Revolutionary general Horatio Gates proved his incompetence in the Southern Department, losing at Camden and personally outrunning his routed forces. Recruits were few. Money and supplies were running out or nonexistent. The revolution could die out by simply going bankrupt. That meant General Washington had to go for broke in 1781. He was lucky that factors beyond his control fell into place. And he was skilled enough to take advantage of that change in fortune.

Comte de Grasse was going to take twenty ships of the line—about a quarter of the French fleet—along with 150 transports to the Caribbean. He was to deliver supplies to France's Spanish allies there, as well as threaten Britain's island holdings, protected by Rodney's ships. Washington was disheartened to hear the French were not available to help him move on New York, for him the strategic prize. That did not mean de Grasse was inflexible. He was already in communication with Rochambeau via letters carried by a lone French frigate. They developed a different strategy, and it required that the army and the fleet work together. They knew Cornwallis was in Virginia. With Pennsylvania and New Jersey firmly in Continental hands, the British had no way of supporting or supplying Cornwallis by an overland route. It had to be by sea, and seizing Chesapeake Bay would sever that connection. Rochambeau listened to Washington about New York, then tactfully persuaded him of the advantages of marching to Virginia, supported by de Grasse's fleet. To Washington's credit, he saw the opportunity as well.

And Rodney saw it, too.

The admiral of the Leeward Station penned his misgivings, pointing out Cornwallis's vulnerability to a naval cutoff. He sent his message to New York via mail packet, to educate Arbuthnot and Clinton about the situation. But the British admiral and general, who were not on speaking terms, never got the message. An American privateer had intercepted the packet only two days out from New York.

De Grasse had already left the Caribbean with his fleet. Rodney, acting on his own initiative, dispatched his pugnacious subordinate Admiral Samuel Hood to reconnoiter the entrance to the Chesapeake with fourteen ships of the line, in hopes of stopping the French if they were found there. There was no sign of de Grasse when Hood pulled up by the entrance of the Chesapeake in late August. Even though de Grasse had left first, the Frenchman had chosen a difficult passage between the Bahamas and Cuba, which slowed his progress but cut a shorter course to the Virginia Capes. De Grasse arrived just as Hood pulled into New York to confer with the new admiral on station, Sir Robert Graves, who had replaced Arbuthnot.

The Complex Duet of Land and Sea

One of the peculiarities of naval warfare is that it is so often intertwined with events on land, as dominance in one sphere can reinforce or hinder the other. This campaign would prove the rule.

As Cornwallis fortified Yorktown, and as de Grasse and Hood raced for the Chesapeake, Rochambeau moved his army from Newport to join Washington at White Plains, New York. The joined forces crossed the Hudson and marched south through New Jersey. Washington was vulnerable to a strike from New York should Clinton bestir himself. To fool the British general, Washington ordered large bread ovens to be built in New Jersey, just across from Staten Island. This fooled Clinton into thinking that Washington would be basing his army there for a final push on New York. Washington and Rochambeau crossed the Raritan River and headed south, leaving Clinton clueless. It wasn't until the joint force reached Philadelphia that Clinton realized Cornwallis was the target.

The Franco-American force marched to Head of Elk, Maryland, at the northern end of Chesapeake Bay, to be met by French transports and frigates ready to take them to Virginia. De Grasse's fleet was at anchor by the entrance of the great bay, near present-day Norfolk. Washington had won the race. And de Grasse had brought gold to pay for American operations, as well as 3,000 more troops for Rochambeau. After picking up a few more ships in the Caribbean, the French fleet now numbered twenty-eight ships of the line.

Now it was time for the British to react. The better admiral, Hood, was junior in rank to Graves, now in command of the fleet.

The objective was to defeat the French and relieve Cornwallis at Yorktown. Clinton also promised to send another 5,000 troops to Cornwallis, who now had 7,500 men under his command. Combine these two forces and Cornwallis would have enough men to bring Virginia to heel and cut the colonies in half.

Clear Decks for Battle

On September 5, Graves arrived, only to see a forest of masts where none should be. De Grasse was expecting the French squadron from Newport, Rhode Island, now under the command of Admiral de Barras and carrying the French siege artillery. But the flags on the approaching ships were British, so no luck there. It was 8 A.M. De Grasse could not order his ships out until the tide turned. By noon, the tide began its rush out to sea. The French fleet cut its anchor cables and slipped out, with the British twelve miles offshore. Graves had the "weather gauge"—he had the enemy in front of him and the wind at his back. He could choose when to attack. De Grasse's only options were to stand and receive the attack or run away.

Graves signaled his nineteen ships to "form line." His flagship *London* was in the line's middle. Graves ordered his fleet to turn east, bringing the British battle line ahead of and parallel with the French.

Now Graves wanted to make a right turn to close the distance with the French and bring them to battle. But how to turn? Graves wanted all the ships in his line to turn right at the same time. He had instructed his captains before the battle to make a right should they spot the half-red, half-white signal flag flying from the top of the *London*'s mainmast. But his captains interpreted the signal to mean "turn in succession"—as each ship reached the spot where *London* turned, that ship would turn as well. Frantic, Graves signaled each of his ships individually to turn right.

It was now 3:45 P.M. and not a shot had been fired. Graves maintained his signal "form line" but then added the flag for "close action." As "form line" was flying from his mizzenmast, his captains obeyed, ignoring "close action." It was coming up on 4:15 P.M. before Graves realized his mistake and ordered "form line" hauled down. Now the twelfth ship in Graves's line turned out and untied its sails to stop and open fire. This threw the rear of Graves's line out of order, as succeeding ships now had to steer around the stopped ship. Again, Graves raised the flag for "form line." Five minutes later, Graves had that signal hoisted down, replaced by "close action." All these orders, followed by counter-orders, were creating disorder.

It was 4:30 in the afternoon! The French and British warships had been in sight of each other for more than eight hours. The ships in the British van were opening fire, even if the center and rear divisions could not. Graves ordered *London* to turn out of line and bear down on the French. But the ship ahead of him also untied its sails to stop and fire. *London* was now on a collision course. The captain ordered the flagship steered around the stopped vessel, but that threw the line out of order again, as the following ships copied *London*'s course—away from the French.

By the time Graves re-formed his line and resumed action, an hour had passed. Only ten of his nineteen ships had opened fire, targeting only eleven of the twenty-four ships in de Grasse's battle line. Graves once more hoisted "form line" followed by "close action." It is hard to say whether it made any difference. By 6:30, the two fleets were on divergent courses, and there was not enough daylight left to change course and bring the whole fleet to bear down on de Grasse. The more aggressive Hood could only watch his superior bungle a chance to beat up the French. The ships of Hood's rear division never fired a shot all day.

The ships that did fight managed to inflict some damage. The French *Diadem* took twenty hits and lost 120 seamen. The British *Terrible* looked as bad as her name and was too far gone to repair. The British set fire to her to keep the ship out of enemy hands. All told, the British suffered 90 killed and another 25 wounded. French personnel losses were higher. But that made no difference. If the French could not be defeated or destroyed, the Royal Navy would fail to link up with Cornwallis, abandoning his force to defeat.

Graves and de Grasse maneuvered their fleets around the mouth of the Chesapeake for several days, like circling boxers looking to land a good punch. Nothing came of it. While all this shadowboxing was going on, de Barras arrived from Newport with his eight ships, the siege guns, and engineers. The smaller fleet slipped past the Virginia Capes, anchoring safely in the Chesapeake. De Grasse broke contact and sailed in as well. When Graves brought his fleet in, his lookouts now estimated more than thirty-six French warships in port.

Now Washington had the assets to besiege Yorktown—French engineers to outline the trenches and emplace the French siege guns that could breach the earthworks protecting Cornwallis's forlorn force.

It was easy for Graves to take the counsel of his fears while he was outnumbered two to one. Back to New York the British sailed, even though Hood was still spoiling for a fight.

The Rest Is History

The experienced French army settled down to besiege Yorktown, a craft that the Americans learned very quickly. By September's end, Cornwallis was cut off on land by encircling entrenchments manned by French regulars and Continentals, suffering constant bombardment by artillery. By October 19 it was over, as Cornwallis sent an officer to enemy lines to ask for terms.

News of the expected loss of Yorktown still came as a shock. Great Britain was juggling too many fires all at once, as it had to fend off France, Spain, and the Dutch. Losses had to be cut quickly. Prime Minister Lord North resigned after Parliament voted to limit the British Army's operations in America to defense only. Under the new government, headed by the Marquess of Rockingham, British and American representatives met in Paris to hammer out terms for the war's end and America's sovereignty.

Cornwallis could not be blamed for the naval defeat that sealed his fate. That fault rests with Graves. He tried to fight the Battle of the Chesapeake in two ways: by obediently following Fighting Instructions by forming line-ahead and by calling for a general melee by ordering close action. He accomplished neither.

The Battle of the Chesapeake stands out for its irony. It was the most decisive naval battle in American history, since its direct outcome meant British defeat and the birth of the United States. Yet not a single American ship, nor a single American sailor, was involved. Not a single ship was sunk on either side.

The Royal Navy suffered defeat by not winning the battle. The French fleet enjoyed victory by not losing it.

THE SHOALS OF TRIPOLI

The Philadelphia *and the First Barbary War, 1803*

BY PAUL A. THOMSEN

Without a decisive naval force we can do nothing definitive, and with it, everything honorable and glorious.

—President George Washington, 1732–1799

The United States Navy is often remembered as having the capability of projecting power and terror into the very heart of rival nations. Less than two hundred years ago, the American navy, in fact, consisted of a few frigates and a complement of ill-experienced sailors with barely enough firepower to watch the North American coastline. Believing his sailors were capable of far greater endeavors, in 1801 President Thomas Jefferson ordered the American navy to cross the Atlantic and suppress the pirate Barbary States, a coastal region of North Africa. There was, however, one little problem: the American military institution actually knew relatively little about their enemy's home territory. Before long, this oversight and one captain's untempered zeal sorely humiliated the United States Navy and humiliated the Jefferson administration.

Jefferson first warned his contemporaries in the 1780s about the dangers of unchallenged international piracy to American commerce. With a little planning, they had countered, a small, ragtag band of untrained yeoman farmers had managed to defeat the British Empire. Pirates, they said, would be no problem. At the time, American maritime commerce was also far too small to justify the expense of developing a navy. Still, Jefferson would not let the issue die. In 1786 he attempted to mitigate the issue of cost by trying to bring America into "an association of the powers subject to habitual depredation" with Portugal, Venice, Naples, Denmark, and Sweden, in order to protect essential trade routes. The idea, however, fell to pieces when some questioned what England or France might think of this alliance. It was, after all, easier to offer tribute and deal with individual incidents of piracy than risk antagonizing either the major powers or their thrift-minded constituents.

Sadly for American merchants, the Barbary pirates of Algiers, Morocco, Tripoli, and Tunis were looking to the United States with just those very thoughts. In this climate of pirate tolerance, American ambassadors and other poor nations tried to mitigate piracy by supplying the pirate nations with "annual gifts" of tribute. Nations who failed to offer tribute often saw their ships become instant prey for the pirates. If these ships were caught, the pirates habitually demanded a hefty ransom as penalty in exchange for the seized ship and crew. If the ransom was not paid, the hostages were sold into slavery and the nation's other ships were made into special targets. For the pirates and their state benefactors, this strategy was traditionally far easier and potentially more lucrative than tempting fate by attacking French and British vessels. Eventually, however, the pirate states came to see this parlay of international maritime security as their means of obtaining grand fortunes through an exponential escalation of demands.

If the Americans were willing to pay $25,000 as a gift, they began to think, then why wouldn't they be willing to pay another $225,000 if we threatened them a bit?

Shortly after assuming the presidency, in 1801, Thomas Jefferson had his first official confrontation with piracy in which he refused to pay tribute to the pirate coalition of Tripoli. When the Barbary state declared war on the United States, Jefferson responded by ordering the American navy into the Mediterranean Sea, telling Congress, "The style of the demand admitted but one answer. I sent a small squadron of frigates into the Mediterranean. . . . The bey [the ruler of Tripoli] had already declared war in form. His cruisers were out. Two had arrived at Gibraltar. Our commerce in the Mediterranean was blockaded, and that of the Atlantic in peril. The arrival of our squadron dispelled the danger."

To a limited degree, this served to enhance the meager reputation of the fledgling American navy. The first naval skirmish between the American navy and the pirates ended with the capture of a Tripolitan cruiser by the small American schooner *Enterprise*, at no cost of life. Later, pirate ships often turned and ran at the first sight of the American flag. Still, Jefferson's war was fraught with difficulties for the navy. First, the United States Navy had only a few active vessels to patrol a large region of enemy activity. In 1800, the United States Congress had mandated that the American navy stand at a peacetime size of six active frigates. It would, therefore, take time to build new ships and teach the crews, forcing the American navy to regularly send squadrons to tour the enemy waters. Second, the navy was now navigating hostile waters it had not mapped, fighting against an enemy it could not accurately count an ocean away from reinforcements should the enemy put up an organized resistance to its presence. Luckily for the American sailors, the Barbary pirates acted largely autonomously, but this too created new problems. As individual pirate vessels either were successfully subdued or fled, these initial naval victories also bred overconfidence in the American sailors, promulgating a dangerous climate of risk-taking and false feelings of invincibility. Finally, the successful counterthreat of the American frigates on the high seas encouraged the pirates to stay closer to the safety of their better-known and more heavily guarded coastal waters, daring the frustrated American sailors to chase them into the range of their state's fortress cannons. Eventually these problems converged with American Captain William Bainbridge ordering his frigate *Philadelphia* into the heavily armed and unmapped enemy harbors of Tripolitania.

In 1803, the United States Navy detailed a squadron of frigates under the command of Commodore Edward Preble to tour the Mediterranean in search of Barbary pirate activity. His flotilla included two frigates, the *Constitution* and the *Philadelphia;* the brigs *Argus* and *Siren;* and the schooners *Enterprise, Vixen,* and *Nautilus.* It was larger and more versatile than the previous squadrons, and Preble hoped the smaller vessels could occupy fleeing pirate vessels, which would buy enough time for the frigates' guns to be brought into range. If the enemy fled toward the coast, the smaller vessels were supposed to be able to follow the enemy more closely, which would leave the frigates to provide support fire safely out of range of shoreline guns. At least, that was the theory.

Under orders to blockade the coast of Tripoli, Preble spread out his force to look for potential enemy activity. Shortly thereafter, Captain Bainbridge, on the *Philadelphia,* ordered the *Vixen* off to canvass the area. On October 31, the crew of the *Philadelphia* spotted a pirate vessel running along the nearby shoreline. Anxious for battle, Bainbridge directed his crew to pursue the enemy.

Within minutes, the frigate's sails were filled by the stiff Mediterranean autumn winds and it closed with the now-fleeing quarry. Bainbridge, however, soon realized that the waters they were sailing through were far too shallow for the safety of his ship. He promptly ordered the *Philadelphia* to turn back to sea, but it was already too late. Suddenly the crew was thrown to the deck as the frigate lurched forward and came to a complete stop. They had run aground on one of many uncharted reefs in the area.

Over the next several hours, the captain and crew of the *Philadelphia* struggled in vain to free the ship from the reef, but every attempt seemed only to make the situation worse. They tried in vain to fill the sails with wind. They threw the ship's stores and some of the guns overboard, but the vessel still would not budge. Desperate, they even attempted to lighten their load by cutting away the frigate's foremast. This too failed. Moreover, the *Philadelphia* began listing to one side. Just then, when it seemed as if the situation could not get any worse, Bainbridge spotted a large force of Tripolitan gunboats about to descend upon the helpless ship and take their revenge for months of privation. His sailors tried to man the guns, but the *Philadelphia,* now listing high out of the water, spoiled their aim. As there was no hope of reprieve or rescue, Bainbridge surrendered his frigate and his crew to the enemy.

The capture of the frigate sorely wounded the American war effort. Upon hearing the news, Preble flew into a rage at the notion that a United States Navy captain would surrender his ship and his crew to pirates. Worse, the ship's captain and crew were being held in some unknown dungeons to await ransoming. The commodore's mood darkened still further when he received word that the stuck ship had been pulled off the reef by a fleet of Tripolitan vessels and placed at the very center of Tripoli Harbor's defense system. According to a later congressional report, "The United States' frigate *Philadelphia*, of forty-four guns . . . was got off, without material damage, and . . . was moored in the harbor of Tripoli, within pistol shot of the whole of the Tripolitan marine, mounting altogether upwards of one hundred pieces of heavy cannon, and within the immediate protection of formidable land batteries, consisting of one hundred and fifteen pieces of heavy artillery. It is stated that, besides this force, there were encamped at the time, in the city and its vicinity, twenty thousand troops, and that upwards of one thousand seamen were attached to the fleet in the harbor." Hence there was no way to rescue the crew and the American fleet had no hope of sailing safely within range of the *Philadelphia* to sink her.

As a matter of honor, the commodore also could not leave the frigate in the hands of the enemy. However, one of his adjutants, Stephen Decatur, had a plan. Decatur, captain of the schooner *Enterprise,* had recently captured an enemy ketch, the *Mastico.* Under cover of darkness, Decatur explained to Preble, the ketch, renamed the *Intrepid,* would slip into the harbor with a minimal crew, close with the captured *Philadelphia,* destroy the ship, and hopefully make for open waters before the enemy could react.

With Preble's blessing, at about ten o'clock on February 16, 1804, the *Intrepid* drew near the *Philadelphia.* As Decatur had hoped, the ketch was mistaken for a pirate vessel by the Tripolitan gun crew manning the captured frigate. Subsequently, Decatur and his seventy-man crew of volunteers charged onto the frigate's decks and, taking the pirate crew by surprise, recaptured the ship. According to Decatur's later account, the plan worked so well that he could have sailed the *Philadelphia* out of the harbor before the enemy could respond, but the captain had other orders. Preble had specifically instructed the boarding party to set fire to the ship's "gun-room, berths, cockpit, storerooms forward and berths on the berth deck" and to blow out her bottom. Once the enemy crew had been eliminated, Decatur ordered the crew to carry out the commodore's instructions. When the fires reached the rigging and sails, Decatur and his crew reboarded the *Intrepid* and made once more for the open sea.

Although Decatur's actions had limited the collateral damage caused by the capture of the *Philadelphia,* Bainbridge's mistake had cost the United States dearly in both military assets and political clout. The war had already incurred a million-dollar financial burden for the American nation, with little gained in return. Moreover, a United States frigate, the pride of the American navy, was now a smoldering ruin in an enemy harbor. With a diminished force, in the summer of 1804 Preble was forced to rely on a small flotilla of gunboats loaned out of pity by the Kingdom of the Two Sicilies to actually hurt Tripoli. Still, no matter how many pirate ships they caught or successful raids they launched, Tripoli never caved to the pressure of the American navy. Rather, the loss of the *Philadelphia* ensured that no matter how long combat operations lasted, the United States would lose the political underpinning of the war. Faced with the prospect of losing three hundred citizens to slavery or death, on June 10, 1805, the Jefferson administration agreed to pay the pirates $60,000 for their American prisoners, with the stipulation that the money paid be referred to as ransom and not tribute.

The loss of the *Philadelphia* in the First Barbary War due to Bainbridge's zeal served as a valuable lesson for the United States Navy, teaching both humility and the importance of accepting reasonable limits. After the War of 1812, Preble, Bainbridge, and Decatur were once more tasked with suppressing the Barbary pirates, and in less than a year, the American military managed to finally drive the Tripolitan government into submission. This time the Americans took care to watch for the jagged rocks and shoals.

NELSON'S MASTERPIECES

The Nile and Trafalgar, 1798 and 1805

BY ROLAND J. GREEN

England expects that every man will do his duty.

—Horatio Nelson, 1758–1805

Horatio Nelson might have had a page or two in naval history even without his stellar victories. Born into the family of a prosperous country parson, he had "interest" (connections) for a naval career from birth—a maternal uncle was a prominent naval officer. So when he wanted to go to sea, at age twelve, he did so, although not without dire prophecies about his fate.

Those prophecies almost came true on an arctic expedition when he was fourteen. Out on the ice, he fired his musket at a polar bear—and missed. The bear charged. Nelson clubbed it with his musket. The ship's guns opened fire, frightening off the bear before it had a chance to cost Britain her greatest naval captain.

With both interest and ability on his side, Nelson rose rapidly. He made captain at twenty-one, survived yellow fever in Central

America, and commanded frigates in the American Revolutionary War.

After the war, he was stationed in the West Indies. There he earned the ire of local merchants for trying to strictly enforce various trade regulations. He won a more favorable response from Frances Nisbet, a young widow with a son. They married in 1787. When Nelson's tour of duty was over, the family went home to England and settled down to a half-pay existence.

This came to an end in 1793, when England and revolutionary France went to war. Nelson soon received command of the sixty-four-gun ship of the line *Agamemnon,* which he praised highly. (Nelson always praised the ships and men under his command; egotistical as he was, he believed in "loyalty down.")

Nelson served in the Mediterranean in his new command, as France and Britain struggled for control of the historic sea. An alliance with Spain gave the French an edge, and Nelson lost sight in his right eye in an attack on Corsica. Fortunately the damage was only to the optic nerve, and he never had to wear a patch, only a green eyeshade over his good eye to prevent strain while he was doing paperwork.

By 1797, Nelson was a commodore under Admiral Sir John Jervis and distinguished himself at the Battle of Cape St. Vincent, off the coast of Portugal. Rather than showing headlong boldness, Nelson seems to have been following discretionary orders from Jervis when he took his flagship *Captain* into the Spanish line to keep two sections of it from joining. He also took as prizes two Spanish ships of the line, personally leading the boarding party that took the first.

This action earned him promotion to rear admiral, a knighthood, much glory, and an admonitory letter from Lady Nelson (as she now was). She asked him not to lead any more boarding parties, but rather to leave that sort of thing to captains.

It took more than an indignant wife to keep Nelson out of the forefront of battle. In July 1797, he lost his right arm in an attack on the Spanish Canary Islands. He was quick to learn to write with his left hand, and pronounced himself fit for sea duty by the end of the year. It was just as well, because another challenge to Britain was emerging in the Mediterranean.

The Campaign of the Nile

Napoleon Bonaparte had been hatching a plan to conquer Egypt. It would be a cheap victory (or so he appears to have thought) but would give the French command of the eastern Mediterranean, if they had a strong enough fleet to keep it. It might even allow for a French base in the Red Sea on the trade route to India—as if they didn't have a perfectly good one at Mauritius.

But increased French influence in the East could only harm Britain and endanger trade with India. Nelson, now commanding a large portion of the Mediterranean Fleet, had a priority task—halt Bonaparte.

Nelson got off to a shaky start. While cruising off the French coast in May 1798, his flagship *Vanguard* ran into a squall. Neither Nelson nor his flag captain seems to have been at his best, and the flagship damaged her masts—at the same time that Bonaparte's expedition was passing close by.

Nelson's luck held. Reinforcements arrived, *Vanguard* was re-rigged, and the British set off on the trail of the French. Once Nelson was sure the French hadn't sailed out into the Atlantic, he knew the only way they could have gone was east.

Unfortunately his scouting frigates had scattered and did not rejoin him quickly, so it was a long and frustrating chase. Nelson himself complained that if he died now, "want of frigates" would be found written on his heart. He had one advantage—with all of his ships of the line within signaling distance, he could go immediately into action at full strength.

He put the wait to good use, however. He had an exceptional group of captains, most destined to rise to fame, flag rank, or both, and he regularly hosted them at dinner. Nelson was a charming and intelligent host with his fellow professionals (with landsmen he tended to be a bit full of himself), and the table talk seems to have ranged over everything that might help them beat the French. Those dinners led to the emergence of the "Band of Brothers," a cohesive command group rarely equaled on land or sea and one that knew aggressiveness and initiative would be rewarded.

Bonaparte was not wasting time. He landed his army in Egypt, defeated a Mameluke-led army, and then marched on Cairo. He stuffed the transports into the harbor of Alexandria but left his fleet sitting in Aboukir Bay, in the Nile delta. This was *not* a good idea, with a first-class enemy hot on his trail.

Nelson sighted the French fleet in Aboukir Bay on August 1, 1798. He immediately cleared for action and with a favorable northerly breeze came down on the enemy. He had ten 74-gun ships and one 50-gun; French Admiral Brueys had his 120-gun flagship, *L'Orient,* twelve other ships of the line (all larger than Nelson's), and four frigates.

Unfortunately, Brueys had also quite literally left his fleet at loose ends. Neither the van nor the rear of his crescent-shaped line was close enough to shore to prevent an enemy's passage, and he'd put no heavy guns ashore to cover either channel. The French had also left wide gaps between individual ships, rather than anchoring them bow to stern and linking them with cables. And some ships had so much clutter below, they could barely clear their inshore guns for action—*L'Orient* had turpentine, paint, and oil lying about.

Even without these advantages, the British probably had the edge in pure firepower. Their gunnery tactics emphasized rapid fire at close range into the enemy's hulls, killing men and smashing guns. The French had also abolished the expert corps of *canonniers marins* as a relic of aristocracy and hadn't spent enough time at sea to train replacements.

The British had recently adopted the carronade. This short gun, light for its caliber, could be mounted on slides higher in ships than the heavy truck guns. Over a short range, it could throw heavy round shot or devastating loads of grape and canister with antipersonnel effects that can well be imagined.

The battle was actually decided in the first hour. Captain Thomas Foley, in the lead ship, *Goliath,* saw the wide channel at the head of the French line and boldly took his ship around to the inshore side of the French line. The rest of the British fleet either followed him or worked their way down the seaward side, so that one French ship after another was caught between two fires.

Not everything went that smoothly, of course. Thomas Troubridge's *Culloden* ran aground, and her very able captain spent a maddening night trying to get his ship afloat and into the fight. The British *Bellerophon* overshot her planned opponent and ended up engaging the huge French flagship, easily twice her strength. *Bellerophon* was dismasted before Nelson's *Vanguard* came up on the seaward sound to take a hand. *Bellerophon* then drifted off into the night with nearly two hundred casualties.

The French gunners promptly grazed Nelson's forehead with a grapeshot, and he had to go below to the surgeon. He probably had a concussion but was back on deck in time to see the high point of the battle.

L'Orient was on fire. As the flames spread, the crew started going over the side and ships near her started edging away to avoid what was coming. At around 10 P.M. the flames reached the magazine and the huge ship erupted like a volcano. She took down with her, among other things, the looted treasures of the Knights of Malta and both Captain Casabianca and his son, the famous boy who stood on the burning deck in Felicia Hemans's venerable poem.

The fighting came to a halt for about half an hour. Many eyewitnesses were too stunned to move, and none of them forgot the sight. Some British sailors simply fell asleep beside their guns. Others were too busy rescuing drowning Frenchmen or putting out fires started by bits of flaming wreckage.

After firing resumed, it continued with diminishing intensity until dawn. By that time the British had destroyed or captured eleven French ships of the line and two frigates. The commander of the French rear, Admiral Pierre de Villeneuve (destined to encounter Nelson again), took his two ships of the line and two frigates out to sea, and with only one ship in fighting trim, the British could not pursue.

The British hardly needed to do more. The French had lost their fleet, Bonaparte was stranded in Egypt, and nine thousand Frenchmen were dead, wounded, taken prisoner, or stranded ashore with the army. British casualties were about one-tenth of France's.

Britain and her allies were ecstatic. Nelson was elevated to the peerage.

A Semiromantic Interlude

Nelson could have conducted himself better during the next two years of mopping up after the Nile. Unfortunately, he fell in love with Emma Hamilton, wife of Sir William Hamilton, British ambassador to the Court of Naples—and let it be said, she fell in love with Nelson. Their affair was the talk of the Mediterranean, but Sir William, a classic eighteenth-century complaisant husband, may have looked benignly on the prospect of a younger man being there to take care of the rather feckless Emma. Nelson was not so chained to Emma that he didn't manage more of his usual competent work at sea. The British rounded up the waifs and strays from the Nile, liberated Malta, and blockaded the French army in Egypt. They did not bag Bonaparte, who sneaked home in a frigate and made himself dictator.

The French victory at Marengo in 1800 brought peace to the lands around the Mediterranean. Nelson and the Hamiltons were both called home and traveled overland in a triumphal progress.

The reception in Britain was less ecstatic. Nelson's colleagues gave him the cold shoulder and Lady Nelson simply walked out. (Possibly Nelson's request that she be friendly toward Lady Hamilton was the last straw. One of the admiral's less endearing qualities was a tendency to what can only be called chutzpah.)

Early in 1801, Emma bore the newly promoted Vice Admiral Nelson a daughter, Horatia. She was presented first as the child of one of Nelson's colleagues, then as his "adopted daughter" (a taradiddle Victorian historians swallowed hook, line, and sinker). Before further embarrassment could descend on the little ménage, Nelson was called back to sea.

The new crisis arose over the League of Armed Neutrality, an alliance of Sweden, Denmark, Prussia, and Russia to defend the trade rights of neutrals, rights which the British had been rather flagrantly violating in the name of enforcing the blockade of France. The British suspected the League of being a potential threat to their own vital trade in naval stores (timber, sailcloth, cordage, tar, etc.) and decided on a preemptive strike.

The striking force would be a fleet under Admiral Sir Hyde

Parker, an elderly mediocrity. Nelson would be his second, because at that point Jervis did not trust him with an independent command.

The fleet sailed on March 12, arrived off Copenhagen on March 30, and went straight into battle. Nelson had very little to do tactically, except impress (read: kidnap) a number of experienced Baltic pilots to guide his inshore squadron down a channel that was less exposed to the city's powerful forts. (The pilots could have done a better job; several of Nelson's ships ran aground.)

After that it was a brutal pounding match, with heavy casualties on both sides (900 British; 1,600 Danish). The Danes came so close to outpounding the British that Parker hoisted the recall signal for Nelson's squadron. Nelson, either stubborn or with a better sense of how the battle was going, engaged in a masterpiece of creative insubordination. He held up his telescope to his blind eye and said, "I really do not see the signal."

The Danish fleet surrendered, but peace was not signed until Nelson had to threaten to burn the prizes "without having the power to save the brave Danes who have defended them." After that, all fell into place. It helped that Czar Paul of Russia had been assassinated on March 24. Sir Hyde Parker went home; Nelson took over the fleet and finished disarming the League of Armed Neutrality with a speed and thoroughness that suggest diplomatic gifts as well as tactical ones.

He was praised in Parliament and called home. He had only one more period of sea service that year, leading an abortive assault on the French invasion fleet concentrated at Boulogne. He had his usual bad luck with amphibious operations—the attack failed miserably—but at least he wasn't wounded.

Then he and the Hamiltons retired to his new country estate, while the war-weary empires of Britain and France negotiated the Peace of Amiens, signed late in 1801.

The Campaign of Trafalgar

What ought to be called the Truce of Amiens lasted only until the spring of 1803. Britain refused to return Malta to the French. The French refused to evacuate the Low Countries. So war came again, in early 1803.

Hostilities found the British navy in less than ideal shape. Earl St. Vincent had chosen the interval of peace as the time to root out corrupt practices among the timber merchants who had supplied the naval dockyards. The timber merchants replied with a boycott of the navy. Construction and repairs ground to a halt.

St. Vincent left the Admiralty. Timber deliveries resumed, in a slightly more honest fashion. The British fleets took to the sea at reduced strength, looking one way for reinforcements and the other for French topsails.

Fortunately Napoleon (which we shall now call him, although he wasn't crowned emperor until 1804) was fixated on building up his invasion fleet. One hundred sixty thousand of the best troops in the world were camped at Boulogne, waiting for the order to embark. That would come when France's Mediterranean Fleet had broken out, joined the ships at Brest, and either drawn off or (dream on!) defeated Britain's Channel Fleet.

They might not have enjoyed what followed even if they could have gained control of the channel. The landing barges had absorbed enough men and matériel to rejuvenate the French, without being very maneuverable or seaworthy. When a squall blew up during a review of one landing squadron, two thousand men drowned before their emperor's eyes. What would have happened in mid-channel hardly bears thinking about.

Even with three days of good weather (unlikely in the English Channel even in summer and unimaginable the rest of the year), once the French lumbered up to the landing beaches their troubles would not have been over. Apart from British heavy ships that "surged" (as we would now say) from every channel and North Sea port, the inshore squadrons would have been waiting. Able to maneuver in shallow water, they were intended to stop French privateers but could easily have switched to French landing barges. And the British had enough army and militia forces ashore to probably halt all the seasick Frenchmen who made it to land.

Of course, there's always an element of luck. The British were being careful to see that it stayed on their side. Their basic strategy fulfilled the requirements of KISS (Keep it simple, stupid). The Channel Fleet would blockade its opposite number in Brest. The Mediterranean Fleet would blockade Toulon. A small squadron would blockade the base at Rochefort on the Bay of Biscay. If any French squadron came out, the British would try to stop it in its tracks. If the French escaped, the British would follow them to the ends of the earth.

Nelson never had to do that. He left Lady Hamilton (now a widow) and Horatia in the spring of 1803 to take command of the Mediterranean Fleet, flying his flag in *Victory*. This three-decker had always been a popular flagship during her forty-year career because of her excellent sailing qualities.

The next two years may have been the happiest of Nelson's life. He had a good ship under him and a good friend, Sir Thomas Hardy, as flag captain. He had good ships and crews, and he was making them better. He was well supplied with frigates, fresh vegetables, and spare spars. He would even have a worthy opponent on the day of battle.

That day did not come in 1803, or in 1804. In the latter year, Villeneuve did get out and sail to the West Indies, with Nelson in such hot pursuit that the French had very little time to damage British commerce. They sailed home to Toulon and the status quo ante.

While cruising on blockade, Nelson developed his plan for his next battle. He also seems to have been a disciple of KISS, because his plan left very little room for misunderstandings.

He would take the weather gauge (the side from which the wind was blowing). He would sail down on the enemy in two strong columns, plus a reserve squadron if he had enough ships. His two columns would break through the enemy's line and engage it at close quarters, and the enemy would have to sail slowly into the wind. Meanwhile, any reserve squadron would either engage the enemy's van or catch a portion of the enemy fleet between two fires if a British squadron needed help.

Matters grew more complicated toward the end of 1804. Spain allied herself with Napoleon, which brought the Spanish fleet into the naval equation. And it deserved some respect—the ships were well designed and often well built, and the officers brave and sometimes skilled. But too many of the sailors were inexperienced, and too many of the gunners had been drafted from the army's artillery.

The British also lost their First Lord of the Admiralty (the civilian head of the navy) over a financial scandal. However, they found a first-class replacement in Sir Charles Middleton, a retired naval officer. Elevated to the peerage as Lord Barham, he has been given credit for brilliant strategic innovations that won the Trafalgar campaign. He certainly deserves much credit, but mostly for having the sense to follow the old adage "If it ain't broke, don't fix it."

Nelson was chasing Villeneuve across the Atlantic, this time with an inferior force. But he was ready to fight the French to the finish, even at the cost of his own fleet, if he could cripple Villeneuve's. Villeneuve lifted the blockade of Martinique (a French privateer base) and recruited several Spanish ships of the line. Then the transatlantic derby was on again.

This time it ended when Villeneuve met Sir Robert Calder's British blockading squadron off Cádiz, the major Spanish naval port. With fifteen ships against twenty, Calder took two Spanish prizes but in poor visibility let the rest slip off. But instead of bringing out the Spanish fleet and sailing for the English Channel, Villeneuve himself dove into Cádiz.

The result was a tempest on both sides of the channel. Napoleon was growing doubtful about the invasion, but here was a French admiral sabotaging it by flagrantly disobeying orders! He ordered Villeneuve replaced by an Admiral Rosily, who hadn't been to sea in twenty years.

The British Admiralty and public were also outraged. British admirals had done better against much longer odds. Calder was recalled and never went to sea again. Fortunately, he was replaced by Nelson, whose squadron joined the blockade, and who made the grand gesture of sending Calder home in his former flagship. This deprived the fleet of a three-decker, but it had seven more, and Nelson was confident that his twenty-seven ships could beat what he thought were thirty-six (actually, thirty-three) in Cádiz.

He was so confident that he took *Victory* for a brief home leave, to see his family and consult with the Admiralty. After three weeks, did he slip quietly into his barge on Portsmouth beach at dawn, or did he depart amid a tumult of cheers and adulation? All we can say for certain is that Nelson loved the cheers.

He did get a warm welcome when he rejoined the fleet off Cádiz on September 28. He took over from Vice Admiral Cuthbert Collingwood, a great fighting seaman and a master of gunnery, but rather dour and closemouthed. Nelson was quite the opposite—although it may be doubted that his captains were wild with joy over the attack in two columns (which didn't leave enough ships for a reserve squadron). They knew that the lead ships in each column would receive a heavy raking fire. They also knew Nelson's reputation, and that he would be leading his column in

Victory. And they would not have been too unhappy about one of Nelson's most famous (and sound) tactical maxims: "No captain can do very wrong who lays his ship alongside that of an enemy."

Ashore, the allies were trying to hammer out a plan of action without hammering on one another. The Spanish did not like their guests, whom they considered regicides and atheists, as well as rude and greedy. The French did not like the wretched Spanish accommodations for the sick of both fleets, the condition of the Spanish ships, or the shortage of food and naval stores.

The hinterland of Cádiz was also in the grip of plague and overrun with bandits. This was a backhanded blessing for Villeneuve, as his putative successor was stranded in Madrid. Rosily refused to go on without a strong army escort, which the Spanish were taking their time about gathering.

So Villeneuve was free to supervise his captains in getting their ships ready for sea and working out a plan of action. The consensus that emerged was to sail into the Mediterranean, land the troops to reinforce the French in Italy, and wait for Napoleon's orders, which were even then being drawn up.

Nelson had a line of frigates watching Cádiz, positioned to relay anything that happened in the port to *Victory* in about an hour and a half. On October 18, Nelson learned that some of the allied ships had their topsails set.

On the 19th, some were in the outer harbor.

On the 20th, the whole allied fleet was at sea, heading for the Straits of Gibraltar in three columns. Sighting Nelson, Villeneuve had no choice but to turn back toward Cádiz and form a somewhat ragged line of battle. The very able Spanish Commodore Churruca is supposed to have said, "We are lost. The French admiral does not know his business."

The two fleets remained in sight of each other that night.

Entire books have been written giving blow-by-blow accounts of Trafalgar. I recommend Dudley Pope and Oliver Warner—I am not even going to try to imitate them in this brief space.

Nelson's tactics at Trafalgar were actually almost as simple as those at the Nile. As planned, he formed his fleet into two columns, with him commanding the left or windward column of fifteen, and Collingwood to leeward with twelve. Each admiral headed his column in his flagship, but Nelson had two more three-deckers in close support while Collingwood was alone in *Royal Sovereign*.

The weather was nearly fair, with a light overcast and such soft winds that some ships could barely keep moving. Nelson noted a swell from the west that predicted a storm, made a tour of his flagship, then went to his cabin. A devout member of the Church of England, he composed a prayer that hoped the British fleet would show "humanity in victory." Then he wrote farewell letters to Emma and Horatia and an amendment to his will leaving his mistress and child as a legacy to his country.

After that, he went on deck and ordered the most famous signal in naval history: "England expects that every man will do his duty." The reception to this last bit was less rapturous at the time than it has been since. A good many in the fleet, of all ranks, grumbled that Nelson already knew perfectly well they were going to do exactly that.

One later signal is often ignored by historians. "Prepare to anchor at close of day" came directly from Nelson's suspicion that it was going to blow that night. It did, and the more ships anchored, the fewer lives lost.

The allied fleet opened fire around noon. Collingwood was quicker into action and laid his flagship alongside a Spanish three-decker, *Santa Ana*. The two big ships pounded each other into wrecks, with some help from passing friendly vessels, and the Spanish flag came down. But by then *Royal Sovereign* didn't have a stick standing, so Collingwood transferred his flag to the frigate *Euryalus,* from which he could send signals.

Nelson's flagship came under fire at about 12:24 P.M. and sailed into what Nelson described as "too warm work to last long." She had fifty casualties before she broke the line just astern of *Bucentaure* and practically wrecked Villeneuve's flagship with a single broadside of fifty double- and triple-shotted guns and a heavy carronade crammed to the muzzle with canister.

Victory then ran alongside the French two-decker *Redoubtable*—and never was a ship more appropriately named. Under her bantam-sized captain, Jean Lucas, she fought a yardarm to yardarm action, close against *two* three-deckers (after Nelson's next astern *Temeraire* came up).

Call it three-to-one odds, which Lucas tried to redress by using sharpshooters, grenades, and firebombs to clear *Victory*'s spar deck so that he could board. He never quite brought it off, but his crew fought until five-sixths of them were killed or wounded and their ship was sinking under them.

One sharpshooter killed Nelson, putting a ball into his left shoulder that passed down through his chest to break his spine. He was carried below, drawing a handkerchief over his face to avoid alarming the crew.

He took three painful hours to die, asking for as long as he was lucid about how the battle was going. Captain Hardy brought periodic bulletins. At one point he informed Nelson that the British had taken fourteen prizes, but Nelson said he'd bargained for twenty.

He almost got his wish. By the time he died, at 4:30 P.M., eighteen allied ships were prizes, and half an hour later a nineteenth, the French *Achille,* blew up. One French squadron was making for the open sea, to be captured a few weeks later. Only ten allied ships of thirty-three would ever see Cádiz again.

The British had not done everything right, let alone everything they wanted to do. They had not broken the allies' line or cut them off from Cádiz. As one British sailor put, "They fought us pretty tightish for French and Spanish"—too tightish to be simply swept away. Concentrations of each side's ships against a single enemy were common and usually wrecked their targets. But British gunnery was superior, and hardly a single British captain failed to get close enough to an enemy to do lethal damage. Nor did some French and Spanish—the British had at least three ships dismasted besides *Royal Sovereign.*

Trafalgar was bloodier than it need have been because Nelson's last order, to anchor, was not properly carried out. The storm blew in that night, and continued blowing for nearly four days. Fourteen of the eighteen prizes sank or wrecked on the rocky coast, although some of them may not have had anchors, cables, capstans, or able-bodied crews to work these.

The British needed on one hand to sail their own ships, and on the other to save the prisoners aboard the doomed prizes. They sometimes did so at the cost of their lives but answered Nelson's call for "humanity in victory" on the grand scale.

British casualties reached 2,000 killed and wounded. Allied casualties ran over 10,000 dead and prisoners (many of the prisoners wounded), not counting the dead and wounded landed at Cádiz. And while the dead washed up on the shore, HMS *Pickle* was sailing for England with a dispatch that would spread equal portions of grief and jubilation across the British Isles.

This chapter has mustered most of the mistakes on both sides but needs to mention Napoleon's real whopper. Simply, he tried to build a mighty navy *and* a mighty army, without having the resources for both and without knowing how to use the navy. If

Kaiser Wilhelm II had read this lesson correctly, World War I might have been very different—or might not have been at all.

And to the question that any English-speaking (above all, English) reader may ask—*was* Nelson the greatest admiral in naval history? Certainly, he is a front-runner. All those battles he won and the example he set helped build British naval supremacy, and that supremacy built the foundation of the world we live in today, two centuries after Nelson's death.

The Romans gave triumphs and thrones to generals who helped their civilization. Perhaps Nelson needs a statue up there with some of them.

REMEMBER THE *MAINE*!

Naval Battle of Santiago, July 3, 1898

BY WILLIAM TERDOSLAVICH

A good Navy is not a provocation to war.
It is the surest guarantee of peace.

—President Theodore Roosevelt, 1858–1909

The spark that started the Spanish-American War was struck when the battleship *Maine* was blown up in Havana Harbor on February 15, 1898. The war ended just five months later when her sister ships destroyed the Spanish naval squadron based at Santiago, Cuba.

On the face of it, the Spanish-American War was a complete and decisive victory for the United States. It marked the birth of a new world power at the expense of an old one. Reading the history books today, that victory seems to have been inevitable. But in the heat of the moment, it was not a sure thing. Spain began the war from a position of weakness, but believed that with a different strategy they had a chance to force a stalemate with the United

States. The realism needed to pull that off was trumped by a romantic fatalism, ensuring Spanish defeat.

Fear the Spanish Navy!

Following the loss of the *Maine,* American public opinion was whipped into a frenzy by newspapers run by Joseph Pulitzer and William Randolph Hearst. The ensuing diplomatic crisis resulted in Spain breaking off relations with the United States on April 23 and declaring war. The United States responded in kind two days later.

The war's opening was marked by the U.S. Navy's opportunistic victory at Manila Bay, as a squadron commanded by Commodore George Dewey wiped out the Spanish squadron based there in about four hours.

On the east coast of the United States, the navy had more to do. One mission was to escort troop ships bound for Cuba. This would be done by two battleships, an armored cruiser, several protected cruisers, and fifteen lesser vessels, all based at Key West, Florida. Designated as the North Atlantic Squadron, the force was placed under the command of Rear Admiral William T. Sampson.

The next mission was protecting the east coast from Spanish naval raids. This may sound a bit weird to the reader of today, but the war did trigger a serious panic that Boston or New York might be shelled. The protection mission was entrusted to the Flying Squadron, Commodore Winfield Scott Schley commanding. This force was based at Hampton Roads, Virginia, with two battleships, an armored cruiser, two protected cruisers, and several auxiliary cruisers.

The battleship *Oregon* was ordered to proceed from Bremerton, Washington, to the east coast via Cape Horn, the southern tip of

South America. The Panama Canal was not built yet, though its necessity was becoming clear.

President William McKinley declared a blockade of Cuba in late April. This cut off the Spanish army from reinforcement and formed a cordon that the Spanish fleet would have to evade or fight.

As the U.S. Navy pulled over stray merchantmen and raided the Cuban coast, the army activated V Corps. Units began concentrating at Tampa, Florida, the closest port to Cuba that also had a rail link to the rest of the United States.

As the Americans busied themselves, Spain had to make some strategic choices. The newly constructed warships *Pelayo* and *Emperador Carlos V* were held back for the First Squadron, which would protect Spain proper.

Second Squadron was formed under the command of Vice Admiral Pascual Cervera y Topete. Assigned were the *Vizcaya* and *Almirante Oquendo*. Cervera took his squadron to Portugal's Cape Verde Islands, off the coast of West Africa. By mid-April, he received the cruisers *Cristóbal Colón* and *Maria Teresa*. Added to these were three destroyers and three torpedo boats. But the *Colón* lacked her 10-inch main gun, and all the ships were cursed with defective 5.5-inch guns and faulty ammunition. Cervera entreated his superiors to supply everything his ships lacked. The government in Madrid lacked the common sense to do so.

Spain had options. The Second Squadron could be stationed in the Canary Islands, a Spanish possession off the coast of North Africa. As a "fleet in being," this force would have compelled the U.S. Navy to either scatter its ships to defend all the east coast ports, cross the Atlantic to blockade the Canary Islands, or seek decisive battle there. The last two options would play to Spain's strength, as the Americans would not have a base nearby to support their fleet. The logistic ships needed to support a fleet in distant seas did not exist yet.

No one in Madrid was thinking along these lines. Cervera pestered his superiors for clear orders, or at the very least clear guidance, about his mission and the strategy he should pursue. The best he could get from his government was an understanding that the war was already lost. The most that could be hoped for was a defeat, a second Trafalgar, to provide a glorious redemption for the expected loss of Cuba.

This was a plan?

Ship for ship, there was no way the under-resourced Spanish fleet was going to outfight the U.S. Navy, whose fleet tonnage outweighed the Spanish navy by two to one. Seeking any fight was Spain's biggest mistake. Politically, Spain had to make some kind of stand to show it was fighting for possession of its overseas colonies, even if Cuba was in rebellion.

Being a good officer, Cervera accepted his mission after making his protests known. Basing the Second Squadron in Portugal's Cape Verde Islands was possible, thanks to a diplomatic understanding between Madrid and Lisbon. A clever American diplomat stationed there bought up all local coal supplies, preventing Cervera's squadron from taking on fuel. By late April, Cervera was ordered by the Ministry of Marine to proceed to Puerto Rico and Cuba to reinforce Spanish forces. Portugal compounded this urgency by officially declaring neutrality, giving Cervera twenty-four hours to clear port, ready or not.

Mission: Impossible

"Not ready" was the more accurate condition of Cervera's squadron. Chugging along at seven knots, Second Squadron made the 2,150 miles to Martinique in eleven days. *Vizcaya*'s bottom was thick with seaweed and barnacles, slowing her speed. The destroyers had to be towed part of the way. The more short-range torpedo boats and supply ships were sent back.

Citing neutrality, French authorities in Martinique refused to allow Cervera's ships to take on coal. Cervera could make for Puerto Rico, four hundred miles away, to replenish his ships at San Juan. But the Americans had shelled the port, so he was unsure whether his arrival would be contested. He could set course for Curaçao in the Netherlands Antilles, where a Spanish collier with five thousand tons of coal should be waiting. Or he could burn every lump of coal steaming for Santiago de Cuba, twelve hundred miles away. Cervera set course for Curaçao.

There was no collier waiting there. Dutch authorities allowed *Vizcaya* and *Maria Teresa* to take on six hundred tons of coal. Then, citing neutrality, they ordered Cervera out.

By this time, the Caribbean islands were linked by telegraph, so the U.S. Navy knew about Cervera's arrival at Martinique. Protecting the east coast became moot. Schley's squadron was shifted from Hampton Roads to Key West, then dispatched to Cuban waters to keep an eye out for Cervera's arrival.

Cervera could put in at Havana, Cienfuegos, Santiago, or San Juan in Puerto Rico. The Americans were about, so Cervera had to factor in the risk of interception. Santiago was the only port where he knew the Americans were not, so there the Spanish squadron went. The Flying Squadron was off Cienfuegos when Schley received orders to go to Santiago. This he did with all deliberate leisure, standing well out to sea to receive messages via packet boat. It was on this distant station that Schley received word from one of his auxiliary cruisers that it had intercepted a collier bound for Santiago. Could that mean the Spanish fleet had finally arrived? Schley ordered his squadron to close with the shore, and sure enough, the *Cristóbal Colón* was spotted guarding Santiago's harbor entrance. Cervera had gotten past Schley.

There were only six hundred tons of low-quality coal available at Santiago. Cervera needed more than four thousand tons to replenish. The port of Santiago was woefully underequipped to move what coal it had in bulk to his ships. The Americans had intercepted a much-needed coal shipment. The fleet was going nowhere. The U.S. Navy began its blockade. It was now late May.

Use the *Merrimac* While Monitoring Santiago

Schley showed he could dither when action was needed. His boss, Rear Admiral Sampson, acted quickly once he arrived with the fleet. A pair of fortresses guarded the harbor entrance and could shred any warship that dared force an entrance. Sampson could plainly see he could not repeat at Santiago what Dewey had done at Manila.

Sampson decided to block the harbor entrance by sinking a ship in the narrowest reach of the main channel. The collier *Merrimac* was tapped for the job. On June 3, assistant naval constructor Richmond Pearson Hobson took on a crew of six men and a stowaway to guide his temporary command on a one-way trip. At 3 A.M., he rang up nine knots to begin his approach on Santiago harbor entrance, some two thousand yards distant. With five hundred yards to go, a Spanish picket boat began firing on *Merrimac*'s rudder. Other Spanish guns opened up. Hobson cut his engine and glided his ship to the right spot. The bow anchor dropped fine. The plan called for the anchored *Merrimac* to use the outgoing tide to swing her perpendicular to the channel. A stern anchor would be dropped to hold her in position while her crew would explode ten charges to sink the ship.

Hobson put the wheel over to swing *Merrimac* across the channel, but the helm did not answer. The Spanish had shot the rudder to pieces, blown away the stern anchor, and taken out the wiring needed to blow the charges. *Merrimac* drifted, took more hits, then sank in shallow water. Hobson and his crew jumped into the water, miraculously unharmed. The Spanish were impressed with their courage nonetheless and sent a picket under a white flag to inform Sampson that Hobson and his crew were safe and being well cared for.

Plan A did not work for Sampson. It was time for Plan B.

Send in the Marines!

Ships of this day relied on coal-fired steam engines for propulsion. Refueling was a grueling ordeal in which the crew turned out to manhandle sacks of coal into the ship's bunkers. After that, the able-bodied seamen shoveled coal from fore to aft, then to the engine room to feed the greedy boilers that raised steam for the engines. Moving coal between ships at sea was risky, so Sampson sought a nearby harbor where this could be done safely, thus supporting the blockade. Forty-five miles east of Santiago was Guantánamo Bay. Seizure of the bay and its shores was assigned to the First Marine Battalion, a provisional unit made up of guards from various east coast navy yards. Embarked aboard the transport *Panther,* the marines were escorted by the cruisers *Marblehead* and *Yankee.* The force was landed on June 8.

This was a far cry from amphibious operations in World War II. There were no defenders waiting to shoot at the marines. The nearest Spanish garrison was based ten to twelve miles away. Upon getting word that the marines were ashore, the Spanish countered by quickly seizing a ridge with a good view of the bay.

What followed was four days of aggressive skirmishing that did not dislodge the marines. By June 12, Cuban rebels came through with information about a major buildup of Spanish troops six miles away at Cuzco. About two hundred marines marched to clear out the village, with the dispatch boat *Dolphin* providing offshore supporting fire. The battle was quick. The Spanish were driven off.

But most important, Stephen Crane of the *New York World* covered the fight. The marines were portrayed as heroes, and the rest became history—and legend. Before Guantánamo, marines served as shipborne infantry or as dockyard guards. The Corps had just lost a nasty bureaucratic fight where it tried to provide gun crews for the navy's warships. Winning at Guantánamo gave the marines a new mission—and an image.

With Guantánamo secured for coaling, Sampson got down to the dirty work of blockade. During the daytime, twelve warships took up station four miles offshore, forming a semicircle eight miles long to cover the entrance to Santiago. At night, six warships stood closer to shore, while one battleship aimed its searchlight at the harbor entrance. Ships would peel off in ones and twos to chug to Guantánamo, take on coal, then return to resume their boring but vital duty—waiting for the Spanish squadron to come out. It would take a land battle to make that happen.

Charge!

The war changed its complexion once V Corps was landed at Daiquiri, near Santiago, on June 22. Major General William Shafter's forces picked their way through several chains of hills east of Santiago, perhaps not with the greatest tactical acumen. Obscure men like Leonard Wood, Theodore Roosevelt, and John J. Pershing made their reputations in these battles. The end result was V Corps closing in on Santiago by early July. If they captured the port, they would also capture the fleet. Cervera had to do something.

Cervera had lent crew members to fight as naval infantry. Now they were recalled to their ships and ordered to make all preparations for getting under way. The best Cervera could do was order his ships to scatter in different directions, hopefully confusing the U.S. Navy and thus allowing some ships to get away. Spanish lookouts noticed a gap in the American blockade line to the west, as the *Brooklyn* was out of position. The opening move would require a pawn to be sacrificed. And that would be Cervera's flagship, the *Maria Teresa*.

On the morning of July 3, Cervera got the drop on the U.S. Navy. Only five heavy ships and two armed yachts were on patrol outside of Santiago. The *New York* went off to the east at twelve knots, conveying Sampson to a meeting with Shafter at Siboney. The *Massachusetts* and several escorts were off to Guantánamo for coal.

Cervera steamed out around 9:30 A.M., his ships making ten knots, eight hundred yards apart. *Maria Teresa* led, intent on taking on *Brooklyn,* closely followed by the *Vizcaya, Cristóbal Colón, Almirante Oquendo,* and the destroyers *Pluton* and *Furor.*

Maria Teresa bore down on *Brooklyn.* It was a game of chicken. *Brooklyn* blinked, turning east with six hundred yards to go before collision. But this put her in the way of *Texas,* which backed engines to stop short. Now there was a wide gap in the western sector of the blockade line. Through this hole steamed Cervera's squadron, all ahead full.

The Americans gave chase, maintaining no particular formation. It was going to be a running gunfight, with the Americans pouring on the coal to make speed.

Iowa opened fire, hitting the stern turret of *Maria Teresa*. *Colón* replied, putting two shots into *Iowa*. *Brooklyn* and *Texas* opened fire, scoring more hits on *Maria Teresa*. The shell impacts caused fires to break out. Cervera ordered *Maria Teresa* turned to shore, running her aground and striking her colors at 10:35 A.M.

Iowa, Oregon, Indiana, and *Brooklyn* then concentrated their fire on *Almirante Oquendo*. A fire broke out in the ship's torpedo room, threatening the magazine. The captain ordered the ship to turn to shore, running her aground within sight of the *Maria Teresa*.

The last ships out were the destroyers *Pluton* and *Furor,* which were engaged by the armed yacht *Gloucester.* Both Spanish ships were taken out of action by 10:50 A.M., even though each of them outgunned the yacht.

Only *Cristóbal Colón* and *Vizcaya* were left. *Vizcaya* scored a lucky hit on *Brooklyn,* ripping through one of the sponsons housing a 5-inch gun, killing one sailor. But the *Brooklyn* was luckier, landing a shot on *Vizcaya*'s bow, setting off a torpedo in the forward tube. The explosion blew off the *Vizcaya*'s bow. Another 8-inch hit from *Brooklyn* mauled her superstructure. Fires spread throughout the ship. The captain ordered hard right and beached the *Vizcaya,* leaving the *Cristóbal Colón* to carry on.

The *Colón* was steaming west at fifteen knots, its closest pursuer being *Brooklyn,* some six miles behind and making twenty knots, her black gangs shoveling coal like madmen to maintain steam. Not far behind was Sampson aboard *New York,* also making twenty knots for the past two hours. *Texas* and *Oregon* were not far behind, with *Oregon* now using her good coal to get a better burn in her boilers.

The race was not *Colón*'s to win. By 12:20 P.M. her speed began to slacken. The Americans caught up. *Oregon* opened fire with her 13-inch guns, followed by 8-inch fires from *New York* and *Brooklyn*. Seeing the Americans a mile behind and gaining, Captain Jose de Paredes ordered *Colón* to run aground some seventy-five miles west of Santiago. The great chase was over as of 1:15 P.M. The

Spanish flotilla was destroyed, with no loss to the U.S. Navy. The battle was no contest.

The Price

Spain suffered the total loss of Cervera's squadron, with 323 men killed and 151 wounded out of a total crew of 2,227 officers and seamen. About 1,700 entered captivity, with another 180 or so escaping into the Cuban hills after their ships were beached. The United States lost no ships, suffering only one dead and two wounded. Santiago fell in due course to V Corps, but battle losses had whittled the strength of the army's 20,000-strong unit by 10 percent, and tropical diseases disabled yet more.

The United States picked up Puerto Rico and Guam in secondary operations. The Philippines turned on American occupiers, who waged a ruthless counterinsurgency, subduing the islands by 1902. The lengthy trip by the *Oregon* around South America renewed the demand for a canal through Central America. Spanish-American War veteran President Theodore Roosevelt delivered, engineering a rebellion that prized Panama from Colombia. The massive multibillion-dollar construction of the canal was not completed until after he left office.

Only decisive naval victories made this outcome possible. But one must wonder whether Spain could have prevented such a decisive defeat if it had chosen differently. American strategy depended on winning battles. Keeping "fleets in being" in the Canary Islands and the Philippines would have denied the Americans the chance to fight them. The longer the war went on, the more American popular opinion would have been taxed by the lack of results. Popular support is the political fuel needed by a democracy to fight a war. Its decline would have made it harder for the United States to keep the war going, perhaps allowing Spain to seek an armistice or a negotiated peace.

Spain chose a more foolish course of action, pursuing a strategy based on battle, playing to American strength instead of minimizing Spanish weakness. Winning battles scores points in war. And Americans love keeping score.

TSUSHIMA

Japan vs. Russia, 1905

BY DENNIS SHOWALTER

The surer of himself an admiral is, the finer the tactical development of his fleet, the better his captains, the more reluctant must he necessarily be to enter into a melee *with equal forces, in which all these advantages will be thrown away, chance reign supreme, and his fleet be placed on terms of equality with an assemblage of ships which have never before acted together.*

—Alfred Thayer Mahan, *The Influence of Sea Power upon History, 1660–1783*

Tsushima, fought on May 27–28, 1905, is generally and legitimately accepted as one of the greatest naval battles of history, ranking with Trafalgar, Jutland, Midway, and the Philippine Sea. Tsushima is unusual in the context of naval history because it was a battle of annihilation, of the kind projected by Alfred Thayer Mahan but seldom approached, much less achieved. Of the three dozen Russian ships that participated, only three reached Vladivostok harbor. Japanese losses and damage were inconsequential.

Tsushima was the first battle of modern ironclad fleets—

Santiago in 1898 was just a stern chase. Tsushima was the only battle of the pre-dreadnought navies on which so much thought and treasure had been lavished in the previous quarter century. Tsushima was also a battle of navies purchased as much as constructed. By this time the dominant man-of-war, the successor to the eighteenth-century ship of the line, was the battleship. It had evolved to a common type: twelve thousand tons, four 12-inch guns, eighteen knots speed, and the equivalent of today's nuclear carrier in terms of relative complexity. The lesser ships of both Russia and Japan, the cruisers and destroyers, were domestically built. But every one of the major Japanese combatants, four battleships and six armored cruisers, was foreign-built, with Britain, France, Germany, and Italy contributing. The four new battleships that were the core of the Russian Second Pacific Squadron had been built in Russian yards, but to a locally modified version of a French design.

In Japan's case this policy was a consequence of a still physically limited construction capacity. Not until 1909 would the first Japanese-built true battleship be commissioned. Constrained to purchase externally, the Imperial Japanese Navy bought the best, from British yards when possible, and ordered upgrades in armor, armament, and engines that improved their purchases significantly over their Royal Navy counterparts. Russia had the construction capacity, but its designers' abilities lagged behind their European counterparts. So did the efficiency of their navy yards. The result was that by the 1890s, indigenous Russian battleships ended up over budget, overweight, and over deadlines to a point where the ones that participated at Tsushima bore the nickname "self-sinkers."

Turning from material to personnel, until the Industrial Revolution it was axiomatic that sailors were born, not trained. Engines and long-range guns, however, put traditional seamanship at a discount. Shoveling coal was the same in a factory or a stokehold.

Russian sailors were conscripts serving for three years, a deliberate mixture of rural and urban—the latter were considered more likely to be influenced by radical ideas. A third were illiterate, which handicapped training in technical fields. Pay was low, food abysmal, promotion prospects negligible. The officer corps was drawn from the entire spectrum of society, but their professional development was along specialist lines. That could be a problem should, for example, a communications specialist be given a navigator's responsibilities in an emergency.

The Japanese navy was manned by a mix of conscripts serving for eight years and long-service volunteers motivated by tradition and patriotism. Most of them were literate. Training was intense, especially in gunnery, but pay was double the army's; living conditions were good and promotion to petty officer a prospect. Enlisted men, moreover, were treated respectfully; the random harshness often associated with Japanese military discipline was a later development. Japanese officers were trained at Etajima. Established by a British training mission, its standards were so high that fewer than 10 percent of applicants were admitted. Its culture was pervasively British; the Imperial Navy's wardroom behaviors and uniform styles closely followed British patterns. That acculturation, ironically, did much to develop the assumption that Japanese could imitate but not innovate, which cost so many British and Allied lives in 1941–42.

Tsushima's strategic background was conditioned by the Russian Empire's turn-of-the-century determination to establish itself as a Pacific power. In naval contexts that meant major redeployments, to the Siberian bay of Vladivostok and even more to the newly established base of Port Arthur on China's Liaotung Peninsula, "leased" at gunpoint in 1898. By 1905 this was at best a forward position, with its landward defenses still developing and insufficient docking in the facilities to support a large modern naval force.

Redeployment continued nevertheless, with Russia's most modern ships dispatched in ones and twos to the new frontier. By the outbreak of war the result was a "squadron of samples," seven battleships of five different designs, whose tactical cooperation would have been a challenge for a far more worked-in command and personnel than was the case when the shooting started. From the beginning the Japanese navy, operating in its home waters and from its peacetime bases, held an edge that after two unsuccessful surface actions led the Russian command to accept blockade and await developments.

These developments were dominated by a successful, albeit extremely costly, Japanese siege that eventually led to the capture of dominating gun positions and the destruction of the Russian squadron in what amounted to target practice. The Japanese, however, did not escape unscathed. Two of the six battleships with which they began the war were sunk by Russian mines within a few days of each other. Keeping the sea in all weathers improved already high crew quality but wore down ships at a high rate—it later became a rule of thumb that one year of wartime deployment equals three years at sea during peace. And Japan had no way to replace its big-ship losses.

Admiral Heihachiro Togo coped in part by moving his armored cruisers into the battle line. That class of ship had developed in the 1890s largely for commerce raiding and trade protection. Heavier than battleships and a knot or two faster, their lighter armor and smaller guns—usually around 8-inch—were de facto arguments against integrating them directly into the line of battle. But needs must, and Togo began by attaching two of them as a fast division of his depleted battle squadron. The other four, under Rear Admiral Hikonojo Kamimura, were also intended to participate in a main battle when it occurred. In the interim they proved their worth at the Battle of Ulsan (August 14, 1904), ending the career of Russia's three-cruiser Vladivostok Squadron, which had been hindering Japanese transports and supply ships in the Yellow Sea since the war's early days.

It was a favorable sign, especially since a relief force was in the process of fitting out in Russian ports. The Second Pacific Squadron has been excoriated as "the fleet that had to die" in so many accounts that it can be difficult to separate wheat from chaff in evaluating its prospects and progress. Its core were four *Borodino*-class battleships. Still fitting out, they were unable to undergo gunnery or engineering exercises before sailing; their quirks and qualities remained to be discovered en route. The other three battleships were at best obsolescent. The Naval Ministry kept adding even older vessels to an already heterogeneous mix. The crews were a mixed bag of green conscripts and unhappy recalled reservists; the officers were a correspondingly mixed bag.

The squadron's commander, Vice Admiral Zinovy Rozhestvensky, was highly regarded as a gunnery expert and staff administrator. He needed every ounce of his ability to provide his ramshackle force with even rudimentary training as it steamed toward Cape Horn and then into the Far East. His problem was exacerbated by the constant need to recoal ships whose inefficient engines burned quantities of fuel huge by later standards. "Coaling ship" in any navy was a dirty, sweaty, unpopular task, even when the officers took part—emphatically not the case in the Second Pacific Squadron. It did much to nullify Rozhestvensky's efforts to develop reasonable levels of skill and pride in his big-ship crews.

Yet when all was said and done, the squadron made a favorable impression as it passed Singapore on April 8, 1905, creating telegraphed headlines across the world. Its arrival alone gave Russia's naval image a welcome boost. But to what end? Port Arthur had surrendered on January 2. With the fleet and the fort gone, Rozhestvensky had one viable option: break through or bypass the Japanese and make for Vladivostok. The problem there was that the squadron lacked enough coal to make the run. Colliers were on their way—but they were accompanied by an ad hoc Third Pacific Squadron whose ships were so useless Rozhestvensky had literally been trying to evade them for months.

Again, needs must. On May 8 the ostensible reinforcements reached the Russian anchorage in French Indochina's Cam Ranh Bay. Togo had had five months since Port Arthur's surrender to refit his ships and rest his crews. The only question was which route the Russians would take north. Togo decided to await the Russians in the Straits of Korea—the shortest line between the two points of Cam Ranh and Vladivostok. Even then it took the Russians two weeks from their departure date of May 14 to reach the battle zone.

Rozhestvensky's deployment for the run through the straits was as much administrative as tactical: modern battleships on the right, older battleships on the left, everything else in the middle. The only real chance of success was for the Japanese to fail to make contact. Togo and his staff, not for the last time in Japan's naval history, developed a complex plan of action. It began with torpedo craft striking the Russian columns before they entered the straits. A series of night attacks would prepare the way for the decisive gun duel, to be followed by pursuit, driving the survivors onto minefields newly laid outside Vladivostok.

In fact, the Russians evaded contact until 3 A.M. on May 27. The main Japanese fleet sortied two hours later, guided to the Russians by wireless reports from light cruisers scouting ahead. Togo took his time closing. Not till 1:19 P.M. did the Japanese flagship lead the First Division, four battleships and two armored cruisers, across the Russian column, then initiate a turn in succession that brought the Japanese across the Russian T at a range of 6,500 yards. The advantage of position was accompanied by the risk of exposing each ship to Russian fire as it turned. But the damage was minimal: more straddles than direct hits. The Japanese, first using high-explosive shells, then switching to armor-piercing as the ranges closed, fired at rates the Russians could not match and began to score decisively.

Oslyabya, leading the column of older battleships, was first to go under, at around 2:25 P.M.: the first battleship to be sunk by gunfire, turrets silenced, armor belt stripped away. *Suvorov,* leading the other column, was reduced to a shambles, communications knocked out, steering disrupted, crew demoralized. Her following sister ships, *Borodino* and *Aleksandr III,* were set on fire within twenty minutes.

By this time Rozhestvensky was disabled by a shell splinter in his skull. Neither of his senior captains knew it—not that it made much difference. The *Aleksandr III* initially tried to lead the dissolving fleet north. Togo swung back to pound the battleship; Captain Nikolai Bukhvostov responded with a full-ahead charge toward Togo's fleet as *Borodino* led the Russians in a turn south, attempting to evade the raking Japanese fire. Smoke and poor light temporarily shielded the Russians, but the Japanese quickly overtook them as they attempted to continue north. The Japanese were guided this time by Kamimura's armored cruisers, sent ahead by Togo to regain contact. *Aleksandr III*'s luck ran out around 6:30 P.M. Disabled by a Japanese salvo, she sank a half hour later, with no survivors. *Borodino* staved off torpedo attacks until 7:30 P.M. Togo ordered the action to be broken off. One of his captains decided it was easier to fire the shells in his guns than unload them. A shell hit *Borodino* and started a magazine fire. The ship blew up; there was only one survivor. *Suvorov,* which had gamely kept up with the movements of her sisters, had fallen to a torpedo-boat attack thirty minutes earlier, leaving 20 survivors.

The commander of Third Pacific Squadron, who had spent the day at the rear of the formation, now took the lead and ordered a course to Vladivostok. But during the night Japanese torpedo craft savaged the Russian survivors in a series of close-range attacks. Some ships sank. Some scuttled themselves. Others broke away, seeking escape on their own. By the morning of May 28 the remnants were only three hundred miles from Vladivostok. Then the light cruisers found them and Togo closed in, encircling the Russian squadron, then opening fire at long range. At 10:30 A.M. the admiral surrendered his three surviving battleships. Japan's naval supremacy in the Far East was sealed. It would endure for forty years.

Tsushima's consequences covered a broad spectrum. In specifically naval terms, the effective performance of the Japanese armored cruisers gave the dreadnought battle cruisers of the next generation more credibility as elements of a battle line than they merited. The Russian capital ships that surrendered were the last major warships—indeed the last warships except small auxiliaries—to lower their flags in the face of an enemy. By World War I, navies had collectively, unofficially, and no less decisively adopted a principle of "no surrender."

Tsushima, in the context of the Russo-Japanese War, symbolized Japan's position as a major power. That gain, however, proved ephemeral compared to the requirements for sustaining Japanese greatness. An economy already strained to the limit was burdened by large foreign loans. Increased military and naval requirements added to the strain on a still largely agricultural population. The Western powers continued to compete financially in Manchuria. China remained virtually immune to Japanese penetration on any level. The result was an increasing development of a concept of

Asian regionalism, with Japan as its focus: a kind of Asian Monroe Doctrine based on coexistence and coprosperity, secured and guaranteed by Japanese military power.

In an even broader context, throughout Asia Tsushima became a watershed. It wasn't just that an Asian power defeated a European one. That had, after all, happened before. But at Tsushima, Japan had played the West's game with the West's tools—and triumphed decisively. A new precedent had been set, one that would be implemented time and again across the Pacific, ending—perhaps only temporarily—on the roof of the U.S. embassy in Saigon on April 30, 1975.

CATCH ME IF YOU CAN

Flight of the Goeben, *July–August 1914*

BY WILLIAM TERDOSLAVICH

> *War is the province of chance. In no other sphere of human activity must such a margin be left for this intruder. It increases the uncertainty of every circumstance and deranges the course of events.*
>
> —Karl von Clausewitz, 1780–1831

There is a thin gray line between escape and destruction. Sometimes it is as narrow as an hour on a clock or as short as a mile over the horizon. The German battle cruiser *Goeben* sailed that tricky course.

Some call the ship lucky, but its captain, Admiral Wilhelm Souchon, made his luck. Souchon used his cunning to keep *Goeben* and its escort, the cruiser *Breslau,* one step ahead of destruction at the hands of the British Royal Navy. It also helped that not all the sea hounds chasing him were as daring or smart. Little did Souchon know that his accomplishment would have an outsize impact on the course of World War I.

A Modest Ship for a Modest Station

The *Goeben* was not the most powerful or the biggest ship that ever sailed the Mediterranean. It displaced only 23,000 tons. It had only ten 11-inch guns arrayed in five turrets, at a time when first-rate ships were starting to pack 14-inch and 15-inch artillery. Being a battle cruiser meant the designers had sacrificed some armor for speed. Ideally, the *Goeben* could zip along at twenty-eight knots, but the ship was slowed by a couple of knots due to worn engines. The key attribute of the battle cruiser was that it was armed like a battleship, so it could easily outrun and outgun any vessel of a lesser class.

The *Goeben* had only the light cruiser *Breslau* for an escort. *Breslau* could keep up, having a top speed of twenty-seven knots, but she weighed in at only 4,500 tons and packed twelve 4.1-inch guns—making her little better than a destroyer on steroids. *Breslau* was new to the Mediterranean, while *Goeben* had been on station for two years without a visit to the drydock. Her hull needed a good scraping and her boiler tubes desperately needed replacement, both maintenance issues that robbed the ship of some speed.

During peacetime, the *Goeben* "showed the flag," its presence confirming Germany's political interests in North Africa and the Mediterranean. Showing the flag is harmless in peacetime. When war is declared, however, a political statement can become a target.

When Archduke Franz Ferdinand was shot in Sarajevo in June 1914, *Goeben* was making a port call at Haifa, in the eastern Mediterranean. Souchon knew war was imminent and his ship badly needed refitting. He shifted base to the Austrian port of Pola (now Pula, Croatia), in the northern Adriatic to take delivery of new boiler tubes sent from Germany. From July 10 to 28, Souchon worked his crew hard to replace four thousand tubes on the *Goe-*

ben's twenty-four boilers. Berlin issued a war warning while work was under way. With the overhaul unfinished, Souchon weighed anchor and made for Brindisi, on Italy's heel, to rendezvous with *Breslau*. During the passage, Germany declared war on Russia, and Russia's ally France was expected to declare war on Germany. Should the Triple Alliance be activated, Souchon's division would operate with the Austrian and Italian fleets to fight the French fleet.

Italy was still neutral and was constrained by international law when it came to aiding the warships of belligerents. *Goeben* needed a fresh load of coal to be truly war ready. Souchon could find none in Brindisi, nor in Taranto, and finally he ended up in Messina, Sicily, where he could take it directly from any German merchant ships docked there. On the night of August 2, *Goeben* weighed anchor and put out to sea. Souchon had no orders but wanted to be ready to fight the French should war begin. His timing was good.

Mother, May I . . .

On August 3, Berlin and Paris exchanged declarations of war. *Goeben* was in a good position to mess with the French fleet, now covering the movement of XIX Corps from the North African colonies back to France. If the *Goeben* could get past the escorts, it could sink the troop carriers.

The situation was clear for the French but confusing for the British. They were not yet at war with Germany. On August 4, German troops crossed into Belgium to execute the wide, flanking march that would get them to Paris. Britain took exception to this, issuing an ultimatum calling for the withdrawal of German troops by midnight, or else.

Souchon now had to consider his position. Britain had stationed a trio of battle cruisers in Malta—the *Inflexible, Indomitable,* and *Indefatigable.* Each displaced eighteen thousand tons and could do twenty-five knots, making them lighter and slower than *Goeben*. But each ship packed eight 12-inch guns. With the British squadron able to bring thirty-six guns against *Goeben*'s ten, Souchon had a reason to treat this threat with some respect. Four armored cruisers rounded out the British deployment—*Defense, Warrior, Black Prince,* and *Duke of Edinburgh*—along with four light cruisers and sixteen destroyers.

Admiral Sir Archibald Berkeley-Milne commanded this fleet. He can be best described as a competent officer who knew how to follow orders. But the orders he received were anything but competent. Mission number one was to work with the French to protect the passage of XIX Corps, but mission number two was to bring *Goeben* to battle. Berkeley-Milne was also ordered not to engage superior forces, but to choose the best moment to fight. These were the instructions issued on July 30 by Winston Churchill, Lord of the Admiralty (the equivalent of the American secretary of the navy). And Churchill was quick on the telegraph key. On August 2, he ordered Berkeley-Milne to keep two battle cruisers on *Goeben*'s tail. Then, on August 3, Churchill added another mission: keep an eye on the entrance to the Adriatic, but also keep an eye on *Goeben*.

With the *Goeben* sighted at Taranto on August 2, Berkeley-Milne peeled off *Indomitable* and *Indefatigable* from the Adriatic patrol to rush to the waters south of Italy, leaving the four armored cruisers under the command of Rear Admiral Ernest Troubridge. Berkeley-Milne figured the *Goeben* was making for Gibraltar, to exit the Mediterranean and make its way back to the German High Seas Fleet, which was ready to contest British naval mastery in the North Sea. But contingencies and contrary orders were pulling Berkeley-Milne's fleet in different directions.

While this war dance was going on peacefully in the Mediterranean, Germany and Turkey signed a defensive alliance against Russia, also on August 2. Souchon later got the order to proceed to Constantinople. Perhaps training the *Goeben*'s guns against Germany's new ally might induce the Turks to actually go to war. But Souchon was busy at the moment, that August 4. Close to the shores of Algeria, he was eager to shell Philippeville and Bône before obeying orders.

The Chase

This proved to be a big mistake. Shelling two French colonial ports did nothing to hinder the movement of XIX Corps back to France. Instead, Souchon telegraphed his location to the British. Within hours, Captain Francis Kennedy, commanding *Indomitable* and *Indefatigable,* spotted *Goeben,* headed east at twenty knots. The British battle cruisers were steaming west at twenty-two knots, closing the distance.

Aboard *Goeben,* Souchon and his crew watched nervously as the British battle cruisers steamed past, expecting to receive fire. The British ships kept their turrets fixed forward and aft. About ten thousand yards past *Goeben,* the British battle cruisers turned to follow. Kennedy could not order his ships to open fire until war was declared. The Germans had no idea when that would happen. No one was taking any chances. Souchon rang the engine room: full speed, bringing the ship up to twenty-four knots. Kennedy kept station behind him. His ships were designed to reach twenty-five knots, but the battle cruisers had been at sea for a couple of years and were also slowed by the lack of a refit.

Kennedy radioed a terse message: *Goeben* was in sight. Word came back from Churchill in London: "Very good. Hold her. War imminent." The hounds were on the fox's tail. But they were not allowed to bite just yet.

Churchill assumed *Goeben* was steaming west to harry the French; he did not know that it was steaming eastward. He wanted Berkeley-Milne to have the authority to open fire without waiting for a declaration of war, should the *Goeben* fire on the French. Prime Minister Herbert Asquith wanted to put this to a cabinet vote. Time was now being wasted when action was urgent. All the trigger-happy Churchill could do was seethe quietly.

All Kennedy could do was to maintain the chase. The light cruiser *Dublin* now joined, posted on *Goeben*'s right, just beyond the German ship's gun range. By 3 P.M., it looked like the British were gaining slowly. An hour later, the Germans were pulling ahead. *Dublin* kept up the chase as the British battle cruisers fell behind. By 7:30, *Dublin*'s captain could see only *Goeben*'s smoke on the horizon. By 9 P.M., even that trace vanished from sight as night fell.

At midnight, the British ultimatum to Germany reached its deadline. With no reply from Berlin, Germany and Britain were now at war.

It's Okay to Shoot Now!

The morning of August 5 found *Goeben* and *Breslau* back in Messina, looking for more coal. Italy was still neutral, which meant Souchon had little time to refuel or he would risk seeing his warships interned for the duration of the war. Between a collier and the hapless German liner *General,* Souchon's crew and the liner's passengers all wielded shovels to get the coal from the deck to the bunkers below, moving 1,500 tons of the stuff in about twenty-four hours.

Souchon got word that Turkey was looking to maintain some degree of neutrality and might not permit passage through the Dardanelles Straits, which connect the Mediterranean with the Black Sea. Austria would not be lending assistance because it was not at war with France, and Italy was staying out of the fight, so there would be no joint Italian-Austrian operation against the French. Berlin had no instructions for Souchon, who was left to use his judgment.

Souchon made his decision on August 6. With all options foreclosed, he ordered his ships to sea. Destination: Constantinople. "I hope to carry the Turks with me in a war against their traditional enemy, the Muscovites," Souchon later wrote.

Berkeley-Milne still thought the *Goeben* would be making for the French convoys, so he kept his battle cruisers at Malta, ready to intercept. He could have taken his ships into Messina to destroy the German warships, Italy's neutrality be damned. But Berkeley-Milne was directly ordered to respect Italian neutrality. Italy was not honoring its alliance commitment to Germany and Austria, so why provoke them into doing so?

Berkeley-Milne could have stationed his ships to blockade Messina, thus containing *Goeben,* which would have risked destruction if it tried to slip past again. Sadly, Berkeley-Milne was no Souchon, never mind another Lord Nelson. The only ship near Messina to contest *Goeben*'s passage was the light cruiser *Gloucester,* Captain Howard Kelly commanding. It was like dispatching a puppy to stalk the fox.

Packing a pair of 6-inch guns, *Gloucester* could take on *Breslau* but was no match for *Goeben*. *Gloucester* sulked outside *Goeben*'s gun range, maintaining contact as Souchon left Messina, steering north by east toward the mouth of the Adriatic.

But that was not where Souchon was going.

At around 10:45 P.M., Kelly radioed to Berkeley-Milne and

Troubridge: *Goeben* was changing course, heading south. At midnight, Kelly radioed again: *Goeben* now headed southeast, toward Greece.

Troubridge was on station, south of Corfu and in a position to intercept *Goeben* with *Defence, Warrior, Black Prince,* and *Duke of Edinburgh*. Each ship displaced about fourteen thousand tons. Altogether the ships could present twenty-two 9.2-inch guns, and the eight destroyers could make torpedo attacks. Had *Goeben* and *Breslau* gone for the Adriatic, Troubridge would have ambushed them. The planned battle would have been fought at close range, negating *Goeben*'s advantages in gunnery and speed. Troubridge poured on the coal, coaxing nineteen knots out of his squadron, intent on giving battle in the morning somewhere off Greece. Maybe if the *Goeben* were intercepted at dawn's early light, the British might have a chance.

This plan troubled Captain Fawcett Wray of *Defence,* who was Troubridge's flag captain. Wray understood gunnery and knew that *Goeben* could use its superior speed to maintain a standoff distance of sixteen thousand yards and pound the British with no worry of return fire. Wray wanted Troubridge to change his mind. The Admiralty order noted that the British should not engage a superior force. Didn't *Goeben* and *Breslau* fit that definition?

Interception was expected around 6 A.M.

With two hours to go, Troubridge decided to call it off. He radioed Berkeley-Milne that his force would not engage the *Goeben*. Six hours later, he got a reply: Intercept! By this time, Troubridge was nowhere near *Goeben*. After breaking off the interception, he had pulled into the Greek port of Zante so his destroyers could take on coal.

Souchon's luck was holding.

While Troubridge called it quits, Kelly hung on stubbornly. *Gloucester* was still shadowing the German ships, maintaining contact and radioing position reports. Souchon was taking this shadow seriously, figuring it was the vanguard of a larger force. Off-duty crew members were called to station, handed shovels, and told to get to work moving coal into the boiler rooms. *Goeben* needed more speed. Souchon detached *Breslau* to rough up *Gloucester*, but Kelly got in the first shots. At 1:30 in the afternoon, *Gloucester*'s two 6-inch guns opened fire on *Breslau*, range 11,500 yards. The shots fell short. *Breslau* returned fire, the shells falling about thirty yards away from *Gloucester*. Kelly ordered more speed and closed his range to ten thousand yards, readying a broadside. That is when the fox turned and bared its teeth. *Goeben* sent its eleven-inch shells crashing into the sea near *Gloucester*. A hit from any one of them would sink the ship.

Kelly backed off, maintaining contact outside *Goeben*'s gun range. By 4:45 P.M., Souchon reached Cape Matapan. Round this landmass and the Germans would leave the Ionian Sea for the Aegean. Kelly's orders forbade pursuit past this point. With *Gloucester* running low on coal, Kelly reluctantly broke chase. Hopefully Berkeley-Milne was nearby with the battle cruisers, ready to fight *Goeben* and *Breslau*. But the big hounds were nowhere near the fox.

Expectations for Nought

Berkeley-Milne was still in Malta with his three battle cruisers. Eight hours after Kelly's last radio message was received, the force weighed anchor and steamed out at twelve knots, headed east. Berkeley-Milne was still convinced *Goeben* and *Breslau* would double back to attack the French. Then he got word from the Admiralty: Austria had declared war on Britain. Concentrate the fleet. Berkeley-Milne turned north to link up with Troubridge's squadron. Now that patrol across the entrance of the Adriatic mattered! Four hours later, the order was countermanded. A contingency order had been issued by mistake—Austria had not declared war against Britain. Berkeley-Milne untangled his doubts from his mistakes twenty-four hours later, then resumed an easterly course into the Aegean, speed ten knots.

Souchon was a wily one. He had wired ahead of his departure from Messina to charter a collier in Piraeus, the port city of Athens, to rendezvous with his ships in the Aegean. Once together, the trio of ships made for Denusa, a small, insignificant island populated by a few Greek fishermen. Greek neutrality be damned, Souchon lashed *Goeben* to one side of the collier while *Breslau* tied up on the other side. Out came the shovels and the crewmen to begin the frantic work of manhandling tons of the black fuel into the bunkers. Lookouts were posted on Denusa's peak, keeping an eye out for the British. Radio silence was maintained. The liner *General* also rendezvoused with the squadron. It was August 9. Souchon dispatched *General* to Smyrna (now Izmir) to cable the German ambassador in Constantinople: arrange for *Goeben*'s passage into the Dardanelles with Turkish permission, if possible.

Souchon was not going to wait for an answer. He was gambling that the Turks would say yes. At 3 A.M. on August 10, *Goeben*'s radio room picked up British radio signals, growing stronger. The British were now in the Aegean, trying to pick up *Goeben*'s trail.

Goeben and *Breslau* pulled out of Denusa, setting a northerly course, speed eighteen knots. By day's end, both ships had reached Cape Helles, marking the entrance of the Dardanelles. Souchon ordered his crew to battle stations. Had the Turks gotten his message? Would they open fire? Should he shoot first and fight his way into the straits?

Souchon kept his cards close to his vest. Facing a Turkish fort, *Goeben* ran up its signal flags: Request pilot.

Two Turkish destroyers came out and hoisted flags: Follow me. The fox had outrun the hounds.

Turkish Delight

Turkish defense minister Enver Pasha had to make a decision when the phone call came from the fort that German warships requested permission to enter the Dardanelles. Turkey would be taking sides, depending on how he decided. Permission granted was his reply, followed by an order to open fire on any British warships trying to enter the straits.

A British request to have the German ships disarmed was rejected. On August 16, the Germans finessed Ottoman neutrality by "selling" the *Goeben* and *Breslau* to Turkey, now renamed as the *Sultan Selim* and *Midilli,* respectively. Souchon now found himself as Turkey's chief admiral, while his crews exchanged their caps for fezzes and moved church services from Sunday to Friday.

It was a clever move. German diplomats took advantage of Turkish resentment against Britain for keeping two Turkish battleships that were already built in British shipyards shortly before the war began. Those ships entered the Royal Navy out of necessity as the *Erin* and the *Agincourt,* with Turkey getting no compensation. By "buying" the *Goeben* and *Breslau,* the Turkish government served revenge as a cold dish to the British. But Turkey was still not in the war.

With Enver Pasha's connivance, Souchon weighed anchor one more time in late October, taking his two ex-German ships and a few Turkish warships into the Black Sea. Without a declaration of war, the squadron opened fire on the Russian port of Odessa. This caught the Turkish government by surprise, but they were not in a position to disavow the action when *Goeben* returned, its 11-inch guns ready to shell the capital. Enver Pasha was playing the warship off against his own government, getting Turkey into the war as a German ally.

The Dardanelles were closed. Russia was now cut off. Odessa was the only Russian port left to export wheat or import war supplies after Germany pretty much shut down the Baltic Sea, cutting off St. Petersburg from the outside world as well. (Murmansk and Archangel were not major ports yet, still too marginal to make a difference.) Without the ability to trade wheat for arms, Russia would spend the rest of the war fighting with one arm tied behind its back. All this was the outcome of *Goeben* reaching Turkey, Churchill lamented in his memoirs. The *Goeben* "brought more slaughter, more misery and ruin than has ever before been borne within the compass of a ship."

Back at the Admiralty, finger-pointing began. Troubridge faced a court of inquiry but was acquitted that November because he followed the order "not to engage a superior force." The decision rankled the more bloody-minded captains and admirals of the Royal Navy, who prized action before discretion. Like Troubridge's, Berkeley-Milne's career was finished, and he too never got another sea command. American naval historian Arthur Marder got the best measure of Berkeley-Milne by quoting him as saying, "They pay me to be an admiral. They don't pay me to think."

The Troubridge acquittal shook up the Royal Navy. From that day on, damn the odds, no British captain ever turned his back on the enemy again.

A BEACH TOO FAR

Gallipoli, October 1914–January 1916

BY WILLIAM TERDOSLAVICH

Time is everything; five minutes make the difference between victory and defeat.

—Horatio Nelson, 1758–1805

Landing an army on a hostile shore is the most complex operation one can undertake in war. When the invasion is unopposed, the beach becomes a gateway to victory. Post some defenders to contest the landing and the shore can become a dead end of defeat.

Before Gallipoli, unopposed amphibious landings were the norm. There was no doctrine that outlined what to do when making an amphibious landing against an actively defended shore.

A nation cannot defend every mile of its shoreline. There are not enough troops in any army to do that. In the past, beaches were left uncovered because of that reality, so any landing would be a surprise. The countertactic to this was to place outposts to spot the invasion when it happened and report back to headquarters. A reserve would then be dispatched to fight the invading force ASAP.

Great Britain found out the hard way that the Turks were prepared when it attempted to seize the Gallipoli Peninsula during World War I. This presumed shortcut to victory promised to take Turkey out of the war, reopen the Dardanelles Straits, and restore trade with Russia via its Black Sea port of Odessa. The British ran into the dead end at full speed, losing soldiers and ships at a horrifying rate, with bloody failure the only outcome.

We tend to look at amphibious invasions from the viewpoint of World War II, with infantry packed in landing craft hitting the beaches, amply supported by naval gunfire and aircraft. But we should instead view the World War II landings through the prism of Gallipoli. The equipment and the techniques used in modern amphibious warfare had not been invented yet. British soldiers would go ashore much as their predecessors did in the 1700s or 1800s, from rowboats moving from ship to shore. This method is fine if the landing is unopposed, but it can be problematic if people are shooting at you.

The lesson many took away from the failure at Gallipoli was that amphibious invasions don't work if they are opposed. It was a damnable legacy that military planners struggled to overcome as they worked on methods to restore amphibious warfare to strategy's bag of tricks. Everything that went wrong there was a problem that had to be solved, by doctrine, training, new equipment, new tactics, and new methods, before you could engineer a World War II–style amphibious landing.

Serving Turkey

The German battle cruiser *Goeben* and her escort, the light cruiser *Breslau,* altered the face of World War I when they sortied under the Turkish flag in October 1914 to shell the Russian port of

Odessa. Britain took exception to neutral Turkey shelling an ally and threatened war if Turkey did not back down. The ultimatum was ignored. Britain declared war, and with that, Turkey became an active German ally.

The western front was becoming stalemated as armies on both sides took to the trenches. Losses were heavy. First Lord of the Admiralty Winston Churchill saw a shortcut out of the mess: land an army on the Gallipoli Peninsula and, with the support of a fleet, march to Constantinople and take Turkey out of the war. The scheme did not get any support from War Secretary Lord H. H. Kitchener, who felt that troops were better used fighting Germans on the western front than attacking a secondary enemy in some sideshow action. That left the Royal Navy to go it alone.

The Dardanelles are only two miles wide at the Aegean entrance at Cape Helles, then guarded by several Turkish forts mounting sixteen heavy and seven medium-range guns. Once past the forts, the straits widen to four miles, only to shrink to less than a mile at the Narrows, between Kephez and Chanak, about fourteen miles in from Cape Helles. At this bottleneck, the Turks placed seventy-two heavy guns and laced the waters with eight belts of mines.

To run this gauntlet, Vice Admiral Sackville Hamilton Carden was given Britain's newest battleship, *Queen Elizabeth* (eight 15-inch guns) and the battle cruiser *Inflexible* (eight 12-inch guns). Added were twelve British pre-dreadnought battleships, eight of which were due to be scrapped in fifteen months, making these vessels expendable. Rounding out the force were four older French battleships. Then-neutral Greece allowed this odd fleet to base at Lemnos, an island just sixty miles away from the Dardanelles.

The plan was methodical. First, use long-range gunfire to destroy the forts guarding the entrance to the Dardanelles. Land two battalions of Royal Marines at Cape Helles to finish off any positions that were missed. Proceed up the Dardanelles to the Narrows. Again using long-range gunfire, destroy Turkish gun positions on the European and Asian shores. The covering fire should allow trawlers with civilian crews to sweep the mines in the Narrows, thus allowing the battleships to steam all the way to Constantinople. That should force Turkey to quit the war.

The first bombardment on February 19 took place too late in the day, with subsequent bad weather preventing further operations for a week. The operation resumed on February 25, and again the next day, with Carden taking his task force all the way to the Narrows, minus the *Queen Elizabeth*.

The *QE* was a brand-new battleship at the time. Her guns were not yet test-fired and calibrated. This would be done by "live fire" against Turkish targets, but the Admiralty did not want massive volleys to wear out the gun barrels so soon (not an issue with the older battleships). However, the Royal Navy had no way of calling and correcting "indirect fire"—fire delivered at targets you can't see from the gun's position. *QE* would simply anchor outside of the Gallipoli Peninsula and fire in. Later in March, *QE* would participate in the effort to force the Narrows. But in this session, it would play a minor role.

Armored battleships could shrug off hits from shore guns, but the minesweepers proved too vulnerable. Chugging against the current they were little better than sitting ducks. They could not clear the mines under fire, despite repeated attempts.

Carden fell ill from exhaustion and was replaced by his second-in-command, Rear Admiral John de Robeck. On March 18, de Robeck would take the direct approach, steaming up to the Narrows, guns blazing. Cruising forth in line abreast were *Queen Elizabeth, Agamemnon, Lord Nelson,* and *Inflexible*, flanked by *Prince George* and *Triumph*. In the second line were the French battleships *Gaulois, Bouvet, Suffren,* and *Charlemagne*. Waiting outside the straits were *Vengeance, Irresistible, Albion,* and *Ocean,* ready to relieve the French line, while *Cornwallis* and *Canopus* would escort the minesweepers in for the final action.

At 11 A.M., *Queen Elizabeth* opened fired on the Turkish forts at a range of fourteen thousand yards. Other ships joined in as they made range. *Gaulois* took one hit below the waterline, forcing her retirement. Despite suffering hits from many Turkish guns, de Robeck's force incurred few casualties and maintained fire. But by 2 P.M., the Turkish situation had become critical. Fire slackened as guns were knocked out, demoralized gunners gave up their stations, and phone lines were cut.

De Robeck ordered the French to retire and his reserve battleships to take their place. Steaming south, *Bouvet* struck a mine in an undetected belt laid parallel to the southern shore. The ship capsized and sank in two minutes, taking down more than six hundred men. *Inflexible* hit the next mine, causing flooding in her forward compartments, forcing her withdrawal. Fifteen minutes later, *Irresistibl*e hit a mine, losing power as her engine rooms flooded, leaving her adrift. Around 6 P.M., *Ocean* also hit a mine, sinking afterward. Failing to force the Narrows, the British exited the Dardanelles. Though replacements were promised, de Robeck did not renew the attack. Ships alone could not do the job. An army was needed to take Gallipoli and silence the Turkish guns from the land.

The Army Is a Projectile Fired by the Navy

The Gallipoli Peninsula is fifty-two miles long, connecting to Turkey's European portion at Bulair. There the peninsula is only three miles wide. Moving south, Gallipoli widens to twelve miles before tapering off to end at Cape Helles. It is mixed terrain, flat in places, punctuated by ridges and thousand-foot rises, with beaches edged by cliffs. Roads there were not good or plentiful. This ground was to become a battlefield.

Control of the operation passed from the Royal Navy to the British Army. Kitchener tapped his former chief of staff from the Boer War, General Ian Hamilton, to take command of the force, consisting of the Twenty-ninth Division, plus the Australia and New Zealand Corps (ANZACs). The force was assembled at Lemnos but had to backtrack to Alexandria, Egypt, seven hundred miles away, to rearrange cargoes for combat. That would take a month. Operational security was bad. Turkish spies learned a lot just by reading Egyptian newspapers.

Now that the British had made it obvious they were gunning for Gallipoli, the Turks turned time into a weapon. Defense Minister Enver Pasha turned to General Liman von Sanders, head of the five-hundred-strong German military mission, to take command of the Turkish Fifth Army, charged with defending the peninsula.

Turkish generals thought that relying on the terrain would be good enough for defense. Good landing beaches were few, so why not post a division to cover each one? Von Sanders chose to concentrate his forces in several central locations, dispatching them to "flood the zone" the moment any British showed up at an invasion beach. (The Germans would use this tactic again in the next war.) He then put Turkish troops to work on improving the roads to enable quick marches to threatened sectors.

By the time preparations were finished, von Sanders deployed the Fifth and Seventh divisions to cover Bulair. He posted the Ninth and Nineteenth divisions farther south on the peninsula. The Third and Eleventh covered the Asian shore at Besika Bay and Kum Kale. Each division was positioned inland, leaving a few small units overlooking the invasion beaches to act as tripwires.

Hamilton was a generally competent officer, having gained his experience in many of the British Empire's little colonial wars that punctuated the nineteenth century. He was commanding the largest amphibious force in modern history, but he was executing the operation with no previous experience or doctrine to guide him.

Doctrine is essentially a rulebook that tells troops how to do something. Troops train to employ the precepts of the book. For amphibious warfare, that doctrine would spell out how far offshore transports would anchor, how to load the assault boats, what supplies to bring, in what order troops should land, how fire support should be delivered, who would be in charge when the boats went to shore, who would be in charge on the beach—pretty much all the details needed to execute a particular type of warfare.

Troops were not trained for ship-to-shore movement. Supply ships were not "combat loaded," with the most essential supplies at the top of cargo holds and the least essential at the bottom. There were no specialized landing craft or portable radios, and support by naval gunfire would be dodgy at best.

The narrow waters of the Dardanelles lacked the space needed for transports and landing boats to operate in sufficient numbers. Worse, the boats could be fired on by Turkish artillery emplaced on the heights overlooking the straits. The invasion would have to take place from the open seas on the Aegean side, and from there the options Hamilton had to choose from were few.

Landing the force at Bulair made the most sense (and von Sanders feared this option the most). Take the three-mile-wide neck and Gallipoli is cut off from Turkey. The invading force could easily defend the bottleneck against Turkish counterattack while a second force could be sent south to roll up the artillery forts overlooking the Narrows. Hamilton turned down this option after surveying the Bulair invasion beach from the bridge of a cruiser.

He saw a swamp overlooked by a high ridge—terrain that favored the defense.

Hamilton opted for a dual landing, putting the Twenty-ninth Division ashore at five small beaches at Cape Helles and the ANZACs halfway up the peninsula at Ari Burnu. Landing forces would then have to rush the heights overlooking their landing beaches to win their battles. A French landing of 16,000 troops at Kum Kale, on the Asian side of the Dardanelles, would be a feint to draw off Turkish troops who could reinforce defenders on Gallipoli.

Putting forces ashore was going to require improvisation. Flat-bottomed landing craft with drop ramps did not exist in 1915. Instead, steam-powered tugs would tow strings of rowboats packed with infantrymen. They would cast off just beyond the surf line and row in. To get two thousand men onto the beach at Cape Helles quickly, the collier *River Clyde* was converted into an improvised landing ship. The vessel would beach and drop two gangways from bow to shore. The infantrymen would sally forth through ports cut into the ship's sides and make for the gangways.

April Foolishness

On April 25, Hamilton sent his forces ashore. The *River Clyde* beached as planned, facing three hundred Turks with rifles and machine guns. As soon as the first British Tommies made their way forward, the enemy opened fire. Fallen men clogged the exits, bunching up their followers into nice, large targets. The clear blue Aegean waters ran red with blood. Despite this setback, the Twenty-ninth Division made it to shore, with four of its columns barely taking the first chain of hills overlooking the landing beaches. These half-mile gains came nowhere close to taking the commanding height of Achi Baba, some seven miles away. Slow to leave the beaches, the Twenty-ninth became bogged down by increasing Turkish resistance.

Farther north, the ANZACs accidentally landed a mile north of their intended beach, thus dodging the barbed wire and Turkish infantry waiting for them. Von Sanders ordered the Turkish Nineteenth Division, Colonel Kemal Pasha commanding, to block the ANZACs, who were tasked with seizing the heights of Chunuk Bair and Sari Bair. Kemal Pasha committed his entire division, advancing through the same broken terrain that slowed his enemy. It was enough to keep the ANZACs from cutting the peninsula in half. They were hemmed into a salient only one thousand yards deep, barely holding the first string of hills overlooking the beach. Stuck fast, the Aussies and Kiwis dug in.

Lack of leadership cursed both landings, as forces advanced off the beaches with no sense of urgency. Hamilton did not sack any commander for "lack of drive"; he always believed that the officer on the scene knew more than the general back at headquarters. This worked badly at Gallipoli, as Hamilton was ill-served by slow subordinates who could not seize an opportunity if you placed it in their hands.

The Turks were proving tougher than expected, and their generals were equally hardheaded. Take Kemal Pasha, whose command blocked the ANZACs. When asked about how he led, he responded that he did not order his men to fight—he ordered them to die. This point was proven all too well on May 19, when 30,000 Turks went "over the top" against ANZAC positions. The Turks lost 10,000 in exchange for 600 defenders, regaining little ground. The Turkish generals were willing to pay any blood price to keep the British and Commonwealth troops at bay.

Office Politics

Stalemate at Gallipoli, running on three weeks at this stage, led to finger-pointing in London, with Churchill in the hot seat. It had been his idea to seize the Dardanelles, and he had been given the responsibility, but not the power, to get the job done. Now the effort had seized up. Churchill wanted to fix the problem but others in government wanted to fix the blame. On May 13, the crisis worsened when a Turkish destroyer fired a torpedo into the elderly battleship *Goliath,* taking about 570 of its almost 800-man crew to the bottom. First Sea Lord Jackie Fisher recalled the *Queen Elizabeth*.

This decision had the effect of taking a ship away from where it could do little good and reassigning it back to the Grand Fleet based at Scapa Flow/North Sea. There the Royal Navy waited for the German High Seas Fleet to sortie into the North Sea seeking decisive battle. (Such a thing eventually happened in 1916, with less dramatic results.) The key to winning this anticipated battle was always having more battleships handy than the Germans did.

Fisher tired of working with the meddlesome Churchill and resigned on May 15. Prime Minister Asquith refused to accept the resignation. As the political crisis worsened, it was becoming clear to Asquith that he would have to take the Conservatives in as coalition partners. But the price would be high. Opposition leader Andrew Bonar Law wanted Churchill out of government. This was payback for Churchill crossing the aisle from the Conservative to the Liberal side in the House of Commons years before. Asquith fired Churchill to appease Bonar Law and form the coalition. Fisher then pressed for more power to run the navy as he saw fit, making the next first lord irrelevant. Seeing that war was too important to be left to the admirals, Asquith found his backbone and fired Fisher.

This did not help anyone back in Gallipoli. In late May, a U-boat torpedoed the old battleship *Triumph* at Suvla Bay. The old battleship *Majestic* also suffered a torpedo hit and sank. Onshore, the situation remained a bloody deadlock.

Kitchener sent three more divisions to Hamilton, but that only reinforced the suffering. British and ANZAC troops fought vermin and disease as well as Turks. Practicing good hygiene in the trenches was impossible. The unwashed troops soon found their uniforms infested with lice, whose bites made them itch. Worse, some of those lice would also transmit typhus, which was deadly.

The lack of latrines turned the trenches into open sewers. The filth would find its way into the food and water the soldiers consumed, making them sick with dysentery. That, in turn, spread more dysentery.

Dead bodies left between the lines rotted in the hot sun, adding their stench to the bright, sunny days. On the Turkish side, life was no better, as dead soldiers were incorporated into the earthworks protecting their living comrades. May bled into June, which sank into July, finally oozing into August. Fourteen Allied divisions now faced sixteen Turkish divisions. Something had to be done.

Double or Nothing

Kitchener doubled down again, sending IX Corps, with two fresh divisions, to Gallipoli. Hamilton planned to land the corps at Suvla Bay, just north of the ANZAC position. The British at Cape Helles would attack uphill to keep the Turks from shifting units north. The ANZACs would also try to attack out of their positions to support IX Corps, which Hamilton tapped to deliver the main effort to take the heights.

The British attack on Cape Helles made minor gains but fixed the Turkish defenders in place. The Australians and New Zealanders had it worse, suffering horrendous losses as they made frontal attacks against high ground held in force. The thrusts toward Lone Pine Ridge and Sidi Bair produced casualties, not results. One Australian brigade lost 1,700 men out of 2,900. Another battalion lost three-quarters of its men.

One column had better luck—the Sixth Gurkha Battalion took the ridge at Chunuk Bair. They had the Turks on the run, having reached the top. The road south to Achi Baba was clear. If the Australians reinforced this attack, the Turks would be outflanked. But this was not an age when portable radios existed, so no one higher up knew of the breakthrough. Preplanned naval fire put six 12-inch shells into the Gurkhas, destroying their charge.

The golden opportunity lay with IX Corps, General Sir Frederick Stopford commanding. Twenty thousand men landed on the beach, facing only three weak Turkish battalions and outnumbering the defenders ten to one. All Stopford had to do was rush his troops uphill to take the Anafarta Gap, turning the Turkish position that kept the Australians bottled up. Stopford stopped at the first slope. Hamilton was quick to visit Stopford, urging him to hurry. This had no effect. Von Sanders quickly rushed two Turkish divisions to Suvla Bay from Bulair, now that he no longer needed to cover Gallipoli's vulnerable neck. The next day, the hills above were packed with Turks. Subsequent attacks out of the Suvla position cost the British 40,000 casualties in two weeks, again showing no gains.

August rotted into September. The British and Commonwealth troops maintained the bloody stalemate, dying into October. Their failure to take the Dardanelles convinced nearby Bulgaria that the Allied cause was not promising, so they entered the war on the German side come October 14. Greece too joined the Entente in response. One French and one British division were pulled out of Gallipoli and sent to Salonika, opening the Macedonian front against the Bulgarians.

Two days later, Kitchener replaced Hamilton with General Sir Charles Monro, a western front general who had always doubted the wisdom of taking Gallipoli. His conclusion was no surprise—pull the army out. "He came, he saw, he capitulated," wrote Churchill in his diary. By November 7, Bonar Law gave Asquith a good shove, declaring that the troops must be withdrawn or Asquith should resign. Asquith chose withdrawal. The evacuation began that month. Come December, 120,000 men pulled out of the Suvla/ANZAC beachhead. Come January 1916, Cape Helles was evacuated. Turkish troops refused direct orders to charge what remained of British positions. Why attack and die when the enemy was finally running away?

It Was Churchill's Fault

Gallipoli was supposed to be an economy-of-force operation in a secondary theater, expected to produce outsize results. It took eight and a half months to produce strategic failure. Turkey was not knocked out of the war. No supply line was restored to Russia. Bulgaria became a German ally, which drove Greece to join the Entente to forestall invasion by Bulgaria.

About half a million British, French, Australian, and New Zealand troops were cycled through this meat grinder. More than half of those became casualties, with 50,000 killed in action. Turkish casualties were between 250,000 and 350,000, which is only a guess given poor record keeping. The Turkish army was never the same again, fighting on in Palestine, in the Caucasus, and in Mesopotamia with decreasing forces of increasing mediocrity.

The high body count affected Australia grievously. An obscure journalist named Keith Murdoch broke the story on how inept British generals fought to the last Aussie. Mourning and outrage forged a nation, turning Englishmen down under into Australians.

Kemal Pasha went on to become Kemal Ataturk, the founder of modern Turkey after war's end. He did not have an easy start, having to fend off an attack by Greece, then overturning every vestige of Ottoman rule to forcibly modernize his country. The bad experiences of World War I were enough to keep Turkey from allying with anyone in World War II.

Gallipoli also destroyed reputations. Kitchener's expertise was no longer unquestioned. Fisher was retired. Hamilton was out of the army, becoming a principled pacifist. And Churchill left government to do his penance in the trenches of Flanders for six months, serving as a reservist major in his home regiment. Churchill's name became synonymous with failure.

Churchill reentered the cabinet later in the Great War as Minister of Munitions, eventually heading the Colonial Office and even the Treasury. Yet the Dardanelles hung around his neck like a dead albatross, lending a stink to his political career. This single failure followed him around like an unwanted shadow, undermining his credibility, mocking his later successes. "Searching my heart, I cannot regret the effort. It was good to go as far as we did. Not to persevere—that was the crime," Churchill said, looking back. He was not able to exorcise the Gallipoli demon until 1940, when he became prime minister at last and rallied his nation to face Germany—again.

DECISION BY INDECISION

The Battle of Jutland, 1916

BY ROLAND J. GREEN

When I am without orders and unexpected occurrences arrive I shall always act as I think the honour and glory of my King and Country demand. But in case signals can neither be seen or perfectly understood, no captain can do very wrong if he places his ship alongside that of the enemy.

—Horatio Nelson, 1758–1805

The keel of the Battle of Jutland was laid almost a generation before the battle was fought. Its principal cause was the decision of Imperial Germany to build a navy large enough to rival Britain's.

This unwise decision had several fathers. One was Kaiser Wilhelm II, who had more faults than virtues but was also the supreme autocrat. When he wanted a navy, he got one. His principal naval adviser, Admiral von Tirpitz, had strategic plans for a larger German navy. Finally, German heavy industry supported the idea, to create larger domestic markets.

Tirpitz's basic strategic concept went by the name of the Riskflotte (Risk Fleet). The idea was that if a major naval power (say, Britain) fought a naval war with an inferior coalition (say, France and Russia), they would probably win. But they might be so weakened that a Germany with a substantial (not necessarily superior) fleet might be able to exact colonial concessions. And colonies were a big part of Germany's drive for a place in the sun.

The Riskflotte strategy made very little sense at the time and none whatever for most of the century since it became a major factor in causing World War I. It was the kind of strategy that depends on one's opponent either being too obtuse to see what fate is being planned for him or lacking the resources to respond to it.

The British were neither obtuse nor weak. They cleared their diplomatic flanks by making alliances with Japan (1902), France (1904), and Russia (1907). They also turned the world's largest and most efficient shipbuilding industry to producing a fleet of unprecedented size, including the new all-big-gun battleships of the dreadnought type.

The British also played a purely strategic card. The German war plans included attacking British squadrons off the German coast with mines, submarines, and their fast (but short-range) torpedo craft. Attrition would reduce the British fleet until the Germans could sail out at their chosen moment and meet it on comparatively favorable terms.

What sank this strategy was the German assumption that the British would play into their hands. Instead, in 1911, the British abandoned their traditional "close blockade" to revive an even older strategy, the "distant blockade." British squadrons would now wait in North Sea and English Channel ports until they learned the Germans were putting to sea. Then they would sortie at much closer to their full strength. Once at sea, the British would block the Germans at the channel and the northern end of the North

Sea—the German High Seas Fleet's only two routes to the open ocean from which it so grandly took its name.

War came in 1914. The British rounded up the German overseas squadrons and raiders. German U-boats and mines drew blood from the British, and the British replied in kind.

Both sides raided each other's coastal waters, and the German battle cruisers bombarded British coastal towns. The British battle cruisers caught them at it in the Battle of Dogger Bank in 1915. The Germans came off the worse but learned important technical lessons.

Each fleet sortied at times, for training and in the hope of bringing a portion of the other fleet to battle with their own full strength. Nothing happened except near misses. North Sea visibility was too uncertain, and the art of coordinating the movements of dozens of ships by wireless was a work in progress.

The British did gain some real advantages. New battleships (some armed with 15-inch guns) increased their superiority. Their submarines penetrated into the Baltic Sea, forcing the Germans to look over their shoulders at their Baltic trade routes. Codebooks that the Russians recovered from a sunken German cruiser let the British organize a code-breaking office called Room 40 to read the High Seas Fleet's mail.

Finally, the British had the edge in leadership. The Germans had the superb Franz von Hipper leading their battle cruisers, but the High Seas Fleet had one timid commander and one who was dying of cancer. They finally got something like what they needed in Reinhard Scheer, in early 1916.

By then, however, Sir John Jellicoe had methodically (the only way he knew) polished the Grand Fleet into a formidably trained and disciplined fighting force. His battle cruiser leader, Sir David

Beatty, was more swashbuckling than systematic, but his charisma and aggressiveness were morale boosters.

In the spring of 1916, Scheer planned another battle cruiser raid to the north, but this time the whole High Seas Fleet would be just out of sight behind Hipper. And Zeppelins and U-boats would be deployed across the path of the Grand Fleet, to give warning and possibly even inflict a few casualties on them.

The stage was set, the players were costumed and made up, and the curtain was about to rise on the largest naval battle of World War I.

Bad Luck

Scheer began with bad luck that delayed curtain time. One of Hipper's battle cruisers was in dockyard hands, and neither admiral wanted to lose her gun power. By the time she rejoined the fleet, the picket submarines were running short of fuel and had to come home. Poor visibility in the North Sea also kept the zeppelins virtually blind.

Better luck came with a bit of electronic deception, having a wireless station in Wilhelmshaven use the call sign of Scheer's flagship. So Room 40's code-breakers assured Jellicoe that the High Seas Fleet was still in port, as he ordered the Grand Fleet to sea to foil another of Hipper's raids.

The scouting forces clashed first on May 31, as the British opened fire on German ships inspecting a neutral merchant vessel. The battle cruisers steamed to the support of their scouts, and a running fight ensued, with Hipper heading south with five ships to lure an eager Beatty into range of the High Seas Fleet.

Beatty was a little too eager, as it happened. He had, in addition to his battle cruisers, four battleships of the *Queen Elizabeth* class, with eight 15-inch guns and a speed of twenty-four knots, assigned to him while a squadron of his own battle cruisers was detached for gunnery practice. They would have given Beatty a crushing superiority from the first broadside. But he left them behind to catch up as best they could while he charged off after Hipper, determined not to let him get away again.

As it was, in half an hour Beatty was down to four ships against five. Two of his battle cruisers blew up and sank with nearly all hands. Beatty's flagship, *Lion,* would have gone the same way if the dying turret officer hadn't given the order to flood the magazine.

Beatty's comment on these losses was, "There seems to be something wrong with our bloody ships today." The British battle cruisers were in fact too lightly armored for heavy-gun duels and, worse, flash protection to their magazines was poor. A bursting enemy shell could ignite a powder charge and pass flames down to the magazine. The Germans had encountered that problem and fixed it earlier in the war, and they also had better range-finders and, for the moment, better visibility.

But Beatty's battle squadron was now catching up and starting to hit the Germans. Not long after, a British cruiser saw the southern horizon sprouting the masts and funnels of the whole High Seas Fleet. The cruiser reported this unwelcome development and turned north.

So did Beatty. Now it was his turn to lead Hipper into the jaws of the approaching Grand Fleet. He started off on the wrong foot, ordering his line to turn in succession. By the time the last battleship turned, the German van was in range. The Queen Elizabeths took a pounding, but their heavier armor saved them from fatal damage, and their heavier guns gave as good as they got. Only *Warspite* had to leave the line and go home early.

The two main fleets both suspected that they were about to clash, but they approached each other in some confusion. (The

British seaplane carrier *Engadine* had launched her plane, the first one to ever take part in a fleet action, but it had to land with a broken oil pipe and saw nothing.) As Beatty steered toward where he thought Jellicoe's rear would be, Beatty's orphan squadron appeared, charging Hipper's battle cruisers. They fatally damaged his flagship and the light cruiser *Wiesbaden* but lost one of their own to yet another magazine explosion.

To further compound the confusion, a squadron of British armored cruisers (obsolete ships, with no place in this joust of dreadnoughts, and under an admiral with more zeal than sense) appeared. To finish off *Wiesbaden,* they charged Hipper's battle cruisers, masking Beatty's guns with their funnel smoke. Hipper promptly sank one and crippled two others.

Amid all this, Sir John Jellicoe, on the bridge of his flagship, *Iron Duke,* remained admirably clearheaded. The Germans had to be close enough that it was time to deploy the Grand Fleet from its cruising formation of six four-ship columns to a single battle line. But how to deploy? With the port squadron leading or the starboard squadron?

Deploying to port meant more maneuvering room and less risk of torpedoes. It would also mean longer range—maybe too long, as mist, fading daylight, funnel smoke, and gun smoke stole visibility.

Deploying to starboard might run the weakest battleships of the Grand Fleet straight into a melee with Scheer's strong van. It might also bring the whole Grand Fleet into torpedo range.

Jellicoe probably never thought of himself as "the only man on either side who could lose the war in an afternoon" (as Winston Churchill described him). He wasn't that kind of egotist. But he did know that his first responsibility was to prevent a German victory, and only after that to seek another Trafalgar.

So the twenty-four dreadnoughts filed into a single line ahead—

and Scheer came out of the murk to find it crossing his T. Every British ship was positioned to fire and only a few German ones were able to reply.

The Germans had prudently developed a maneuver to deal with this situation. It was the "battle turn-away"—a simultaneous 180-degree turn by every ship in the battle line, reversing course and hopefully breaking contact with the enemy. The Germans were not blind to the disadvantages of being the weaker fleet.

Like well-drilled soldiers, the High Seas Fleet turned, while its destroyers launched a massed torpedo attack and steamed away. The British met that with a maneuver that they too had practiced—the whole line turning 90 degrees away from the enemy, "combing" the torpedoes. British lookouts sighted enough torpedoes passing too close for comfort, leaving no doubt that the turn was a wise move. Only one British dreadnought, *Marlborough,* was hit, and she was able to stay in line for several hours before leaving for home.

Some partisans of aggressive tactics by the Grand Fleet have suggested that Jellicoe should have turned 90 degrees toward the Germans. This might have brought on a close-range melee, believed by some to guarantee British victory. Jellicoe did not share that belief. Less maneuvering room, friendly-fire incidents, even collisions—quite a list of unnecessary hazards. Above all, it risked reducing the weight of broadside that could bear on the enemy—and for Jellicoe, a gifted gunnery officer, that was the worst possible move in fleet tactics.

Jellicoe certainly had a sounder grip on the situation than Scheer did. Having led his fleet out of immediate danger, Scheer then reversed course and led it back almost the way it had come.

Scheer later said he wanted to resume the battle with his squadrons more favorably positioned, and in the process rescue *Wies-*

baden's crew His critics say he wanted to work around Jellicoe's rear and break for home. Each statement probably contains part of the truth.

What actually happened was Scheer's worst nightmare—the entire Grand Fleet across his path again, and every British ship that even thought it had a target firing as fast as it could. It was the greatest array of heavy naval guns ever to see action. Even German steelmaker Krupp's best armor could not survive such a beating for long.

Some German ships would not have lasted even this long if the fuses in British armor-piercing shells had not been too sensitive. They detonated the shells on contact with heavy armor, producing spectacular fireworks displays but less damage than if they had delayed a moment, allowing the shell to penetrate deep into its target and produce the lethal detonation of an exploding magazine. Hypersensitive British fuses probably saved six or eight German capital ships on the day of Jutland—more than all the other British defects put together.

Scheer did the only thing possible—he ordered another battle turn-away. He also ordered the four German battle cruisers that could still steam to charge the British line without regard for the consequences—even ram, if necessary. By some miracle the battle cruisers survived this "death-ride" and rejoined the rest of the High Seas Fleet, now unequivocally heading for home.

At the height of the uproar, the British *Colossus* took two hits for five casualties. That was all the damage Scheer did to Jellicoe's battle line, which sent several of the latest German dreadnoughts home in need of major repairs.

As the two fleets drew apart, Beatty in the British rear had a clear enough view of the Germans to inflict some damage on the old and slow pre-dreadnoughts in the German rear. He also sent a suggestion to Jellicoe that if the lead squadrons of battleships followed the battle cruisers, he could cut off the whole High Seas Fleet from home.

Vainglory? Trying to compensate for his errors during the day? Or simply a better idea of where the Germans might be going? Regardless, Jellicoe was having none of it. He did not wish to risk a night action (for which he knew the Germans were better trained) with a divided fleet. His goal was to put the united Grand Fleet where it could block the High Seas Fleet's passage through the Frisian Islands into safe coastal waters.

In fact, Room 40 already knew where the Germans were going—the Horns' Reef Passage, which Wilhelmshaven had already ordered swept for mines. The Admiralty had already ordered a destroyer-minelayer to undo that work. But when Jellicoe received the message, he remembered the day's surprises and he was skeptical about Room 40's ability to keep track of the High Seas Fleet.

So the two fleets, literally in the dark, missed a second bout. The British steamed south. The Germans curved around the tail of the British line.

Several British capital ships had clear sightings of German ones but withheld their fire, having no permission from fleet or squadron commanders. The Germans were more flexible and had better luck. One of their cruisers caught a British ship passing the night recognition signal to another with a disabled wireless. So when the crippled British armored cruiser *Black Prince* steamed out of the darkness and flashed the signal to a German battle squadron, they opened fire and blew her out of the water.

No recognition signals were needed when the High Seas Fleet blundered across the destroyers and cruisers at the tail of the British line. That was a melee indeed, fought at sailing ship or even galley ranges. The British lost five destroyers and a sixth rammed a German battleship and came away with twenty feet of the German's bow plating perched on her own mangled forecastle.

The Germans had two light cruisers torpedoed, and another rammed by a "friendly" battleship and afterward scuttled. Just as dawn was breaking, British destroyers torpedoed the pre-dreadnought *Pommern* and an exploding magazine sent her down with all hands. The British drew the last blood by mining the battleship *Ostfriesland,* while the last ship to sink was the damaged armored cruiser *Warrior,* being towed home by that harbinger of navies to come, the seaplane carrier *Engadine.*

The Strategic View

"And what good came of it at last?" to borrow from Robert Southey on the Battle of Blenheim.

The debate on that topic has spilled enough ink to float a small dreadnought, and used up enough paper to keep her records for twenty years. The British Admiralty accidentally started the brawl by admitting all their losses (three battle cruisers, three armored cruisers, eight destroyers), and they could not pretend that the Germans had lost more than one battle cruiser, one pre-dreadnought, four light cruisers, and five destroyers.

This did not look like a Trafalgar. In fact, it smelled like defeat. And British dead were more than twice the German—6,000 versus 2,500. The Germans were and are proud of the way their fleet stood up to the superior British and gave about as good as it got.

"Stand up to" is, however, not the same thing as "defeat." Two days after Jutland, the British could have sent to sea thirty-two battle-worthy dreadnoughts. The Germans might have managed fourteen. They had no hope of even breaking the British blockade, let alone imposing their own on Britain—and victory would require at least one of those actions.

They did try, beginning in 1917, going back to unrestricted submarine warfare at the urging of Scheer, now head of the German navy while Hipper led the High Seas Fleet. It nearly worked. But the United States joined the Allies, the convoy system broke the U-boats, and the AEF landed in France.

Beatty, like Hipper, succeeded to command of his fleet. He was more conservative than expected, not calling for any "wild charge of the battle squadrons," in the words of Arthur Marder. He also threw his weight behind improved fuses, which he got by 1918.

Early in November 1918, the German fleet mutinied, the sailors fearing that they were being sent to sea on a suicide mission. The armistice came. Later that month, the High Seas Fleet went to sea again—to steam into Scapa Flow and haul down its flags. And in June 1919, the Germans scuttled it there.

The High Seas Fleet had gone to that limbo of defeated fleets, and Jutland began its passage there.

THE ODDLY ANACHRONISTIC VOYAGE OF *ADMIRAL GRAF SPEE*

November 1939

BY DOUGLAS NILES

> *The study of history lies at the foundation of all sound military conclusions and practice.*
>
> —Alfred Thayer Mahan, *The Influence of Sea Power Upon History, 1660–1783*

It would become the first major action between surface ships of World War II, yet in a way the mission of *Admiral Graf Spee* and her climactic battle seemed to belong to an earlier age. The accomplishments of the raider, and the final outcome of her mission, were all decided by naval gunnery, not airplanes or even torpedoes. The raider's victims had been taken with almost gentlemanly rules of engagement. Her captain was known even to his enemies as a brave and honorable man who resolved his battles with remarkably little bloodshed. And the ultimate fate of the fast, modern ship was determined as a result of diplomatic niceties and the captain's decision to avoid further casualties, rather than a duel to the death on the open sea.

Perhaps it had something to do with Captain Hans Langsdorff being present at the Battle of Jutland, the only major naval engagement of World War I. That fight, in the North Sea off the coast of Denmark, resulted in a draw; the main outcome was the German high command's realization that the Kaiser's fleet did not stand a chance of surviving in a straight-up battle against the Royal Navy. After Jutland, the German battleships spent the rest of the Great War sheltering in their well-fortified anchorage.

After capitulation at the end of World War I and the signing of the Treaty of Versailles, the entire German battle fleet was surrendered to the Allies. The British took some of the ships to their base at Scapa Flow, north of Scotland, where they scuttled most of them. Even then the sunken fleet proved useful. The sunken hulks of the German ships would serve as breakwaters and anti-submarine bulwarks for the harbor during World War II. One captive dreadnought would go to the United States, where in 1921 it would be bombed and sunk by the revolutionary aviator General Billy Mitchell in his controversial attempts to prove that warships could indeed be sunk from the air.

That same treaty of Versailles, which ended World War I and exacted harsh vengeance against Germany, as part of its provisions prohibited the Teutonic nation from building battleships or any warships greater than ten thousand tons displacement. With typical German tenacity the nation set about building modern vessels within the limitations of the treaty (which would be honored until the start of the Nazi era, in 1933). One innovative type of vessel, specifically designed to compensate for the weight restriction, was termed the Panzerschiffe—literally, "armored ship." Three of these vessels would ultimately be built: *Admiral Graf Spee, Deutschland* (later renamed *Lützow*), and *Admiral Scheer.* Equipped with batteries of 11-inch guns, these warships packed more punch than any heavy cruiser, though they lacked the armored protection of a true battleship. They would become popularly known as "pocket battleships."

While the pocket battleships in reality did exceed the treaty limit of ten thousand tons, they displaced only 10 percent or so more than that mark. Several innovations, including a hull of welded steel plates instead of overlapping plates held together by rivets and a revolutionary array of eight linked diesel engines, provided the ships with good performance and protection while still keeping the overall weight under control. *Graf Spee,* in particular, was technically advanced in another way as well: she was the first German warship to be equipped with radar, an advantage she would employ to great effect during her famous combat voyage.

The Panzerschiffe were some of the very few German military projects of the interwar yet pre-Nazi years; *Graf Spee*'s hull was laid down even before Adolf Hitler and his fascist party came to power. Launched in 1934 and commissioned in 1936, *Admiral Graf Spee* was named after the German nautical hero of World War I who had commanded a flotilla of raiders until its destruction, and his death, in a battle near the Falkland Islands. The admiral's namesake pocket battleship served as the flagship of the Kriegsmarine (German navy) until 1938. During the Spanish Civil War she took part in patrols off the Iberian Peninsula. Near the end of 1938, Captain Langsdorff took over command of the ship. He continued training her crew and making ready for war.

The War Begins

In August 1939, barely ten days before the Nazi invasion of Poland initiated World War II in Europe, the pocket battleship left the port of Wilhemshaven, on the narrow North Sea coast of Germany, and headed north. She was accompanied by the tanker *Altmark,* which carried extra fuel and spare ammunition for *Graf Spee*'s powerful batteries. The *Graf Spee*'s orders were to raid commerce in the South Atlantic after the outbreak of hostilities.

Graf Spee's course took her northward along the Norwegian coast, then west around the Faeroe Islands. From there she hooked west and south into the North Atlantic Ocean, avoiding discovery and steaming steadily south, crossing the equator a week or so after the war began on September 1, 1939. As soon as Britain declared war, and clearly remembering the nation's critical and costly hesitation during World War I, the British implemented a convoy system for their heavy merchant shipping traffic in the North Atlantic. The sparser volume in the South Atlantic, however, was not compelled to sail in protected convoys.

For several weeks *Graf Spee* steamed back and forth in the South Atlantic, still avoiding discovery by the Allies. On September 26, Langsdorff finally received orders to commence his combat mission, and he wasted no time in going to work. On September 30, *Graf Spee* encountered the British flagged merchant ship *Clement* very near to Pernambuco, Brazil (the easternmost point of the South American continent). This 5,000-ton vessel was transporting kerosene from New York to Brazil. The merchantman's crew was allowed to take to their lifeboats before their ship was sunk by the pocket battleship's guns; the Germans then broadcast the position of *Clement*'s lifeboats as *Graf Spee* changed course and churned eastward, toward Africa.

The German raider took her second prize less than a week later, on the other side of the ocean: on October 5 she captured the *Newton Beach,* which was 4,700 tons and laden with a cargo of grain. The merchant ship was taken over by a German prize crew and still accompanied *Graf Spee* several days later as, on October 7, the *Ashlea* (4,200 tons, with a cargo of sugar) was sunk. The crews from both ships were held as prisoners on the *Newton Beach,* then transferred to the pocket battleship when the *Newton Beach* was sunk on October 8.

Still operating in waters off the west coast of Africa, *Graf Spee* took captive an 8,200-ton liner, *Huntsman,* with a cargo of precious tea, on October 10. The Germans used that liner's radio to broadcast a message reporting a false location, claiming the ship had been attacked by a U-boat. In the meantime, the imprisoned crewmen from the last three prizes were placed aboard *Huntsman,* which trailed behind the raider for another week. On October 17, *Graf Spee* rendezvoused with *Altmark,* taking on supplies and transferring the prisoners to the German tanker. After the transfer, *Huntsman* was sunk.

On October 22, *Trevanion,* 5,300 tons and transporting ore, was accosted, her bridge machine-gunned when she tried to broadcast a distress message. The warning was effective and, surprisingly enough, nonlethal. Again the crew was allowed to take to the lifeboats. The pocket battleship, after sinking five English ships, had not killed or even badly injured a single British seaman!

For most of a month, the raider had been working back and forth in the same stretch of ocean, the part of the South Atlantic below the bulge of Africa. Now Langsdorff decided to change his pattern; he steamed southward, then veered east to pass around the Cape of Good Hope. The whereabouts of the *Graf Spee* would remain unknown to the Allies for the next three weeks.

But that was not for lack of effort on the Allies' part. The activities of *Graf Spee* had mobilized a large contingent of British and French naval power, as a series of task groups were dispatched from many ports and ordered to find the German raider wherever she was preparing to strike next. Though both Allied nations possessed fleets of battleships far in excess of anything the

Kriegsmarine could put to sea, most of those vessels dated back to World War I and simply did not have the combination of speed, guns, and armor that would allow them to catch and fight the German pocket battleship. Thus the Allies employed small forces of their most modern vessels to make up these hunting groups, which quickly encompassed the length and breadth of the Atlantic Ocean, except for the far northern waters.

Force L

From mainland France came Force L, with the powerful modern battle cruiser *Dunkerque* as flagship, accompanied by three modern cruisers and a light aircraft carrier. For a time, Force L was also augmented by the British battle cruiser *Repulse* and the Royal Navy aircraft carrier *Furious*. Force L concentrated its search in the North Atlantic, remaining to the west of the European continent. From their base at Dakar in West Africa the French also mustered Force Y, under the flag of the speedy *Strasbourg* (sister ship of *Dunkerque*) and accompanied by the cruiser *Neptune*. Force Y would patrol the waters off the South American coast, generally north of Brazil.

Into the central Atlantic the Allies sent Force X, the aircraft carrier *Hermes* accompanied by several French cruisers. British cruisers *Berwick* and *York* comprised Force F, patrolling in Caribbean and central Atlantic waters, while the powerful Force K, with the fast battle cruiser *Renown* and aircraft carrier *Ark Royal,* steamed for the South Atlantic waters where *Graf Spee* had claimed her October victims.

The far South Atlantic would be the province of two cruiser groups: Force H, based out of Cape Town, including *Sussex* and *Shropshire;* and Force G, coming north from the Falkland Islands, organized around the heavy cruiser *Exeter,* accompanied by three other cruisers. By late October, all of these forces were actively searching the Atlantic, in patterns designed to scour just about every square mile of that vast body of water.

But Captain Langsdorff had thrown the Allies a nasty curveball. On November 15 and 16 *Graf Spee* struck again, sinking *Africa Shell* and capturing *Mapia*—in the Indian Ocean! Having passed around the cape, the German raider had angled north almost as far as the island of Madagascar and took these two ships in the Mozambique Channel between the island and the African mainland. Immediately after these two actions, the pocket battleship reversed course again, passing the southern tip of Africa even closer to the Cape of Good Hope than before and steaming her way rapidly into the South Atlantic.

Once again she started in on the merchant shipping off the southwest coast of Africa. On December 2 she sank *Doric Star* and on December 3 *Tairoa*—both ships closer to the African mainland than any of her previous victims. *Doric Star* was a converted Blue Star liner of more than ten thousand tons, carrying meat and dairy products; her crew managed to get off a distress call and then sabotage the engines before the Germans came aboard. *Tairoa*, eight thousand tons and full of a cargo of meat and wool, also sent a distress message before going down. Once again, Langsdorff captured and sank his prizes without inflicting any fatalities upon the crews.

From here the pocket battleship turned to the west, steaming quickly across the South Atlantic, approaching South America again. Her final prize was the 4,000-ton steamer *Streonshalh,* with a cargo of wheat, sunk on December 7, 1939. After this attack the raider met her supply ship again, taking on fuel and ammunition and transferring more captured British seamen to *Altmark,* which had been waiting far to the south, outside the purview of any of the Allied searching forces.

Graf Spee continued on a heading of west by south, closing on the mainland near the wide estuary of the Río de la Plata, or River Plate, the broad river that flows between Argentina and Uruguay. Here, finally, the German pocket battleship ran into enemy warships. The cruisers of Force G, under the command of Commodore Henry Harwood, now included one heavy—the *Exeter*—and two light cruisers, the *Achilles* and *Ajax*. Having steamed north from its Falkland Island base, the force had been patrolling off the mouth of the Plate. On December 13, British lookouts spotted the raider approaching from the east.

The fight would inherently be uneven, with the Royal Navy ships at a considerable disadvantage. The heaviest guns aboard *Exeter* were a mere 8 inches in bore, while the light cruisers were armed with only 6-inch guns. Countering these, *Graf Spee* had multiple batteries of long-range, powerful 11-inch guns. Knowing he was outgunned, Harwood divided his force and closed in for the attack, with *Exeter* steaming straight ahead while the two light cruisers cut to starboard in an attempt to bracket the raider between their fires.

Although *Graf Spee*'s big guns outranged the British cruisers by close to ten thousand yards, Langsdorff declined the chance to fight a long-range battle and instead set course to close with Force G. This would turn out to be a crucial error. The cruisers maneuvered violently, with the bigger *Exeter* veering along a separate track from *Ajax* and *Achilles,* a tactic that made it difficult for the German ship to concentrate her fire on any one target. As a result, she went after the heavy cruiser first, while the two lighter British ships sped close enough to use their 6-inch guns. The four ships exchanged fire for more than an hour, with most of the meaningful hits being scored by the raider. After eighty minutes of sustained gunnery, *Exeter* had been knocked out of action: all of her main batteries were disabled, and she was on fire from stem to stern. Both *Ajax* and *Achilles* had been pounded to the point where many of their guns were useless, and the latter ship had trouble making speed.

Yet the Royal Navy guns had also inflicted serious damage. Early in the fight one of *Exeter*'s 8-inch shells punctured the raider's engine room, destroying a key component—a filtering system that was necessary to prepare the *Spee*'s fuel for her sensitive diesel engines. The pocket battleship had enough fuel for about sixteen hours of operation, but the filtration system would need to be repaired, in port, before it could again be made operational so that the raider could burn the rest of the unfiltered fuel in her tanks.

Exeter limped away from the fight, burning and barely afloat, and would eventually make the Falklands for repairs. Meanwhile, the light cruisers continued to harass the bigger ship. Langsdorff was particularly worried about a torpedo attack, and he knew his limited fuel supply would be a crucial liability, so he opted to make for the port of Montevideo, in neutral Uruguay. He reached that harbor at midnight, December 13–14. There he hoped to put ashore his wounded and quickly make the necessary repairs.

Victory

The surprised and relieved British sailors in the two light cruisers cautiously followed the pocket battleship almost to the boundary of Uruguayan territorial waters. There they halted, and Commodore Harwood radioed for reinforcements. *Cumberland,* another heavy cruiser that had recently been detached from Force G, arrived shortly. But the rest of the Royal Navy's anti-raider groups remained a considerable distance away.

The Uruguayans, anxious to maintain their neutrality, insisted that the raider could remain in port for only seventy-two hours. Langsdorff planned to comply. Immediately upon docking he released the sixty or so prisoners he'd carried on board, men who had been crewing some of the merchant ships that had fallen to the raider. The German captain, who spoke English well and even shared books in that language with his captives, was universally praised by the men who had lost their ships to his guns. He had, after all, managed the surprisingly humane accomplishment of sinking nine British ships without causing the death of a single merchant crewman. Captain Patrick Dove, of *Africa Shell,* had actually become friends with Langsdorff and would soon write a book about his capture and his time as a prisoner on *Graf Spee.*

The British foreign service pressured the Uruguayans to intern the raider, on the grounds that she was still seaworthy. British naval observers scrutinized the ship from shore, reporting on damage to several turrets and other visible features. They did not suspect the nature of the ship's most serious problem, which lay in the engine room.

But the Brits also practiced some deception of their own. The British consul put out word in the city, very publicly, that a large force of Royal Navy capital ships, including battleships and aircraft carriers, was gathering just over the horizon. Diplomatic niceties came into play, as well, as the Uruguayans wanted the Germans to leave, but restrictions of the Hague convention required that a raider in a neutral port could not leave port for twenty-four hours after the departure of an enemy merchant vessel—that is, any potential target for the raider. The British pushed their ships out of the harbor very gradually, about one a day, all the while clamoring for the Uruguayans to intern *Graf Spee* or else face a challenge to their coveted neutrality.

On December 15 the three dozen slain crewmen of the pocket

battleship were buried in Montevideo's German cemetery. The funeral was notable mostly for the fact that Captain Langsdorff offered the traditional naval salute to the fallen, rather than the familiar Nazi "Heil Hitler!" This was politically risky and a sign of the great prestige the captain and his old-fashioned values had. It is perhaps an additional tribute to the captain's humanity that a number of officers from the ships he'd sunk also attended the funeral.

On the evening of December 17, after a little more than seventy-two hours in the neutral port, *Graf Spee* raised her colors and began to steam down the River Plate toward the ocean. Many observers gathered along the shore to watch her departure, perhaps hoping for a front-row seat to an inevitable naval battle. They were to be disappointed.

In the end, it was Langsdorff's most un-Nazi-like humanity that resulted in his defeat. He'd fallen for the British ruse and believed that *Graf Spee* was going to be massively outgunned when she again sailed into international waters. So the captain had quietly transferred most of his crew to a German merchant vessel in the harbor at Montevideo. With just enough men aboard to operate the engines and steer the ship, he took his raider out of the harbor and into the broad, placid waters of the River Plate.

There the German crew blew up *Graf Spee,* sending her right to the bottom—but in very shallow water. The advanced Seetakt radar system, among other technologies, had been partially destroyed, but the ship came to rest with much of the superstructure remaining above the surface. The sailors of the skeleton crew returned to Montevideo in their lifeboats, where they would be interned for the duration of the war. Several days later, Captain Langsdorff literally wrapped himself in a German flag and committed suicide with a pistol shot to the head; he is presumed to have taken this drastic action in order to prove that he had not ordered his ship scuttled out of any fear for his personal safety.

A final postscript to the voyage of *Admiral Graf Spee* would unfold in February 1940—appropriately enough, with another diplomatic incident. The faithful supply ship *Altmark,* having made a run back to the European mainland around the many British battle groups still patrolling in the Atlantic, was attempting to slip down the craggy Norwegian coast on her way back to Germany. A British destroyer, *Cossack,* chased the supply ship into a fjord. Despite protests from Germany and Norway—both of whom claimed that the ship was unarmed and carried no prisoners—Royal Navy sailors stormed aboard *Altmark* and rescued the prisoners. It was another small triumph for the Royal Navy, one that would have grave repercussions since it was one more argument for Hitler in making the case for an imminent invasion of that northern nation.

In the end, *Graf Spee* attained signal success as a raider and forced a significant mobilization of Allied naval power. Langsdorff was a skilled sailor and an admired captain, but he showed poor judgment and a rather startling lack of tenacity when it came to matching his powerful warship against British guns. If he had sailed back into the ocean from the River Plate, there is no reason to suspect that his raider could not have damaged *Cumberland* every bit as badly as she had mauled *Exeter;* and if he had stood off at a distance that allowed his 11-inch guns to hit at long range, he would have had little danger of suffering another disabling hit. Of course, it is hindsight that shows us there were no other significant Allied naval forces that could have interfered with his operations in the area. But Langsdorff proved himself to be a better man than he was a warrior, and the end of his ship, and his life, provided one small glimmer of hope in a British nation that would soon be reeling from a whole new host of disasters.

THIS IS NO DRILL!

Air Raid Taranto, November 11, 1940

BY WILLIAM TERDOSLAVICH

Never do an enemy a small injury.

—Niccolò Machiavelli

The plan was simple: launch strike aircraft off the deck of an aircraft carrier within two hundred miles of the enemy fleet anchored in port. Fly in low. Line up on the battleships. Release torpedoes to score sure hits. Then fly away.

Sounds familiar, but this is not Pearl Harbor.

The planes are not Japanese.

The battleships are not American.

This is the British air strike on the Italian fleet at Taranto, Italy. It took place more than a year before the Japanese tried the same approach in Hawaii. (And they got that bright idea from the Royal Navy.)

Taranto turned the world of naval warfare upside down. Airplanes could sink battleships during combat. And the Royal Navy continued its tradition of judicious risk-taking to bring the fight to the enemy.

All it took was a few hours to change the naval balance of power in the Mediterranean—for good.

Mare Nostrum

Italy claims the Roman Empire as part of its long history. The Romans once conquered every inch of the Mediterranean shoreline, allowing them to rechristen the middle sea as "Mare Nostrum"—Our Sea. Italian dictator Benito Mussolini conveniently "borrowed" this attitude to justify the rebirth of the Italian navy. It would be based on the battleship. Starting with four World War I–era dreadnoughts (*Caio Duilio, Andrea Doria, Giulio Cesare,* and *Conte di Cavour*), Mussolini added two more: *Vittorio Veneto* and *Littorio,* with a third ship of this class being built when Italy entered the war. This pace of construction taxed Italy's limited economy. But the payoff would be a trio of newer dreadnoughts, each packing nine 15-inch guns.

There would be no aircraft carriers. Instead the fleet would rely on the Italian air force for cover. In a way, this made sense. Italian land-based aircraft could pretty much cover the central Mediterranean. After defeating the British, the Italians would have a free hand running convoys to Libya. There, the Italian army prepared to invade British-held Egypt and eventually take the Suez Canal. Granted, this was a tad unrealistic, but Mussolini always dreamed big before acting small.

At war's start, the Royal Navy was clearly bigger than the Italian fleet. That size was commensurate with the global reach of the British Empire. Ships were posted around the world to protect far-flung interests, so there was no way to concentrate the entire fleet in home waters.

Only part of the fleet would be committed to the Mediterranean. The British naval base at Malta fell within range of Italian airpower, so basing there would be risky. That left Alexandria, Egypt, where the Royal Navy based its Mediterranean fleet: three battleships, one carrier, one heavy cruiser, five light cruisers, and twenty destroyers, all commanded by Admiral Sir Andrew Cunningham. Supplementing this was Force H at Gibraltar: one battleship, one battle cruiser, one aircraft carrier, two cruisers, and as many as seventeen destroyers under Admiral Sir James Somerville. The British had two weaker fleets in the Mediterranean, with a larger Italian fleet between them: six battleships, twenty-one cruisers, fifty destroyers, and more than a hundred submarines.

By the strength of numbers alone, Italy had the local advantage.

Lovers, Not Fighters

The war between the Royal Navy and the Regia Marina (the Italian navy, literally "royal navy," too) began with several whimpers instead of one good bang. In August 1940, Force H steamed out to support the transfer of the battleship *Valiant,* the aircraft carrier *Illustrious,* and two anti-aircraft cruisers to Alexandria. Tagging along was a merchant convoy carrying several hundred tanks for the British Eighth Army in Egypt. Prime Minister Winston Churchill wanted the armor to get there in a hurry instead of taking the long way around Africa.

Nearing Sicily on the night of September 1, Force H turned back to Gibraltar, leaving the *Illustrious* task force to rendezvous with the Mediterranean Fleet just south of Malta. On September 2, the Mediterranean Fleet received a spotting report that the Italian fleet was nearby, at roughly equal strength. Was it coming forth to do battle? No. It was going back to Taranto, located between the "heel" and "toe" along Italy's southern edge.

The same thing happened again in late September. Cunningham sailed the Mediterranean Fleet to Malta with reinforcements for its garrison, taking two battleships, a carrier, and a gaggle of escorts. Between Crete and Malta, the Italian Fleet was spotted by aerial reconnaissance—five battleships, eleven cruisers, and twenty-five destroyers, about a hundred miles to the northwest. And this overwhelming force was steaming away from the British. Cunningham assumed there would be no threat, so he pressed on to Malta to drop off the troops.

The Italians were not pressing their advantage.

This led to British scheming, of course. And the schemer was Rear Admiral Lumley Lyster, a member of Cunningham's staff. Recon flights out of Malta kept Taranto under constant surveillance, gathering information on the positions of barrage balloons and the presence of anti-torpedo nets, as well as keeping an eye on which ships were in port. Using this information, Lyster studied how to attack Taranto using carrier-based aircraft.

On November 10, one of those Malta-based recon flights struck gold. Pilot officer Adrian Warburton brought in his twin-engined Martin Maryland low and fast, buzzing Taranto harbor as Italian anti-aircraft guns opened up all around him. He counted all six Italian battleships in port. And he made it back to Malta alive to pass on the news. If a twin-engine Maryland could survive a low-level daylight romp over Taranto harbor, then the carrier *Illustrious*'s strike package should do just as well at night.

Cunningham had already postponed the mission once. He had hoped to strike on October 21—Trafalgar Day for the Royal Navy. But the *Illustrious* suffered a small fire and was unready for the mission. Now recent news showed all six Italian battleships in

Taranto. That made the mission worth doing the next night, November 11—Armistice Day. This might seem like a cruel joke, but this night mission needed moonlight. The date fit the bill.

The Mediterranean Fleet weighed anchor and steamed out of Alexandria harbor, headed north. Cunningham's force reached the waters west of Crete at dusk on the 11th. *Illustrious* was detached with her destroyer escort, now setting course westward toward Taranto.

Stabbed by Swordfish

The *Illustrious* packed an unlikely punch—twenty-one Fairey Swordfish. These were not like the sleek, all-metal monoplanes operated by Japanese or American navies. The Swordfish was an open-cockpit biplane with a crew of three, a top speed of around 140 mph, and a strike radius of 270 miles. In the Pacific, this obsolete plane would have been dead meat on the wing for any Wildcat or Zeke.

But a Swordfish could carry either bombs or its main weapon, the single aerial torpedo it could launch against a warship. The only weapon that could oppose the Swordfish was the anti-aircraft gun. Germany and Italy lacked aircraft carriers, so forget about a fighter combat air patrol (CAP) over the fleet that could beat away the attack. Thus British naval air strikes could not be opposed "in kind" by the enemy.

Britain had an operational monopoly on aircraft carriers and was playing this advantage to the hilt. *Illustrious* turned into the wind to launch at 9 P.M., sending up its first wave of Swordfish; a second wave followed about an hour later.

Lieutenant Commander Kenneth Williamson led the first flight of twelve Swordfish, half the planes carrying bombs and the other half torpedoes. Reaching Taranto at 11 P.M., the flight divided. The bombers peeled off and stayed high, circling to the south and east of Taranto harbor. Two of the Swordfish began dropping flares to illuminate the target, then began dropping bombs on the oil storage tanks on the shoreline. This drew the attention of searchlight crews and anti-aircraft guns, which ignored the next four bomb-laden Swordfish. Those planes began plinking at the cruisers and merchant ships at anchor.

Williamson brought his six Swordfish in from the west in two flights of three, thirty feet above the water. Anti-aircraft fire brought down Williamson's plane, but he did manage to release his torpedo, which ran straight and true toward the *Conte di Cavour,* slamming into the battleship's left side. Another plane in Williamson's flight managed to score a hit on *Littorio,* also on the ship's left side. The second three-plane flight also came in from the west, but on a more northerly track, banked around a balloon barrage, and lined up for their runs. One torpedo hit the *Littorio,* this time on her right side. The Swordfish then regrouped and headed back to *Illustrious.*

One hour later, Lieutenant Commander John Hale brought in his flight of nine Swordfish on the same flight path, following the same plan. Four bombers peeled off and stayed high—two dropping flares for illumination, then bombs for distraction on the same waterfront targets. Again, searchlights and anti-aircraft guns searched high for the current threat. Meanwhile, Hale came in low from the west. The *Littorio* suffered one more torpedo hit, while the *Caio Duilio* took her first torpedo hit. One Swordfish was lost, and the rest of the flight returned to *Illustrious.* With all planes recovered by 3 A.M., the carrier turned around and headed back to the embrace of the Mediterranean Fleet.

Once Bitten, Twice Shy

With just twenty-one aircraft firing eleven torpedoes, the Royal Navy whittled down Italy's battleship strength by half. *Conte di Cavour* never returned to service again. *Littorio* and *Caio Diulio* were both knocked out for at least six months. The need to match Italian battle strength was diminished, allowing the Royal Navy the freedom to reassign ships to the more vital North Atlantic.

About two weeks after Taranto, Force H sortied from Gibraltar, steaming toward a rendezvous point just south of Sardinia. The Mediterranean Fleet had also left Alexandria, escorting another convoy to Malta and also ready to detach the battleship *Ramillies* and the cruisers *Newcastle* and *Berwick* to the care of Admiral Somerville. As soon as the battleship and two cruisers joined up with Force H just south of Cape Spartivento, the Italian fleet was sighted: battleships *Vittorio Veneto* and *Giulio Cesare,* seven cruisers, and sixteen destroyers.

It could have been an even-money fight—*Ramillies* and the battle cruiser *Renown* against the two Italian dreadnoughts. But Somerville's Force H also had the aircraft carrier *Ark Royal.* Italian Admiral Inigo Campioni thought he would be pouncing on a British force half the size of his fleet, only to find an even-money fight, with the *Ark Royal* as the ace card up Somerville's sleeve. Campioni ordered his fleet to turn tail and run for port, with the British in hot pursuit. Two air strikes launched by *Ark Royal* failed to score hits. The remaining Italian battleships were not worth risking in a fight today, and so would live to fight another day.

Following Taranto, the Regia Marina redeployed its remaining warships to the west coast ports of Naples, La Spezia, and Genoa. The Italian fleet might have retreated for now, but that did not mean it was out of the fight for good.

The British would remain hard-pressed in the Mediterranean. There just weren't enough destroyers for escort duty. Force H and the Mediterranean Fleet would continue escorting convoys and swapping warships via the narrow passages between Sicily and Tunisia. Even the Luftwaffe would get into the act, stationing Fliegerkorps X in Sicily the following January to put the heat on British shipping.

Another battle was needed to settle the issue for good. Who would control the Mediterranean: Great Britain or Italy?

BRITISH DRAMA, ITALIAN COMEDY

Battle of Cape Matapan, March 1941

BY WILLIAM TERDOSLAVICH

It has been quoted that at a prewar diplomatic conference, the Nazi Foreign Minister Ribbentrop "sniffed" to Eden and Churchill that if there was another war, the Italians would be on Germany's side! To which Churchill supposedly replied, "That seems only fair, we had them last time!"

The Italian dream of Mare Nostrum was turning into a nightmare for Benito Mussolini. In November 1940, British aircraft damaged three battleships at Taranto, taking them out of the war when they were most needed. Later that winter, an Italian task force with two battleships turned tail and ran when faced with an equal British force at Cape Spartivento. It was now March 1941. The British were running convoys down the length of the Mediterranean and building up forces in Greece.

So who owned the Mediterranean? Certainly not Italy. And German dictator Adolf Hitler was getting fed up with his Italian ally. What good is a fleet if you don't use it?

Mussolini's prewar decision not to build an aircraft carrier was coming back to hobble his naval ambitions. Granted, the British carriers and their aircraft were not as good as those operated in the Pacific by the Americans and Japanese. But they gave the British enormous striking power against the Italian fleet, which had none. This problem could have been made up by closer cooperation between the Regia Marina and Regia Aeronautica. But the Italian air force believed in fighting its own war and ignored naval entreaties for air cover and strike missions against the Royal Navy.

Then there was the oil.

Italy began the war with a stockpile of 1.8 million tons of bunker fuel. Mussolini figured this would cover ten months of estimated naval operations. But after nine months of real war, Italy had already consumed a million tons of fuel. Mussolini ordered the remaining 800,000 tons to last another twenty months. While fascists like to believe willpower can overcome all obstacles, ships that lack fuel can go nowhere.

Despite all these handicaps, Hitler wanted Mussolini to do something. A Luftwaffe strike on the British fleet in the eastern Mediterranean had allegedly scored mission kills on two British battleships, rendering them useless for now. Would it be too much to ask for the Italian fleet to take control of the central Mediterranean?

A Bold Plan for a Timid Navy

Commander in chief of the Italian fleet Admiral Angelo Iachino began planning a fast sweep of the waters north and south of Crete to interdict the British reinforcement of Greece. The plan relied on six heavy cruisers, two light cruisers, and the battleship *Vittorio Veneto,* the only dreadnought fast enough to keep up with the thirty-knot speed of the task force. The dispersed ships left their berths at La Spezia, Taranto, Brindisi, and Messina, staging their rendezvous in the waters east of Sicily, bound for Crete. The Italians were counting on the Luftwaffe to show up overhead and fill in where the Regia Aeronautica would not. Instead, "air cover" came from a lone Royal Air Force (RAF) reconnaissance plane.

The spotting report quickly reached Admiral Sir Andrew Cunningham, chief of the Mediterranean Fleet. Being bloody-minded, he was spoiling for a fight. So he packed up his bags and his golf clubs and headed for shore that afternoon.

The ruse worked.

Alexandria was crawling with Italian spies, who duly noted the absence of the admiral while his battleships stayed in port. That night, Cunningham sneaked back to his flagship, the battleship *Warspite,* which would be accompanied by the dreadnoughts *Barham* and *Valiant.* According to the Luftwaffe, two of these three ships were supposed to be "out of action"—and the Italians were acting on this information. But the most important asset would be the aircraft carrier *Formidable*—its torpedo-packing planes gave Cunningham the ability to strike at 150 miles' range. This was far beyond the 15-mile range of his battleships' guns.

March 27 was going to see a lot of last-minute changes for both sides. Just as Cunningham's forces sortied that night, the Italians also enacted a change of plan in light of their radio intercept of the RAF sighting report. The sweep to the north of Crete was called off. The cruisers *Zara, Pola,* and *Fiume* were ordered to link up with the *Vittorio Veneto* task force and sweep the seas south of Crete.

Close to 7:30 A.M. the next day, the Italians spotted the British—the cruisers *Orion, Ajax, Gloucester,* and Australian cruiser *Perth.* The Italian cruisers were better—packing heavier guns with greater speed. The British were running away from a superior force. Perhaps the Italians would get in the first shot? Iachino ordered his ships to open fire at a range of thirteen miles. Give chase!

For the next forty-five minutes, the British were running while the Italians were gunning. Then discretion became the better part of Iachino's valor. He ordered the cruisers to return to *Vittorio Veneto*'s side. Commanding the British cruiser flotilla was Admiral Henry Pridham-Wippell, who was just as bloody-minded as Cunningham. Pridham-Wippell turned his force around and gave chase. This may seem reckless, given that the Italian cruisers were the better ships. But Pridham-Wippell understood the value of maintaining contact with the enemy. Lose him and you lose any chance of bringing the fight to him.

Pridham-Wippell's principled persistence paid off. At 11 A.M., *Orion* spotted *Vittorio Veneto*. But Pridham-Wippell's ships were in a bad position. The Italian cruiser force was to the south. The *Vittorio Veneto* was to the north—and opening fire with its nine 15-inch guns. Pridham-Wippell ordered his cruiser flotilla to turn around, make smoke, and run like hell back to Cunningham's fleet. There was no shame in this—the sighting of the Italian battleship was the prize. Swordfish biplanes from *Formidable* now struck at the Italian task force, scoring no hits.

The battle was still in its early stage.

Try Again!

Formidable was living up to its name. The ship launched a second air strike, reaching the Italians around 3:30 P.M. This attack coincided with one the RAF made using conventional bombers. Dropping their loads from on high at a moving target, the RAF scored no hits, while Italian anti-aircraft gunners banged away at the bombers, also scoring no hits. With Italian attention focused on the sky, the *Formidable*'s Swordfish flew in low, barely above the waves.

The *Vittorio Veneto* turned away from the Swordfish. The escorting cruisers leveled their anti-aircraft guns to pour lead on the British. Lead pilot Lieutenant Commander John Dalyell-Stead pressed his attack, letting loose his torpedo at the *Vittorio Veneto* just before his plane was shot down. The fish ran true, hitting the battleship on her left side and punching a hole in the hull. The *Vittorio Veneto* came to a halt, taking on water. Damage control brought the ship back to speed, at first making ten knots, then twenty. It might be enough to outrun Cunningham, whose battleships were only sixty-five miles away and closing.

Formidable was not giving up so easily. At 6:30 P.M., about a half hour after sunset, eight of her aircraft, plus two more from Crete, bore down on the Italian task force. Searchlights dazzled the pilots. Anti-aircraft fire forced them to break formation and take evasive action. That did not stop the pilots from pressing home their attacks individually. A single hit was scored against an Italian warship.

But which one?

Cunningham could break off the action or pursue. His staff offered the counsel of their fears. Going west of Cape Matapan—the southwesternmost feature of the Greek mainland—would bring the Mediterranean Fleet within range of the Italian bombers based on their mainland. Cunningham let his temper show. In *War at Sea: A Naval History of World War II,* Nathan Miller reports him as responding: "You are a pack of yellow-livered skunks! I'll go and have my supper now and see after supper if my morale isn't higher than yours!"

Carpe Noctem

As angry as he was, Cunningham was not being reckless. The night was young. The Italian bombers were not going to fly after dark. That afforded the British one more opportunity to strike. Cunningham was now reaching for his guns.

The latest battle report indicated one Italian ship hit—it had to be the *Vittorio Veneto. Formidable*'s pilots would go after the biggest ship first. And some of Cunningham's ships had radar, which the Italians did not. The advantage in any night action would go to the British, who would "see" first and definitely get in the first shot.

It was sometime past 10 P.M. when the cruiser *Ajax* picked up a blip on its radar screen: ship ahead, dead in the water. Three more blips then showed up on the screen: two large ships and a smaller one escorting. Cunningham ordered *Formidable* to retreat—an aircraft carrier was useless in a gunfight. *Warspite, Barham,* and *Valiant* steamed ahead, screened by the cruisers and destroyers of the task force. At around 10:30 P.M., the destroyer *Greyhound* illuminated the Italian ships with its searchlight. The British battleships opened fire at four thousand yards, which is about point-blank range for a 15-inch main gun. They couldn't miss, and they poured it on.

"One saw whole turrets and masses of other heavy debris whirling through the air and splashing into the sea and in short time the ships themselves were nothing but glowing torches on fire from stem to stern," Cunningham recalled. Only this was not the *Vittorio Veneto* he was describing. It was the cruiser *Fiume,* which along with her sister ships *Zara* and *Pola* became targets for the trio of British battleships. The one-sided gunfight was over in just four and a half minutes. The Italians never fired a shot in reply.

But what happened to the *Vittorio Veneto*?

Cruising to Defeat

When the British staged their last air strike on May 28, they did it within sight of the prize, the *Vittorio Veneto.* Anti-aircraft fire and searchlights disrupted the strike. One British pilot pressed his attack and hit the cruiser *Pola.* In the confusion of battle, however, the stricken target was not identified as a cruiser. On the Italian side, Iachino did not know the *Pola* was hit, either. It was not until 8 P.M.—roughly ninety minutes after the air attack—that he knew the *Pola* was damaged and dead in the water. Iachino detached *Zara* and *Fiume,* along with three destroyers, to render aid to the stricken *Pola.* As the British cruisers were the only enemy warships sighted, the detached cruiser/destroyer force would have been enough to handle them. Sadly, it was the Italian cruisers that became the rubber ducks in the shooting gallery, several hours later. By this time, *Vittorio Veneto* was forty-five miles away from the action. The damaged battleship eventually made port while the British searched for it in vain.

Analyzing the after-action reports, the Italians realized that the British could engage their forces at night, beyond a visual range shortened by darkness. That could only mean the British had radar, which the Italians lacked. The multiple air strikes suffered by the Italian fleet also pointed out the obvious need for an aircraft carrier. Mussolini ordered one up, but again the fascist fetish for willpower overcoming all odds ran into the paucity of Italian shipbuilding capacity. Italy had strained mightily just to double the size of its battleship force before the war started and was not even finished with the job when Mussolini had impulsively declared war on France and the United Kingdom in June 1940. Where was this aircraft carrier supposed to come from? An ocean liner was tapped for conversion, but the refit was not even close to being done by late 1943, when Italy dropped out of the war.

Cunningham missed out on bagging the *Vittorio Veneto*. The Mediterranean Fleet shared that disappointment. Somehow sinking three cruisers and two destroyers wasn't much of a consolation prize. Yet the victory here was strategic, not tactical. The Italian fleet would never again be a worry for the Royal Navy. Yes, the Luftwaffe, the Kriegsmarine, and even Italian naval commandos would all inflict further losses on the British fleet. Britain would make good those losses. The Italians had no hope of replacing theirs.

WHEN A SHORT WAR TURNS LONG

The Life and Death of the Imperial Japanese Navy's Air Service, 1941–1945

BY ROLAND J. GREEN

A gigantic fleet . . . has massed in Pearl Harbor. This fleet will be utterly crushed with one blow at the very beginning of hostilities. . . . Heaven will bear witness to the righteousness of our struggle.

—Rear Admiral Seiichi Ito, 1890–1945,
Chief of Staff of the Combined Fleet, Imperial Japanese Navy

In December 1941, the Imperial Japanese Navy was the world's third largest. It may have been the best. It certainly had the best naval air arm.

Of its 1,500 pilots, nearly all had 600 or more hours of flying time, half of it in the combat aircraft they were flying. Most of the formation leaders had as much as 1,500 hours. The majority were veterans of combat over China, where the Naval Air Service had flown strategic bombing, close support, and air cover missions since the "China Incident" began in 1937.

Their aircraft were fully worthy of their pilots. The A6M Zero was the best carrier-based fighter in the world. The B5N Kate was equally adept at torpedo bombing and level bombing. The D3A Val was at least as good as the notorious German Stuka. The land-based G3M Sally and the G4M Betty had long range and were good high-altitude bombers and excellent torpedo bombers. The Japanese rounded out their strength with several types of seaplanes and the H6K Mavis, a four-engined flying boat with incredible range. All of this was supported by a strong corps of some of the most expert mechanics in Japan.

The carrier-based planes, nearly five hundred strong, flew from nine modern carriers, including some of the best in the world. That was not only three times as many as the United States Pacific Fleet had, but more than the whole United States Navy's carrier strength.

But by the summer of 1945, the Naval Air Service's planes (too many the same early-war types) squatted under camouflage netting and in caves, waiting for their mechanics to prepare them for semitrained pilots to take one last flight, crash-diving into a ship of the American invasion fleet—if they got that far. How the mighty had fallen.

But why?

The Japanese Naval Air Service died from the same cause as so much of the Japanese war effort—faulty grand strategy and a weak economic base. To be brief about the second, Japan had to import practically every essential item of a modern war economy except coal. And in 1944 alone, a fully mobilized American aircraft industry produced almost as many planes (better ones, too) as Japan produced during the whole period of 1942–45.

The Japanese strategic stumble is less well known. Basically, they planned on a short war leading to a decisive battle that would put the enemy in a position that he would not have the political will to fight his way out of.

This strategy meant hitting by surprise, fast, hard, and often. Specifically, it meant preparing a defensive barrier stretching from the Kuriles in the north in a great crescent down to the anchorage of Truk in the Caroline Islands far to the south. Planes, destroyers, and submarines from these bases would hack away at the American fleet (what other one need Japan fear?) until it approached the Home Islands. Then the Combined Fleet would sortie at full strength and so thoroughly crush American offensive capabilities in the Pacific that the United States would seek a negotiated peace.

The concept of a short war has been attributed to the Samurai mentality; to the code of bushido, emphasizing daring and aggression; and to stark realism. The Japanese had not forgotten how narrowly they escaped running out of men and money at the end of the war with Russia, even after winning the decisive battle at Tsushima.

So their main naval striking force, the aviators, were polished to perfection for a short war. The force had once been composed exclusively of graduates of Eta Jima, the Japanese naval academy, survivors of a four-year curriculum that made Annapolis look like a prep school. In 1929 suitable enlisted men were admitted to the two-year flight training course, which washed out about 80 percent of the candidates. Then in 1931 potential pilots were allowed straight in from civilian life.

Having a larger pilot pool helped somewhat, but it also introduced the hierarchical Japanese class system into naval aviation. Physical punishment was allowed; initiative usually was not. This environment was not calculated to produce the best mind-set among the new lower-class pilots.

The planes they climbed into also had a few limitations. None of them had armor or self-sealing fuel tanks. Radios were in short supply, and so heavy and prone to static interference from unshielded ignitions that some pilots refused to carry them. And of course parachutes were bulky and implied an unthinkable willingness to be taken prisoner, and therefore were refused. They could have saved many pilots' lives.

So the Japanese Naval Air Service flew off to an initial victory that slowly turned into doom.

They earned their first triumphs. Pearl Harbor was an attack on a scale that no other navy in the world could have executed until well into 1943. And while survivors were still getting first aid, off in the Philippines air strikes from Formosa (now Taiwan) were devastating American airpower in the islands.

General Douglas MacArthur helped the Japanese cause by failing to disperse his planes despite knowing the war had started. The Japanese fighter pilots who escorted the bombers were flying at extreme range, their fuel-air mixtures leaned out as far as they could go without stalling.

These were apparently amazing feats—but there was a scribble of handwriting on the wall at Wake Island. There, four Marine F4F Wildcats proved their toughness by taking to the air full of holes and not only shot down Japanese planes but damaged a light cruiser and sank a destroyer.

The Japanese went on running wild from Burma to the fringes of Australia. But they were losing as many as two hundred planes a month (army and navy) to operational accidents (read: piling up on a runway hacked out of scrub, ankle-deep in mud, and with a few rocks left for good measure). And pilots who died nosing-over in a pothole were just as dead as those killed dropping a bomb on an Allied warship.

The Indian Ocean saw a lot of that kind of bombing in April, when the Japanese carriers went east. The Japanese carriers also saw what a really determined defense could do—over Ceylon they lost forty to fifty planes.

Worse was to follow. Later in the spring the Japanese divided their carriers, sending two south to cover an attack on New Guinea and getting the rest ready. Warned by the code-breakers, the Americans stop-punched them in the Coral Sea, although losing one fleet carrier against one Japanese light carrier. The real blow to the Japanese was that one of their carriers had her flight deck wrecked and the other lost most of her air group—another dent in the supply of experienced Japanese naval pilots.

So both carriers missed Midway, where they might have turned the tide. As it was, the Japanese lost four carriers—giving them a shortage of first-class flight decks, from which they never really recovered. Many pilots survived, but hundreds of the veteran mechanics were not so lucky—and that was another irreparable blow.

The Battle of Midway also let one other plum drop into American hands. In the Aleutians, a Japanese diversionary raid left a flyable Zero upside down on an uninhabited island. Salvaging it, the Americans got it back in the air and tested it thoroughly. It did not influence the design of the F6F Hellcat (already flying when the Zero crashed), but it did allow the U.S. Navy to learn its opponent's weakness and use its new fighter more effectively.

The Japanese now turned to an advance down the chain of the Solomon Islands, seeking another approach to cutting off Australia. (The Japanese services never agreed on a plan for invading that continent—but then, they hardly ever agreed on much.) They established an air base on the island of Guadalcanal. The United States promptly landed marines to seize the base. The Japanese counterattacked by air, land, and sea.

Guadalcanal

The Battle of Guadalcanal may have decided the Pacific War. It certainly decided the fate of the Japanese Naval Air Service.

Bombing raids from Rabaul and carrier battles at sea took a

toll on Japanese planes and pilots. The Japanese lost about seven hundred planes of all kinds, as well as most of their pilots—and many of the lost pilots were the irreplaceable veterans. The United States lost nearly as many planes, but fewer pilots and crewmen, and the U.S. pilot-training program had plenty of three-hundred-hour pilots in the pipeline, just waiting for their new planes and carriers. The Japanese, on the other hand, were stretched so thin that to send a veteran pilot back to be a flight instructor would deprive a frontline squadron of an indispensable leader.

Meanwhile, Japanese pilot training hours were dropping below two hundred, few of those in combat aircraft. Most of the new pilots were being either siphoned off into new air groups or thrown straight into the maw of the Solomons campaign.

The Japanese evacuated Guadalcanal in January 1943. That ended Japanese strategic offensives in the Pacific. The rest of the year saw no great fleet clashes, because both sides were building up their strength for the next one.

The United States did a better job, both qualitatively and quantitatively. By the end of the year it could sweep the Gilbert and Marshall islands with strikes from five fleet and six light carriers, which then sailed south to eliminate Truk as a working naval base (along with most of the ships in it and all the planes on its runways).

Rabaul

The elimination of Rabaul as a barrier to the advance on the Philippines also proceeded with reasonable speed. The Japanese surface fleet fought aggressively at night, but the United States ruled sea and sky by day and island-hopped steadily "up the ladder of the Solomons." In November 1943, it eliminated Rabaul as a fleet base. In the next few months, it effectively eliminated that base's airpower, which included several replacement air groups intended for the carriers of the Combined Fleet. This blockade ended up trapping yet more pilots and mechanics out of the war as effectively as if they had been in POW camps. From the roofs of their bunkers, they could contemplate new and superior American aircraft such as the P-38 and F4U Corsair swatting the last Zeroes out of the sky.

This did not improve a Japanese situation that was going from bad to worse. Mitsuo Fuchida, who had led the attack on Pearl Harbor, joined the staff of a land-based naval air group intended to defend the Marianas. He was appalled to discover that the group had fewer than two hundred planes and that the average training time for the new pilots was *120 hours*—not enough time logged to let them even fly some of the new planes that were at last reaching the front safely, let alone use them in combat. The mechanics were in equally short supply and equally undertrained, likely to be hopeless with the new planes such as P1Y Frances, D4Y Judy, B6N Jill, and the magnificent long-range flying boat, the H8K Emily.

The Japanese needed more than new planes. They needed flight decks, as they had gained only one fleet carrier in the last year, and they needed fuel for both planes and ships. Unfortunately, while the East Indian oil fields were now producing again, American submarines were taking an increasing toll on Japanese tankers. They were also targeting Japanese destroyers, leaving both convoys and carriers with increasingly thin escorts.

Nor would it have helped Japanese morale to discover that the Americans had a complete set of the plans for the defense of the Marianas, correctly assumed to be the next major objective. Filipino guerrillas had retrieved the plans from a Japanese staff officer who'd swum ashore from a crashed plane.

So when the American Fifth Fleet and a multidivision Marine and Army landing force appeared off the Marianas, the Japanese response held few surprises. The Mobile Force sailed out, with new air groups aboard its five large and four small carriers. Meanwhile, the Americans had systematically eliminated all the Japanese aircraft based on the islands, craft which the Japanese had hoped would be an equalizer, and cratered most of the runways that the Japanese carrier planes were supposed to use for shuttle-bombing operations.

Then the Fifth Fleet positioned itself west of the Marianas and waited for the enemy to come to it. On June 19, 1944, the Japanese came—four massive carrier raids, all of which were intercepted, three of which were nearly annihilated. The Japanese lost three hundred planes to American interceptors and anti-aircraft fire. The Americans had one battleship lightly damaged.

That same day, American submarines sank two of the best Japanese carriers. On the next day the Americans delivered a counterstroke, launching two hundred planes at extreme range and knowing they'd have to return at night.

They sank another carrier and two tankers, in addition to wiping out the few remaining Japanese planes. Then they headed for home. Many ditched for lack of fuel. Many more might have except that Admiral Marc Mitscher, commanding the fast carries, threw caution to the wind and ordered his ships illuminated. That grand gesture saved many plans and crews, and provoked no attacks.

The Battle of the Philippine Sea has been discussed in such detail because it was the greatest carrier battle of all time—and the death knell for Japanese naval aviation. The last carrier force it sent to sea was a diversionary force at the Battle of Leyte Gulf, four carriers with only 116 planes, and they were all sunk or lost.

Then Japan's naval pilots flew into the shadowy land of the kamikazes, where they played an effective role. Certainly many of them must have gone in the same spirit as other pilots who thought that Japan was doomed: life in a defeated Japan would not be worth living, so why not go out doing as much damage to the enemy as possible?

May Americans never have to answer such questions. And may we try not to judge too harshly those who have.

SINK THE *BISMARCK*!

North Atlantic, March 1941

BY DOUGLAS NILES

The Business of the English commander-in-chief being first to bring an enemy fleet to battle on the most advantageous terms to himself (I mean that of laying his ships close on board the enemy, as expeditiously as possible); and secondly to continue them there until the business is decided.

—Horatio Nelson, 1758–1805

The most infamous warship of the Kriegsmarine was the mighty battleship *Bismarck*. She and her sister ship, *Tirpitz,* were at this point the most powerful warships ever constructed by any European or American shipyard. (Only the Japanese built larger battleships, the *Yamato* and *Musashi* both being bigger and having larger—18.1-inch—guns.) The *Bismarck*'s maiden voyage captured the full and undivided attention of the Royal Navy and British high command, up to Prime Minister Winston Churchill himself, and her legendary status echoes down through today. The latter fact is all the more remarkable when one considers that her active career began, climaxed, and concluded all in the course of about a week's time.

Unlike the "pocket" battleships, which, although modern, had their roots in the 1920s, the *Bismarck* was a purely modern vessel, designed, laid down, and launched as World War II took shape and commenced across Europe. Construction was started when her keel was laid in Hamburg during the summer of 1936—shortly before Hitler and the Nazis hosted the International Olympic Games in Berlin. The *Bismarck*'s hull slid into the water in April 1939, right about the time that Germany was breaking the six-month-old Munich Pact by swallowing the nation of Czechoslovakia. Meanwhile, England, belatedly recognizing Prime Minister Neville Chamberlain's catastrophic misjudgment in making that pact, finally began to prepare for the possibility of war. The traditional champagne bottle was smashed onto the warship's hull by the granddaughter of Chancellor Otto von Bismarck, who in 1871 was widely acknowledged as the founder of the German state.

For more than a year, as the war began and Poland, Norway, France, and other nations were occupied by Germany, *Bismarck* was fitted out for operations. She was commissioned in August 1940, at which time her captain, Ernst Lindemann, took command; the next month she began sea trials in the Baltic Sea. Most of her training runs took place along the coastline between Kiel and Danzig. By the end of the year she had returned to Hamburg, where final adjustments based on the sea trials were made.

Bismarck was expected to sail to Kiel at the start of 1941. That port was the main base of the Kriegsmarine, and because of a canal across the base of the peninsula of Jutland (Denmark), it gave German ships access to both the North and Baltic seas, without entailing an exposed voyage through the Skagerrak, the passage north of Denmark and south of Norway. However, British bombers had sunk a German ship in the canal, temporarily closing the passage, so the battleship had to wait in Hamburg for several months.

During this time, Captain Lindemann entertained a visitor, the Swedish naval attaché to Germany, who sent a detailed description of the great ship back to Stockholm. It didn't take long for that description to be leaked to British agents, providing the Admiralty with a significant, and frightening, intelligence bonanza. It seemed clear that the *Bismarck,* with her eight 15-inch guns, great size (860 feet long), and massive armoring, would overmatch any single battleship in the Royal Navy. Furthermore, although this fact was not immediately known, her total of 150,000 horsepower in engines made her faster than all but a very few, and much more lightly armored, British battleships and battle cruisers.

The Voyage Begins

It wasn't until early March that the Kiel Canal was cleared and the battleship made the passage to the fleet's port. She was attacked by British bombers there on March 12, though no damage was inflicted. A little later she ventured eastward to the port of Gdynia, in captured Polish territory near Danzig. (During the war the Germans called the port Gotenhafen.)

Admiral Erich Raeder, in command of the Kriegsmarine, hoped to assemble a massive force of powerful surface ships, dispatching them into the North Atlantic to disrupt Allied convoys and destroy, in gunnery actions, any British task force that dared to challenge it. His ideal was to pair *Bismarck* with her sister ship, *Tirpitz,* and send the fast, powerful battle cruisers *Gneisenau* and *Scharnhorst*—currently anchored in the port of Brest, in occupied

France—along with them. Three heavy cruisers, *Admiral Scheer, Admiral Hipper,* and *Prinz Eugen,* would complete the powerful fleet.

However, the British knew about the battle cruisers in Brest and went after them aggressively. Despite heavy anti-aircraft fire, an airplane-launched torpedo wrecked *Gneisenau*'s propellers and flooded two engine rooms. At the same time, boiler issues put her sister ship, the *Scharnhorst,* out of action. The intended raiding fleet would certainly have horrified the Admiralty into long, sleepless nights, but now both battle cruisers were bottled up in Brest and had suffered damage that would keep them in port for many more months. Additionally, *Scheer* and *Hipper* both sustained damage from the RAF while anchored in Kiel, and *Tirpitz* encountered delays in construction, which forced her to wait until autumn before she could commence operations—though she did join *Bismarck* in Gotenhafen after her commissioning.

Although the strength of the task force was necessarily reduced, Admiral Raeder was determined to order the mission to proceed. He was eager to prove to Hitler that the Third Reich's large investment in surface warships had been a worthwhile expenditure. Admiral Günther Lütjens, who had commanded the German battle cruisers on a successful raid earlier in the war, would command the small task force of *Bismarck* and *Prinz Eugen* for Operation Rheinübung (Rhine Exercise). He brought a staff of more than sixty men, and of course would fly his flag in the new battlewagon. In early May, Hitler toured both of these mighty battleships and asked Lütjens directly if he foresaw any risks in the mission. "None," the admiral replied confidently. He declared that the powerful anti-aircraft batteries on *Bismarck* would be more than enough to protect the ship from enemy torpedo bombers.

Just before she left port, some eighty sailors came aboard *Bis-*

marck to serve as prize crews for potential captured merchantmen, bringing the battleship's complement to 2,221 officers and men by the time she departed Gotenhafen, early in the morning of May 19. The two ships, accompanied by Luftwaffe fighters and bombers as well as destroyers and U-boats, made their way through the Denmark Strait, toward the North Sea. They passed a Swedish cruiser, which duly reported the movement to headquarters in Stockholm. Within an hour or two, that information had been leaked to the British, and the Admiralty began to make preparations to challenge another daring raiding voyage.

The man who bore the responsibility for tracking, stopping, and sinking the *Bismarck* was Admiral Sir John Tovey, at the massive base in Scapa Flow on the northern coast of Scotland. A number of the Royal Navy's battleships were too slow to participate in a search for the modern German warships, but Tovey had command of the very modern battleship *King George V* and the even more recently launched *Prince of Wales*. Both of these ships were nearly—but not quite—equal to *Bismarck* in speed, armor, and armaments. They had batteries of 14-inch guns, compared to the German ship's 15-inch bore, and were not quite so heavily armored in the anti-torpedo "belt" below the waterline. Tovey also had *Hood* at his disposal, a battle cruiser with powerful guns and exceptional speed. Where *Hood* came up short compared to the Nazi battleship was in armor protection, especially on her upper surfaces, which were vulnerable to plunging gunfire and bombing.

Other, older, British ships would also, of necessity, come into play. *Repulse* and *Renown,* battle cruisers even more lightly armored than *Hood,* at least had above-average speed. *Rodney,* one of only two British ships (the other was HMS *Nelson*) that, with her 16-inch guns, actually outgunned *Bismarck,* would also join the search, though she could not come close to the German ship's speed. Aircraft carrier *Victorious* was detached from convoy duty, and the venerable *Ark Royal* was called up from Gibraltar to add another aerial element to the chase.

On May 20–21 the German raiders sped through the Skagerrak, passing around the southern promontory of Norway and steaming up the coast as far as Bergen, where they dropped anchor in Grimstadfjord. Here *Prinz Eugen* topped off her fuel tanks from a friendly tanker; curiously, despite having adequate time to do the same, *Bismarck* did not take on any more fuel.

While Tovey, for the moment, kept his ships at Scapa Flow, he waited for information. The Photographic Reconnaissance Unit (PRU) of the RAF was at this point a relatively new organization, but it was about to prove its worth. The PRU's mainstay was a modified Spitfire, a model stripped of guns and armor and equipped with cameras and extra fuel capacity. On May 21 one of these Spitfires took off from Wick, in northern Scotland, and flew across the North Sea to the Norwegian coast. The pilot spotted *Bismarck* at anchor in the fjord and captured several stunningly clear photographs. Nearby, the *Prinz Eugen* lay alongside a tanker. The next day, in much nastier weather conditions, another PRU flight flew into the fjord just above the waves and discovered that the ships had departed—and one of the great chases in naval history was under way.

Bismarck and her cruiser had slipped out of the fjord just after midnight on the 21st, escorted by several destroyers for a few hours. By dawn, the two massive warships were alone, steaming a northwesterly course. The weather was hazy, with plenty of low clouds, giving the German vessels good cover as they made their run toward the open sea at high speed.

Admiral Tovey had to guess which of three routes the German raiders would take, if they were in fact attempting to break out into the Atlantic. They could have dared to race straight west, passing between the Faeroe Islands and Scapa Flow, but that risky course took them very close to the main base of the British Home Fleet. A second possible route could run north of the Faeroes but south of Iceland; like the first route, this passage lay within easy range of land-based aircraft.

The third route, and the one most often employed by German raiders, was the Denmark Strait, the passage of water between Iceland and Greenland, and this is where Tovey expected Lütjens to make his breakout. The strait was a remote stretch of far-northern waters, where even during the long days of the arctic summer the weather precluded reliable aerial reconnaissance. A minefield blocked off much of the passage closer to Iceland, while the winter ice pack still lay atop the waters for several hundred miles off the coast of Greenland.

For the moment, two heavy cruisers, *Suffolk* and *Norfolk,* endured the unpopular duty of patrolling the Denmark Strait. Even in May the weather was bitter cold, and storms tossed waves high against and over the cruiser's hulls. They were relatively modern ships, but far more suited for duty in tropical waters than patrolling up near the Arctic Circle. Each cruiser was equipped with batteries of 8-inch guns but neither was a match for the *Prinz Eugen,* let alone *Bismarck,* in a gunnery duel. But their task was to scout, not to fight, and their intrepid crews took the mission very seriously.

The navigable passage of the strait was only about twenty-five or thirty miles wide. At 6 P.M. on May 23, a lookout on *Suffolk*'s bridge was stunned by the apparition of a great gray shape slipping out of the fog. Somehow he managed to shout out the sighting of a ship and the bearing; he amended his report to include two ships even before any of his shipmates could react.

In the presence of the 50,000-ton battleship, the 10,000-ton cruiser went to flank speed and raced for a nearby fog bank, vanishing into the murk before *Bismarck* could get off a salvo. *Suffolk* was equipped with a relatively modern radar set and shadowed the Germans along their southwesterly course while remaining mostly out of sight. At the same time she radioed a report of the sighting, which was picked up by *Norfolk* but not by Admiral Tovey, who by then was at sea in *King George V.* The second cruiser plowed through heavy seas to join her sister ship, bursting through the sketchy visibility to come upon *Bismarck* in all her glory. This time the Germans were ready, and *Norfolk* hastily retreated among a barrage of near-misses.

With *Suffolk* to starboard and *Norfolk* to port, the raiders plunged through the strait. The former cruiser had good radar, but her radio was encumbered by ice on the upper aerials; the latter lacked the radar but had a working radio, so at last Admiral Tovey learned of the sighting. The closest British big ships were *Hood* and *Prince of Wales,* then about three hundred miles away and under the command of Admiral Lancelot Holland. Under orders from Tovey, they set off on a converging course at top speed.

Hood was the only battle cruiser in the British Navy. She had been commissioned in 1920, and though limitations in her armor protection had resulted in no similar ships being launched, she had long been touted as a proud and modern ship. She was well known and admired not just in the naval service, but throughout England. Though *Prince of Wales* was the most modern battleship in the Royal Navy, she was not yet fully operational, and in fact had a large complement of workmen aboard who were still putting the finishing touches on her commissioning. Still, she raced forward behind *Hood* under an impressive head of steam, both great ships plowing through rough seas. Their accompanying destroyers had an even rougher ride, frequently disappearing under the waves from the viewpoint of the battleships.

Throughout the night of May 23–24, the great ships plunged through icy seas on a course just north of due west. No crewmen on either of the big ships, and certainly not on the destroyers, got any sleep that stormy night. They received steady updates from the doughty cruisers and by 3 A.M. had learned that they were drawing close to the German raiders. Before dawn Holland had turned his ships onto a southwesterly heading, one that nearly paralleled *Bismarck* but allowed the British ships to gradually close the distance between the two adversaries. The battle cruiser remained in the lead, with *Prince of Wales* trailing very close behind.

The Mighty *Hood*

By the time full daylight reigned the two task forces were less than twenty miles apart, and lookouts in the upper masts and bridges of the big ships could plainly see the enemy. Here Holland issued a valiant, and catastrophic, order: he turned his ships hard to starboard, to steam directly at the flanks of the German raiders, with *Hood* still in advance of *Prince of Wales*. Not only did this take the rear turrets of the two British battleships out of the fight, but it guaranteed that the lightly armored *Hood* would take the first full brunt of *Bismarck*'s broadsides.

Hood fired first, at about fourteen miles of range; the other three heavies joined in seconds later. *Bismarck*'s salvo was stunningly accurate, immediately bracketing the British battle cruiser with a close-set pattern of spuming explosions, with frothing, icy spray shooting high into the stormy air. The Royal Navy's shells plunged farther afield and, making matters worse, one of *Prince of Wales*'s big guns in a forward turret was immediately disabled by a mechanical failure.

The second German salvo scored a hit on *Hood,* amidships, sending up a gout of orange flame. But the ship was not disabled, and in the glow of the flames a new signal became visible on the battle cruiser's yardarm. Apparently realizing the danger of his initial maneuver, Admiral Holland now ordered the Royal Navy vessels hard to port so that they could bring their rear turrets into action and run more parallel to the German ships.

It was likely the last order the courageous naval officer gave, as an entire broadside of *Bismarck*'s 15-inch shells plunged into *Hood*. At least one reached the main and secondary magazines before exploding, and with that blast the proud, sleek battle cruiser simply ceased to exist. Eyewitnesses aboard *Prince of Wales* could scarcely believe their eyes as the violent eruption cast debris, smoke, and fire high into the air above the sea where *Hood* had been.

Hood's ordnance exploded across the surface of the stormy waters, while smoke and flame spumed even higher into the cloudy, windy sky, a pyre that soon merged with the low-lying clouds. *Prince of Wales* came upon the wreckage some thirty seconds later, and by then the forward section of the battle cruiser was all that remained—then even that swiftly slipped beneath the waves. One of the escorting destroyers, HMS *Electra,* steamed for the wreckage, her crew frantically searching for survivors, for lifeboats, rafts, any candidates for rescue. Only three men were pulled from the water; the rest of *Hood*'s complement, more than 1,400 officers and enlisted men, perished with their ship.

And *Bismarck* wasn't through. Now the full fury of those powerful, lethally accurate batteries turned against *Prince of Wales.* In short order His Majesty's battleship suffered a multitude of hits and was forced to turn away from the fight and retire behind a screen of smoke laid by her racing destroyer escort. Though the Germans didn't know the extent of the damage, the British ship had been badly hurt—not just by *Bismarck*'s heavy guns, but by *Prinz Eugen*'s 8-inch batteries and the battleship's secondary turrets of 5.9-inch guns. All of *Prince of Wales*'s main batteries were out of action because of damage or mechanical failure, and a direct hit on the bridge had killed nearly everyone there.

Although many of Lütjen's men wanted to pursue and destroy the *Prince of Wales,* the admiral opted instead to continue with his assigned mission. Captain Lindemann himself vociferously argued for continuing the duel, but he was overruled. It turned out that *Bismarck* had taken three hits, probably from *Prince of Wales.* None of them was disabling, though one blow, forward, had led to flooding of the forecastle. The battleship was down about three degrees in the bow, leaking a little oil, and had a bit shaved off her top speed, though she could still steam a respectable twenty-eight knots. Onboard repairs stopped the leak and allowed the ship to pick up a little more speed.

But the pesky *Suffolk* and *Norfolk* remained just on the horizon, and they continued to trail the raiders as the Germans made their way south. *Prince of Wales* limped along with the two heavy cruisers, and they shadowed the enemy ships. Admiral Tovey, still reeling from the shock of *Hood*'s demise, nevertheless continued the pursuit. He knew his surface ships would not make contact before nightfall, but he ordered a desperate air strike to be launched from *Victorious.*

That carrier's air group consisted mostly of untested youngsters fresh out of pilot school, leavened by a few veteran leaders. They could only make a torpedo attack, flying planes that looked like they belonged to an earlier war. The Fairey Swordfish was nicknamed the "Stringbag": it was a frail-looking biplane with fixed landing gear and a crew of two exposed to the air in an open cockpit. Each aircraft carried a single torpedo, which it would attempt to drop into the water from an elevation of less than twenty feet. With a top speed of around 120 knots, the ungainly aircraft seemed likely to prove a deathtrap in combat operations.

Still, *Victorious* launched her squadron on the evening of May 24, and they boldly challenged the German battleship at dusk. The German gunners were no doubt astounded at the sight of the slow, ungainly planes closing in from several directions, flying just above the water. In a lively but nearly bloodless fifteen-minute engagement, the battleship opened up with all her guns, including the 15-inch batteries—with which she tried to knock down the planes by tossing up huge waterspouts in their path—while the torpedo bombers closed in and launched their "fish." Two of the planes were damaged, slightly, and two of the torpedoes hit, killing one German sailor. The untested pilots somehow managed to return to their carrier in darkness, with every plane landing safely; the green fliers could, with real justification, now consider themselves combat veterans.

Bismarck was not sorely damaged by the torpedo hits, both of which struck her armored belt in its strongest section, but the frantic maneuvering as she attempted to evade the attackers ruptured the repaired hull section in the bow, and she once again took water into the forecastle and lost a bit of speed. In the fullness of the night, Lütjens sent *Prinz Eugen* off on a southerly course, while he directed the battleship to turn west by southwest, toward the coast of France. Her British shadows, forced to zig and zag as defense against U-boats, momentarily lost their target from radar; when they swept back toward the raider's presumed course, the radar screens remained empty.

Free at Last

After thirty-one hours of uninterrupted shadowing, *Bismarck* was loose, and undetected, in the North Atlantic. That news reverberated through the Admiralty, all the way to the prime minister—and even to the United States, where President Franklin Roosevelt, like Winston Churchill, took a close interest in naval matters. Everywhere it was heard, it was a frightening portent of nautical disaster.

Ironically, after escaping his pursuers with brilliant maneuvering, Lütjens made a fundamental mistake by breaking silence during the morning of May 25. He broadcast a detailed account of the Battle of the Denmark Strait and included some analysis on the effectiveness of British radar. Of course, the Royal Navy picked up the broadcast and made a rough fix on the raider's position as a result. However, due to a communications failure, Admiral Tovey got a report that was a reverse of the actual data and concluded from it that *Bismarck* was going to pass near the Faeroes and return to the Norwegian Coast. Consequently, *King George V* and her escorts turned north, steaming away from the German ship.

It wasn't until very late in the day that the mistake was discovered, and a true analysis—that the German battleship was headed for France—was made. Now the search began again in earnest, with Tovey in *King George V* closing in, as well as the doughty *Suffolk* and *Norfolk* resuming the chase. *Rodney*, with her massive 16-inch guns, was operating on her own, and had decks piled high with equipment since she had been headed for a major refit in the United States; now she too turned southward to join in the search.

In the early hours of May 26, a Catalina PBY (patrol bomber) operating from Northern Ireland was directed to extend its search arc southward, in case *Bismarck* was veering in that direction to avoid British air searches. The copilot was an American, a veteran PBY flier who had been secretly loaned to the RAF to train them in the use of the long-range, reliable flying boat. The Catalina's crew spotted a big ship, flew through some clouds, and emerged into clear skies directly above *Bismarck*. The British pilot radioed a report of the contact while the American copilot desperately maneuvered the plane in the face of savage anti-aircraft fire. When the badly damaged aircraft finally limped away, the Royal Navy once again had a detailed and accurate report on the German battleship's position.

A dozen minutes later a patrolling Swordfish from the carrier *Ark Royal* spotted *Bismarck* and was able to stay aloft, out of range, and follow the raider as she steamed toward France. Unlike *Victorious*'s, *Ark Royal*'s aircrews were among the most experienced in the Royal Navy. Still, the stormy conditions were a terrible challenge to flight operations. The forward edge of the flight deck pitched through a rise and fall of 60 degrees, with a forty-knot wind blasting the carrier's bow. Since the Fairey Swordfish would stall below a speed of fifty-five knots, the carrier had to slow her speed enough that the planes wouldn't actually fly backward relative to the ship when they took to the air. This slow speed also served to amplify the vessel's up-and-down lurching.

Nevertheless, a flight of fifteen Swordfish took off in atrocious conditions, found a target, and launched fifteen torpedoes—at the British cruiser HMS *Sheffield,* which had arrived on the scene and taken over the task of maintaining a radar fix on *Bismarck*. Fortunately, that ship—captained by a man with Fleet Air Arm credentials—evaded the attack, chasing the Swordfish away with an outraged rebuke over the radio. The flight commander reported to his captain in chagrin about his perfect attack: "Right height, right range, right cloud cover, and wrong [expletive deleted] ship!"

After 7 P.M. a second attack was launched, by another fifteen Swordfish. This time they flew over *Sheffield* at a height of five thousand feet and got a fix on the German battleship. The squadron split apart, attacking in five sections of three planes each so that they could come at the battleship from different directions. No matter which way *Bismarck* turned, she would expose her broadside to one or more of the attacking sections. The fliers closed in on their target at dusk, dropping almost to the water level and roaring in for a bold attack.

The battleship maneuvered desperately, again firing all of her batteries, trying to evade the torpedo tracks that marked the storm-tossed sea. The fliers could not be sure of their success, given all the splashing and blazing and smoking of the battle, but suspected they had struck at least one, and possibly two, torpedoes into that heavily armored hull. Once again all of the Swordfish survived, and it turned out that they had in fact put two of their fish into the German battleship.

And one of those was a crucial blow, a hit to the starboard rear that damaged the propellers and wrecked *Bismarck*'s steering. She was slowed drastically and lost the ability to steer. Crippled, she could only turn in circles, soon moving onto a northerly course. The watchers aboard *Sheffield* had to beat a hasty retreat as the battleship turned toward them and opened fire; they wasted no time in broadcasting news of the raider's change of course.

This new path took her straight toward the Royal Navy's big gunships, which were closing in at flank speed. The damage was such that the battleship had to slow to eight knots and now just barely moved through the sea. Night fell, and *Sheffield* maintained contact and steadily reported the position of the clearly wounded ship.

Sunk

The next set of British attackers on the scene was a flotilla of destroyers under the command of Captain Philip Vian, who had commanded *Cossack* when she had cornered the *Altmark* in Norway in 1940. Now he had taken the initiative, without orders, to sail toward the "sound of the guns." During the night the raider was harassed by star shells and torpedo attacks from Vian's British destroyers. She remained illuminated throughout the night and suffered additional hits from torpedoes and even from the small-bore guns of the audacious destroyers. *Norfolk,* the heavy cruiser that had chased the raider for so long, arrived during the wee hours and used her lights to guide the massive *Rodney* to the crippled target.

By dawn, *Rodney* had come onto the scene and opened fire with her nine 16-inch guns at about 8:30 A.M. Immediately these big shells began to pound home. Lütjens flashed a final radio message, pledging to fight to the last shell and closing with "Long live the Führer!" His own batteries replied, but *Bismarck* displayed none of the accuracy that a few days earlier had so quickly doomed *Hood.* There was an almost listless quality to the return fire from the slow-moving ship.

Soon *King George V* arrived and joined in the punishment, as both British battleships pummeled *Bismarck* with a relentless barrage of 16- and 14-inch shells. The great ship was gradually pounded into a wreck, smoking and flaming across her superstructure, yet stubbornly refusing to sink. One by one her batteries were silenced, though the German flag still flew from her mast.

It wasn't until the heavy cruiser *Dorsetshire* steamed close and hammered two torpedoes into her hull, then circled around to put two more into the other side, that *Bismarck,* her flag still flying, slipped beneath the waves. The massive battleship settled to port and finally sank by the stern.

Dorsetshire and a few other vessels plucked about a hundred survivors out of the water before the Royal Navy ships were forced to withdraw in response to a U-boat warning. A few more men were rescued by a U-boat and a German weather ship a day or two later. In all, only 107 men out of the more than 2,200 aboard survived the voyage.

Word of the sinking was quickly radioed to Admiralty headquarters in London, where the news produced a sense of relief so profound that it bordered on euphoria. During the morning hours of May 27, Winston Churchill had just concluded an address to the House of Commons when he was passed a piece of paper.

The prime minister rose to his feet again and said: "I ask the indulgence of the House. I have just received news that the *Bismarck* is sunk." Writing about the remark after the war, he concluded, "They seemed content."

THE VALIANT AND VIOLENT STORY OF THE ABDA FLEET

Pacific, February 1942

BY DOUGLAS NILES

The main American naval forces were shifted to the Pacific region and an American admiral made a strong declaration to the effect that if war were to break out between Japan and the United States, the Japanese navy could be sunk in a matter of weeks.

—Hideki Tojo, 1884–1948, General and Prime Minister of Japan

The Japanese military success in December 1941 stunned the Allies across the globe. The Asian nation's accomplishments over a few short days, commencing with the surprise attack on Pearl Harbor in Hawaii, followed by the invasion of the Philippines and Malaya, the seizure of Hong Kong, and the sinking of the proud Royal Navy warships *Repulse* and *Prince of Wales,* amounted to a body of armed work that was almost impossible to comprehend.

By the end of the year soldiers and naval landing forces of the empire of Japan had captured the American base on Wake Island

and were closing in on the great cities of Manila and Singapore. Imperial Japan's army and navy, ably supported by fast, long-range aircraft, seemed to be an unstoppable force of nature, annihilating or sweeping aside their European and North American enemies wherever the latter tried to make a stand.

By January 1942, the U.S. high command was forced to admit that the Philippines were cut off from any possibility of reinforcement or succor. Although more than a hundred thousand American and native soldiers fought to hold on, with the main American battle fleet mostly resting on the seabed of Pearl Harbor there was no prospect of pushing a relief force through to the archipelago any time in the foreseeable future.

MacArthur the Unready

Theater commander Army General Douglas MacArthur, who had been caught flatfooted by the initial Japanese air strikes even though he'd known about the Pearl Harbor attack for hours, finally managed to put in place the long-standing defensive plan: his forces moved into the Philippines' rugged Bataan Peninsula, where they could concentrate their strength behind a stout defensive line. But though the withdrawal itself was accomplished skillfully against stiff opposition, the plan was implemented both too hastily and too late. As a result, vast stores of food were left behind in the capital, Manila, which was occupied by the Japanese on January 2. Half and quarter rations would be the order of the day for the starving troops in their jungle redoubt; even so, they would manage to hold out in Bataan for another three months before entering a hellish existence as prisoners of war for the duration of the long conflict.

By the end of January, the British in Malaya had been pushed back to the island of Singapore. Strong ground forces of the Imperial Japanese Army were prepared to attack the fabled fortress from the landward side, avoiding the massive gun emplacements that had all been installed with their barrels facing the sea. Burma, too, had been invaded, with the attackers moving swiftly in their efforts to close the Burma Road, the only land route connecting the Western democracies with their Chinese ally.

But Japan had entered the war with some serious strategic deficiencies, most notably the fact that virtually all of that small island country's raw materials had to be imported. While some of these imports, notably lumber and coal, could be obtained from captured territory in China, the Philippines, and Malaya, the nation had yet to seize sources for two of the most crucial resources from a military perspective: oil and rubber. However, vast reserves of both of these commodities existed in the territories of the Netherlands (also called Dutch) East Indies colonies, including Burma, the Celebes, Sumatra, and Java.

Not surprisingly, Japan moved swiftly to extend its conquests into these colonies (much of today's Indonesia), which, among other things, formed the last island barrier between Japan and Australia. Japan launched these attacks even before the conquests of the Bataan and Singapore had been completed, but neither of those bases, by this point, was anything more than a defensive redoubt.

In preparation for the campaign against the Dutch colonies, three powerful invasion forces gathered: the Western Force, which would sail from Cam Ranh Bay in French Indochina, and the Central and Eastern Forces, which embarked from the port of Davao, on the southernmost Philippine island of Mindanao. Each force would be escorted by fast heavy cruisers, light cruisers, and destroyers, and carry confident soldiers on an array of transports and landing ships. The Japanese even employed small airborne operations for some of their sudden offensives, though they put little emphasis on paratroops. Even through this point in the war, every objective they attacked, they captured.

Although the Japanese lacked radar on their ships, their cruisers were equipped with catapult-launched seaplanes that served reliably as the eyes of the fleets. Furthermore, the Japanese navy was already proving exceptionally adept in night-fighting, and her ships were armed with the dreaded "long lance," the most lethal torpedo in the world. Technically called the Type 93, this underwater weapon had a range of twenty-two thousand yards and traveled at a speed of fifty knots. It was twice as fast and accurate for almost three times as far as the torpedo the U.S. Navy entered the war with. The long lance packed a tremendously powerful warhead and was propelled by an oxygen-based fuel, a propellant that had been discarded by other nations, including the British, as being far too prone to accidental explosions and much too dangerous to employ on a ship. Yet somehow the Japanese made it work, and work well.

To resist this unstoppable tide of conquest, the Allies cobbled together the few forces they had in the area. Of course, with Holland occupied by the Nazis, there was no prospect of the Dutch colonies getting any assistance from the home country. Their local army formations were mostly formed of native troops of questionable loyalty—and in any event these units would be no match for the invading Japanese in equipment, morale, or numbers.

Though England was of course focused primarily on the war against Germany, she had dispatched some troops and ships to the Far East. The troops, unfortunately, were all bottled up in Singapore or had already been made POWs. The Americans were in a similar fix, with all of their ground troops trapped in Bataan. Like England, Australia had been involved in the war with Germany and had only a bare-bones contingent of home defense forces, together with a few ships.

Yet the four countries did share an interest and a determination to resist, so on January 10, 1942, the American-British-Dutch-Australian (ABDA) command was created. Of necessity, most of the combined force facing the Japanese would have to be naval. After the sinking of the two British capital ships, the order of battle was thin. Two heavy cruisers were available: USS *Houston,* with nine 8-inch guns, and HMS *Exeter,* with a mere six 8-inch guns. *Houston* had been based in the Philippines at the start of the war and together with a flotilla of destroyers had been ordered to escape to the south as the archipelago was overwhelmed. *Exeter* was one of the heroes of the fight against *Graf Spee* in the Battle of the River Plate; she had been dispatched to the Far East as hostilities with Japan grew more imminent.

Several light cruisers also augmented the force, including the Australian *Perth* and two Dutch ships, *De Ruyter* and *Tromp.* Nine destroyers, representing four different nations, all of mixed age and quality, rounded out the ABDA fleet. Though General Archibald Wavell of the British Army was designated as the overall commander of the ABDA forces, tactical command of the battle fleet resided with Rear Admiral Karel Doorman, who flew his flag in *De Ruyter.* Though the Dutch lacked a heavy cruiser, they had the most ships and the most homogeneous force—as well as the defense of their own territory at stake—so Doorman was a logical choice for command.

Disadvantages

The ABDA command labored under some significant disadvantages. The ships of the various nations had never operated or trained together, and each country employed a different system of flags and signals, making coordinated operations extremely challenging. The language problem between Dutch- and English-speaking sailors created a further obstacle in the path of coordinated operations. In addition, the allied force had virtually no airpower to speak of, with the British and American air forces having been destroyed in the early weeks of the war and the Dutch air units, consisting entirely of obsolete machines, easily overwhelmed in the early hours of the Dutch East Indies campaign.

Countering this, the Japanese had not only the scout planes aboard their cruisers, but also an extensive and steadily growing network of bases for their land-based aircraft. Their modern fighter, the Zeke, or "Zero," was an exceptionally capable dogfighter with excellent top speed and range. Their bombers and torpedo planes, while lightly armored, were also fast and possessed great range. Furthermore, Japanese engineering and construction forces were so diligent that often within a few days of capturing a new objective they would have an operating air base established there. As they leapfrogged into the Dutch East Indies, they would make good use of this skill, so that wherever they attacked, they did so under an umbrella of land-based airpower.

As if this overwhelming air strength weren't enough, the fast aircraft carriers of Admiral Nagumo's strike force—the same ships that had launched the attack on Pearl Harbor—were now passing through the area as the campaign reached its climax. This convergence meant that virtually the entire expanse of the Dutch East Indies fell under the uncontested air superiority of the Japanese army and naval air forces. Even as the ABDA command was created, in mid-January 1942, the Japanese offensives commenced, with landings in Dutch territories beginning on January 11.

Invasion

After a series of violent but inconclusive clashes through the rest of that month, the Japanese had seized strong bases on Borneo, Sumatra, the Celebes, and Timor. The key island, and the last holdout, among the Dutch holdings was the island of Java, located to the south of Borneo, east of Sumatra, and southwest of the Celebes. It was here that Doorman decided to base his forces, and here that he would make his last stand, using his fleet as a strike force in an attempt to break up one or more of the powerful Japanese landing forces that, by mid-February, were closing in on Java from the west, north, and east.

On February 19 a Japanese invasion force was spotted in the Lombok Strait, adjacent to Bali and just to the east of Java. This discovery resulted in a sharp fight that ended up with the loss of a Dutch destroyer. That same day Admiral Nagumo launched his carrier air groups against Darwin, the major port in northern and northwestern Australia. The attack (which is featured as the climax of the movie *Australia*) killed nearly 250 people and seriously wrecked the port facilities and supply depots. It left Australia as a nation reeling and fearing an imminent landing on their island continent.

On February 26, Admiral Doorman directed his multinational fleet to the port of Surabaya, which lay on the north coast of Java. His men were exhausted from weeks of patrolling and periods of short combat, but he was returning from a patrol in the Java Sea where he had been unable to find any Japanese. He had sketchy information about the enemy positions and knew that two or three powerful invasion forces were approaching the island; but given the weariness of his crews and the just-concluded unsuccessful search, he decided to anchor in port and give his men a short rest.

Just after his squadron had entered that port on the morning of February 27, a lookout spotted smoke on the northern horizon: at least one Japanese fleet had been located. Immediately fatigue and exhaustion were forgotten as Doorman's ships formed into a column and steamed toward the enemy. The officers and men of the ADBA squadron knew the odds in front of them, and very few of them expected to return from this mission. At best, Doorman hoped to smash up one of the landing forces, perhaps buying a little more time for Java in the unlikely event that somehow, somewhere, an Allied fleet would be able to scrape up a few more ships to reinforce him.

The smoke the Allied sailors spotted on the horizon came from a large Japanese fleet, a covering force of cruisers and destroyers running interference for the vulnerable transport fleet that remained over the horizon to the north. The covering force was commanded by Rear Admiral Takeo Takagi; at first glance, it seemed to match up fairly evenly with Doorman's fleet. Like Doorman, Takagi had two heavy cruisers, *Nachi* and *Haguru*. All the heavies on both sides were equipped with 8-inch guns, but whereas the *Exeter* had only six of these and *Houston* had only six serviceable big guns (three more of these were in a rear turret that had been disabled in an earlier action), the Japanese cruisers each had ten 8-inch guns.

Additionally, both heavy and light cruisers, as well as destroyers, of the Japanese fleet were equipped with the long-lance torpedoes; only the Allied destroyers could launch torpedoes, and their weapons were much less reliable, slower, and packed considerably less punch than the Type 93. Takagi also had two light cruisers and fourteen fast, modern destroyers.

The Battle

The battle was joined shortly after 4 P.M., with the heavy cruisers beginning the festivities with a long-range gun duel. As the two fleets closed, the smaller guns joined in, while Takagi skillfully turned his ships to maintain a blocked position and prevent the ABDA ships from approaching the vulnerable transports. The gunnery action was sharp, but with both fleets maneuvering frantically, very few damaging hits were scored. One of these, however, was an 8-inch shell that exploded in *Exeter*'s engine room, forcing her to limp away, escorted by one Dutch destroyer.

As other destroyers tried to lay a smoke screen to cover *Exeter*'s withdrawal, the Japanese destroyers closed in and launched torpedoes. One long lance struck the destroyer *Kortenaur,* breaking her back and sending her to the bottom very quickly. Destroyer *Electra* made a brave stand against the Japanese destroyers but she was battered to pieces by gunnery and soon slipped beneath the waves.

The rest of Doorman's ships retired with the damaged *Exeter,* temporarily breaking off the engagement, but as soon as night fell the Dutch admiral left the limping cruiser to her own devices and charged back with his surviving ships to make another stab at the Japanese transports. But again Takagi countered effectively, and around midnight the two fleets fought a terrible, confused battle at close quarters. The tropical sea was illuminated by searchlights and star shells, rocked by explosions, blanketed by smoke. HMAS *Jupiter,* a destroyer, blew up in a minefield, and both of the Dutch cruisers, shattered by a combined mix of gunnery and torpedoes, plunged to the bottom, with Admiral Doorman going down with his ship.

Now only *Houston* and *Perth,* together with a few destroyers, remained operational as the Japanese began to land their forces on the island of Java. *Exeter,* escorted by two destroyers, tried to slip away to Australia by escaping around the eastern tip of Java. She was spotted by aircraft and, after being shadowed through a day and night, was attacked by Japanese navy surface ships the next day. All three ships went down, with the loss of all hands.

Houston and *Perth* tried to make an escape to Australia in the other direction, making a run around the western end of Java. Here they ran into the landing fleet of the Western Force, escorted by destroyers and a light cruiser. The ABDA cruisers were greatly outnumbered and could have continued past, but perhaps these brave sailors wanted to strike one serious blow before the end. The two ships charged into the landing zone without hesitation, inflicting serious damage on a number of Japanese destroyers and transports. But in the end they, too, were overwhelmed and sunk.

The Battle of the Java Sea is not terribly well understood, for the simple reason that very few men of the ABDA command survived. Of Doorman's fleet, only four of the old American destroyers managed to escape, limping back to Australia to report that the "Malay Barrier" was solidly in Japanese hands.

"SCRATCH ONE FLATTOP"

Coral Sea Pacific, May 1942

BY DOUGLAS NILES

It is the function of the Navy to carry the war to the enemy so that it will not be fought on U.S. soil.

—Fleet Admiral Chester Nimitz, 1885–1966

The Coral Sea is by all accounts a beautiful and tranquil body of water, tropically warm, lying comfortably south of the equator, protected by geography from the worst of the Pacific Ocean storms. Its sheltered waters are well to the south of the most common cyclone tracks. The western edge of the sea is the east and northeast coast of Australia, with its famous Great Barrier Reef running all of its length in the Coral Sea. To the north rises the tropical mass of New Guinea, while the Solomon Islands and the French colony of New Caledonia straddle the northeastern and eastern edges of the blue, normally placid sea. The island nation of New Zealand rises from the waves to the southeast of the Coral Sea, and there that calm body of water merges into the Tasman Sea between the great landmasses of the Kiwi island and Australia itself. All in all, it seems to be an expanse of sea better suited to diving, snorkeling, and pleasure sailing than military activity.

Yet, during May 1942, the Coral Sea was the site of a landmark battle, a struggle between the United States Navy and the Imperial Japanese Navy that ushered in a whole new era of naval warfare and, for the first time, marked a place where the expansionist intentions of the Japanese empire were thwarted and denied. Up until that month, the course of Japanese conquest had run perfectly unchecked through the central and south Pacific Oceans, across the former European colonies of Southeast Asia, even into the Indian Ocean, which had formerly been, for all intents and purposes, an English lake.

Truly, the tide of conquest had carried Japanese forces to all of their initial objectives, allowing the empire to seize the boundary of its ironically titled Greater East Asia Co-Prosperity Sphere. That territory now stretched from the central Pacific Ocean to South Pacific islands, to the full extent of the Malay barrier, up into Burma and great sections of China and the northeast Asian mainland. In places such as Wake Island, Bataan, and Burma, the Allies had fought savagely against the imperial army and navy, but even when they offered tough resistance, they were inevitably overwhelmed. Never was the confidence of the Japanese high command at a greater pitch, and never was the Allied morale sunk so low.

But the war was far from over, and the Japanese had no intention of relinquishing the initiative. Several tempting objectives presented themselves and were the source of intense debate in both army and naval headquarters in Tokyo. Should the Japanese continue to the west, perhaps seizing Ceylon (now Sri Lanka) in the Indian Ocean and maybe invading the great subcontinent itself? Should they strike south, toward Australia, or southeast, in an attempt to put a physical barrier of Japanese bases between the United States and her ally in the land down under? Or should they push to the east, across the breadth of the vast ocean, to threaten again the huge territory and, thus far, dormant military strength of the United States?

Counterattacks

In March and April 1942, those apparently dormant American forces roused themselves to make a series of blows, none of them strategically significant, against Japanese possessions. Yet the fact that these blows were even delivered was enough of a goad to draw the empire's attention away from India and toward the Australian/American lines of communication. And these counterpunches all had one thing in common: they were delivered by airpower.

The devastating attack on Pearl Harbor in December 1941 had broken the back of the U.S. Navy's battleship fleet, but, in an amazing stroke of good fortune, the American aircraft carriers had been left intact. The new commander of the Pacific Fleet, Admiral Chester Nimitz, had three powerful carriers available to him as the year 1942 commenced. *Lexington, Saratoga,* and *Enterprise,* each a part of the Pacific Fleet, had all been away from port when Pearl Harbor was hit.

Soon *Yorktown,* which had been supporting Atlantic convoy operations before the war, returned through the Panama Canal to bring Nimitz's carrier strength up to four. Each of these carriers was a fast ship, with a complement of seventy-five to eighty aircraft. *Lady Lex* and *Saratoga* were older ships, built on hulls that had originally been laid down as battle cruisers, while *Yorktown* and *Enterprise* were the prides of the modern U.S. Navy. Each carried air groups of three distinct types: Grumman F4F Wildcat fighters, SBD Douglas Dauntless dive bombers (which also doubled as scout planes), and Douglas TBD Devastator torpedo bombers.

To counter these flattops, the Japanese navy possessed six large, modern carriers, all of which had participated in the attack on Pearl Harbor. In the months after the outbreak of war, the Japanese carrier strike force had sailed far to the west, hitting British shipping and installations in the Indian Ocean. They were equipped with air groups of similar size to the American carriers, flying fast, modern planes. The Zero fighter was already famed as a fast, maneuverable interceptor; its quality had come as a rude shock to the Western world. The torpedo bomber type was known as the Kate, and it was much faster than the American TBD. The "Val" dive bombers were not quite so advanced, but all of the Japanese aircraft types had good speed and decidedly longer range than their U.S. Navy counterparts. By late spring of 1942, their aircrews were not only well trained, but also experienced in combat operations.

But the American carriers had not been idle during this period, either. Within a month or so after Pearl Harbor the ships and their aircrews began to blood themselves in a series of raids against Japanese island bases, raids that continued through February and March into the Marshall and Gilbert island groups. No serious damage was inflicted, but the American fliers gained experience and confidence. In one action in particular, while closing in on the major Japanese base at Rabaul, *Lexington* was attacked by a powerful force of Japanese dive bombers, fighters, and torpedo planes. The attackers were destroyed almost to the last plane and failed to score a hit on the U.S. ship.

Doolittle's Raid

The most serious blow to Japanese confidence during this period was far more symbolic than practical, but the symbolism was very powerful indeed. On April 28, sixteen U.S. Army twin-engine

B-25s, normally land-based bombers, took off from the new carrier *Hornet* and dropped a few bombs on the Japanese homeland before flying on to crash-land in China, where most of the fliers were rescued. Like the other raids, this attack inflicted little significant damage. But it was a rude shock to the pride of the Japanese naval high command, under the overall leadership of Admiral Isoroku Yamamoto; in fact, the admiral would personally apologize to the emperor for the nearly unforgivable insult.

And he would make plans to make sure that nothing of the kind could ever happen again. Yamamoto immediately put a complicated operation into motion, one designed to drive a wedge between the American and Australian bases and to further expand the periphery of the Japanese empire south of the Solomon Islands and the island of New Guinea. In short, he would put several fleets into the Coral Sea, seizing the island of Tulagi (adjacent to Guadalcanal, near the southern terminus of the long Solomon chain) and the largest port on New Guinea, Port Moresby, which was only a few hundred miles north of Australia.

The most powerful Japanese base in the South Pacific was now Rabaul, on the island of New Britain. The commander here was Admiral Shigeyoshi Inouye, and he embraced Yamamoto's orders to seize the islands in the southern Solomons and mount an amphibious invasion of Port Moresby. He sent an invasion force, backed up by four cruisers and the small carrier *Shoho,* south along the Solomon Islands chain, with the objective of seizing Tulagi. At the same time, he assembled a much larger force at Rabaul, augmented by two of the Pearl Harbor carriers, *Shokaku* and *Zuikaku,* under the command of Rear Admiral Takeo Takagi. Inouye dispatched it with orders to cross the Coral Sea, landing at and seizing Port Moresby.

The first mistake was made by the Japanese, in that they placed far too much confidence in the security of their naval codes—which, in fact, had been broken by the Americans even before the war began (though this intelligence source had been of no help in revealing the attack against Pearl Harbor, due to the intense security surrounding that mission). But now it gave Nimitz details of the Japanese plan, and he was able to make his countermoves accordingly. He sent *Lexington* and *Yorktown,* under the command of Admiral Frank Jack Fletcher, with an escort of American and Australian cruisers and destroyers to break up the Japanese mission.

On May 3, the Tulagi invasion force reached the island and took control of it against no opposition. At 7 P.M. on that day, an American B-17 bomber based in Australia flew close enough to see that Japanese were landing on Tulagi. The contact report was immediately passed to Fletcher, who set a course with *Yorktown* to attack the landing forces. Staying under a layer of clouds to avoid detection, the American carrier sped northward through the night and launched her planes at dawn. Fletcher was so confident of surprise that he sent only his squadron of SBD dive bombers, not even bothering to send along an escort of F4F Wildcat fighters.

The dive bombers came upon the enemy with complete surprise, dropped their bombs, and returned to report that there was nothing left of the enemy. Still, the admiral was justifiably skeptical of the exaggerated reports of his inexperienced fliers and ended up sending a total of four strikes against Tulagi, eventually sinking three minesweepers and a destroyer. It wasn't a lethal blow, but it was great for the morale of the fliers and of the whole fleet.

Yorktown retired south to refuel and join up with *Lexington.* The next day, May 5, passed with both fleets looking for each other, sending out scouts from the carriers and from land bases in Australia for the Allies, and Rabaul and the Solomons for the Japanese. Still, it wasn't until the evening of May 6 that a solid contact report came in, again from a B-17. Initial reports indicated that two carriers were heading for Port Moresby, and this was the information that Fletcher reacted to.

The next morning he launched a powerful strike of seventy-five dive and torpedo bombers, with eighteen fighters flying along as escort. Instead of finding the Japanese fleet carriers, however, the strike force came upon the smaller, slower *Shoho*. Still, the U.S. Navy fliers attacked enthusiastically, quickly sending the light carrier to the bottom. That prompted one of the American pilots to jubilantly report, "Scratch one flattop!"

But the real action was still to come. Knowing that the U.S. carriers had to be near, Takagi ordered a night attack by dive bombers and torpedo planes. The American fighter pilots of the combat air patrol beat the enemy air groups off in savage dogfights, inflicting heavy losses on the Japanese fliers while suffering very light casualties themselves. In the meantime, given this evidence of U.S. naval vigor, Admiral Inouye ordered the Port Moresby landing force to circle back, delaying the landings at that key target until the American carriers could be dispatched.

The Battle's Climax

Aboard the ships of both fleets, and especially among the aircrews, the night of May 7–8 passed in almost unbearable tension and anticipation. For days the two fleets had been searching for each other's carriers, dancing around with secondary sightings and less important targets. There was a real sense on both sides that the following day would reveal the enemy's fleet carriers, and the battle would in fact achieve a resolution. One veteran pilot, already famous in the U.S. Navy as a boxing champion at Annapolis, was Lieutenant Jo-Jo Powers. He spoke earnestly to his young fliers, reminding them of what had happened at Pearl Harbor. As commander of Bomber Squadron 5, *Lexington*'s SBD group, he personally promised to get a hit on an enemy carrier if he had to "lay my bomb right on her flight deck."

As day broke on May 8, it was the Japanese who made the first contact, as one of their scout planes, flitting between the intermittent clouds, spotted both American carriers; the radioman wasted no time in communicating this information back to the flattops. It was only a few minutes later that a scout from *Lexington* made the reciprocal discovery, so that both carrier groups had an accurate fix on the enemy's location.

All four carriers turned into the wind and began to launch strikes. The two U.S. carriers sent off a total of forty-six Dauntlesses, each with a thousand-pound bomb strapped to its belly. Twenty-one of the lumbering Devastators followed, with an escort of fifteen Wildcats swarming above as a screen against enemy Zeroes. At the same time the Japanese carriers launched a strike of sixty-nine aircraft, following the bearing reported by their early-bird scout. For brief moments during the flight, the pilots of the two sides caught glimpses of the enemy air groups, far away and mostly screened by clouds. Each flier kept his mind on the assigned task, and no shots were exchanged between the strike groups.

The Americans had the distinct advantage of radar in their big ships, and the approaching attack force was discovered at a range of sixty-eight miles. After several days of combat, and with the strike force already winging away, there were only fifteen Wildcats left with the fleet. Some of these were in the air as the standing combat air patrol; the rest were quickly scrambled, engines snarling as they tried to gain enough altitude to challenge the enemy dive bombers. There were a few Dauntlesses on the carriers, too, and they also were sent aloft. Though not heavily armed, they did have wing-mounted machine guns, which were better than nothing.

Lexington and *Yorktown* were relatively close together, both within the ring of their escorts, so the combined force of all the anti-aircraft batteries on the American ships met the Japanese strike force. First came the Kate torpedo bombers, pressing home the attack against the Lady Lex. The well-trained pilots split into two groups, each approaching the carrier from one of the bow angles, forcing her to turn to present a flank against one or the other group. As a result, *Lexington* took two torpedoes in her port side.

The dive bombers came next, harassed by Wildcats and SBDs as they tipped into their dives. Three bombs hit the *Lexington* and another plunged through *Yorktown*'s flight deck. The Japanese paid dearly, however, as more than two dozen of their aircraft were shot down. And since their planes fell among the U. S. fleet, the pilots were lost as well—a grim foreshadowing of what, before long, would prove to be the undoing of the vaunted Japanese carrier air wings.

As the surviving attackers winged away, the crews went to work on their ships. In an amazing testament to the carriers' durability and the skill of the damage-control parties, both ships were not only stabilized, but capable of steaming at speed and even continuing flight operations within an hour or two after the attack.

Meanwhile, the Americans had gotten somewhat scattered by bad weather, but many of the attacking planes came upon *Shokaku;* her sister ship remained concealed by clouds during the attack, which spared her from damage but also prevented her guns from assisting the defense. At first, however, it looked like no assistance might be needed. The Devastators came first, but these slow aircraft, already obsolete, failed to close enough with the target, and none of their fish scored a hit. Then came a group of five dive bombers, plunging through the flak to drop their bombs—all of which missed the frantically maneuvering carrier.

The next group of SBDs had Jo-Jo Powers, commanding officer of Bombing 5, in the lead. He took his dive to the limit, his plane absorbing hits and bursting into flames as he dropped lower and lower. He released his bomb, which plunged through the carrier's flight deck at about the same time that the bold pilot and his gunner crashed into the sea. The rest of the bombers seemed to be inspired by Powers's example and his sacrifice. In short order three more bombs crashed into *Shokaku,* leaving her burning throughout and barely afloat.

As the surviving Japanese aircraft returned to their carriers, they found they could not land on the burning *Shokaku,* and *Zuikaku*'s flight deck was so crowded that many aircraft had to be pushed over the side to make room for the returning strike. In the end, the Japanese lost forty-five out of the seventy-two aircraft that had been operational at the start of the day. The leaking, smoking *Shokaku* would barely make it back to Japan, while her sister ship's air groups were so badly depleted that she would need major replacements before she could resume operations; as a result, both ships would miss the upcoming, and crucial, Battle of Midway.

Victory and Defeat

In the American fleet there was jubilation as the fliers landed to report (erroneously) the sinking of a fleet carrier. That jubilation turned to shock when, in midafternoon, gases trapped belowdecks on *Lexington* exploded, dooming the ship. While the crews abandoned the stricken Lady Lex, and *Yorktown*'s damage control parties worked to keep her operational, Fletcher detached his cruiser covering force to try to interdict the Japanese landing at Port Moresby. These ships were spotted by Japanese navy fliers but managed to maneuver enough to avoid suffering any hits. The enemy fliers didn't stick around long enough to see the cruisers break off the interdiction mission, so Inouye still thought that Port Moresby was defended by a powerful surface fleet.

Both admirals on the scene were shaken by their losses, though pleased to have struck blows against the enemy fleets. The Americans had lost one of their two fleet carriers in the Coral Sea, with the other damaged, so Fletcher decided it was time to withdraw. The Japanese had lost only about half the tonnage of the American ships sunk, but *Shokaku* was in bad shape and *Zuikaku*'s aircrews had been badly depleted. Thus, at almost the same moment that Fletcher gave the order to pull back, Takagi reached the same decision. As the carriers limped away, the invasion force intended for Port Moresby was also recalled.

Coral Sea is perhaps most remembered as being the first naval battle in which the opposing ships never even spotted each other; all of the damage was inflicted by carrier-launched aircraft. And this indeed was a harbinger of so much of World War II and future naval operations. But maybe the battle had an even greater significance, in light of the operations of the preceding six months: at Coral Sea, for the first time in the war, the Japanese had been prevented from completing a mission, from attaining an objective, that they had determinedly set out to achieve.

Perhaps the tide of the war in the Pacific had not actually been turned, yet, but it had most certainly begun to ebb.

MASSACRE UNDER THE MIDNIGHT SUN

The Tragedy of Convoy PQ17, July 1942

BY DOUGLAS NILES

Heroes are made by the times.

—Traditional Chinese proverb

Adolf Hitler's decision to invade and occupy neutral Norway in April 1940 rose out of a clear strategic necessity: the need to secure the transport route for one of Germany's most important foreign natural resources. The Nazis' armament industry needed to manufacture lots and lots of high-quality steel, and that required iron ore in quantities not available within the Reich's borders. The best sources were the mines of northern Sweden, which meant the ore needed to be shipped to German ports.

Some of this ore was shipped directly from small Swedish ports in the Gulf of Bothnia, the northern terminus of the Baltic Sea. However, these ports had limited capacity and, furthermore, the gulf froze in winter, preventing any shipping there. As a result, something approaching half of German iron imports from Swedish mines came through the large, all-weather port of Narvik, in northern Norway. That embarkation point was connected by rail to northern Sweden, and even in summer, when the Gulf of Bothnia was traversable, Narvik remained the most affordable and direct route of transport.

Hitler rightly saw that the shipping route for those ore convoys, down the Norwegian coast in territorial waters, was extremely vulnerable to British interdiction, both by air attack and sea raiding, and by mining. As usual, the Nazi dictator acted aggressively, launching an invasion of that Scandinavian nation even as the Royal Navy was preparing to mine the waters off Narvik and all down that rugged, fjord-marked shoreline. As elsewhere in those early days of the Blitzkrieg, the invasion was a stunning surprise and ultimately successful—though the Allies held out in the truly decisive position of Narvik longer even than they did in France, and in the end only withdrew from Norway because of a failure of morale, not a military defeat.

Following the conquest, Germany established a host of Luftwaffe bases along the Norwegian coast, extending as far as North Cape—the northernmost point in Europe—and around the cape toward Finland; in June 1941, Finland became available for German air bases as well, as she became the Third Reich's ally in the war against the Soviet Union. As a result of this network of bases, German airpower could protect the ore route along the Norwegian coast and even fly as far as England. (In fact, during the Battle of Britain, the Luftwaffe made an ill-fated bomber raid, unescorted by fighters, from Norway against northern England. The Luftwaffe generals were under the impression that all of the British fighters were in the south of the country; they found out, to their chagrin, that they were wrong.)

Another benefit to Germany from the Norwegian conquest developed as the Nazis tried to decide how to use their surface ships. The rugged coastline, channeled as it was with many deep, twisting fjords, provided good anchorage for German raiders. *Bismarck* herself emerged from one of these natural harbors when she departed on her alarming, and ultimately doomed, cruise.

Barbarossa

Norway assumed a whole new strategic significance, however, after the Germans invaded the Soviet Union in the summer of 1941. Immediately Great Britain promised to ship as much aid as possible to the Soviets, and by the end of that year the United States had pledged an even greater amount of Lend-Lease aid to the Soviets, who were fighting for their survival. Two long, overland routes—one through Iran from the south, the other across Siberia from the far northwest—offered some capacity for import. The best, most efficacious, route by far, however, involved shipping the Lend-Lease supplies to the two far northern ports of Murmansk and Archangel. Murmansk was an all-weather port and a shorter trip, but Archangel was a larger city and much more closely linked by rail to the heartland of the Soviet Union. It was the preferred destination when weather allowed.

These cities were much closer to the front than Iran and Siberia and could be reached in a matter of days by merchant ships sailing from Great Britain. Convoys departing from Iceland, Canada, and the northeastern United States could also make the voyage in a relatively short amount of time.

But all of these convoys had to sail around the long Norwegian coastline, and this coast had been transformed by the Germans into a warren of bases for the Luftwaffe, U-boats, and even some of the few remaining German warships, including the battleship *Tirpitz,* sister ship of *Bismarck*. Weather was always an issue in these northern climes, with ice a menace during the winter and endless daylight favoring German air operations in summer. The water was always freezing cold and promised a quick death by hypothermia to any seaman who had to swim away from a sinking ship.

The route was further constricted by several large islands. Spitzbergen, several hundred miles north of North Cape, was always shrouded in ice, but even in high summer presented a barrier to passage farther into the Arctic. To the east, the Soviet island of Novaya Zemlya presented a long north-south obstacle, prevented ships from traveling east of their destinations far from land and then doubling back closer to the Russian coast. A much smaller landmass, Bear Island, stood approximately halfway between Norway and the ice pack and served as a midway mark for convoys traveling to and from the Soviet ports.

Convoys heading for Russia were given designations beginning with PQ and were numbered sequentially. Convoys making the return run were designated QP and usually consisted of ships carrying only ballast, instead of cargo. Convoy PQ1 sailed in August 1941, barely two months after the invasion of Russia, with a dozen more following over the next six months. Convoys PQ1 through PQ12 all made the run with remarkable success, as the Germans did not make a serious effort to challenge these convoys, and only one cargo ship was lost out of 103 to make the voyage.

Convoy PQ13 sailed on March 20, while a day later Convoy QP9 departed Murmansk for the westward voyage. With increased intelligence about shipping departures, and a more vigorous U-boat presence, the Germans sank five ships from PQ13. Convoys PQ14, 15, and 16, sailing in April through June, all encountered enemy attacks, and losses began to rise.

The Battle Escalates

The Germans were determined to shut down the flow of shipping even more effectively. They moved several powerful surface ships into Norwegian ports, most notably *Tirpitz,* based in the central Norway port of Trondheim. She would soon be joined there by the pocket battleship *Admiral Scheer* and the heavy cruiser *Admiral Hipper*. Soviet leader Joseph Stalin wrote directly to Winston Churchill on May 6, pleading and demanding that much-needed supplies be dispatched to the Russians with all possible speed. The prime minister replied that the presence of the German battleship and heavy cruisers now required that each convoy sail with a significant escort of heavy warships. Yet he pledged to make this effort, overruling his admirals, who wished to suspend the convoys until the end of summer, when increasing hours of darkness would provide at least some respite from the enemy searches.

As a result, the largest Lend-Lease convoy to depart for Russia thus far in the war assembled in Iceland during the month of June. Thirty-four merchant ships formed up Convoy PQ17, finally departing on June 27. This was a tremendously dangerous time to travel arctic waters, since there were really no hours of darkness. Storms and fog could hamper visibility periodically, but there was no blessed nightfall to screen vulnerable ships from enemy aircraft. The crews of the merchant ships and their escorts grew fatigued as a result of having to remain on alert twenty-four hours every day, while the German fliers who harassed them were able to return to their bases and get a normal night's (or day's) rest before making another attack.

Befitting its size and the known danger, PQ17 was provided with a great deal of naval protection. A close escort fleet under the leadership of Commander "Jackie" Broome would sail along with the merchant ships, guarding them like shepherd dogs protecting a flock of sheep. Broome had six destroyers, two ships configured for anti-aircraft duties, two submarines, and eleven smaller ships such as corvettes, cutters, and designated "rescue ships." The latter were tasked with picking sailors out of the water after their ships had been sunk—these specially tasked ships freed up the other escorts to continue their combat activities while the convoy plowed onward.

A support force under the command of Rear Admiral Louis Hamilton would also remain close to the convoy, though it would maintain a little more of a free-ranging patrol than the close escorts. Hamilton had four heavy cruisers, including two American ships armed with 8-inch guns, as well as three destroyers.

A threat from the largest German warships, such as *Tirpitz,* would be countered by a powerful task force from the Home Fleet itself. Admiral John Tovey was in charge, with his flag in the modern battleship *Duke of York;* he was joined by the U.S. battleship *Washington* as well as a fast aircraft carrier, making this the first combined U.S.-British fleet action in the Atlantic war. However, Tovey had a double mission: in addition to protecting the convoy, he had to make sure that the German heavies didn't break out into the Atlantic, like *Bismarck* and *Prinz Eugen* had done a year earlier. Because of this task, the battle fleet would have to hang back from the convoy by several hundred miles, and it seemed obvious to all concerned that it would not be able to arrive on scene in time to help in a crisis.

Still, the battleship fleet put to sea on time, departing Scapa Flow on a course that, for several days, would put it between the convoy and the Norwegian coast. Gradually, however, as PQ17 traveled north and east, Tovey and his big ships had to fall back, remaining in position to block or pursue any breakout into the Atlantic.

The convoy's initial progress was good, as it veered as far north as the ice pack would allow. When it finally turned east, it was on a course to pass north of Bear Island, and the crews on merchantmen and warships alike shared an optimism that they would be able to reach Archangel in good order. On July 1 the ships were spotted by German aircraft and several U-boats were discovered trailing the convoy, though the submarines did not move in to attack in the face of the tightly disciplined and vigorous screening force.

The first attack came from the air, late in the day on July 1, as a large flight of He-111s swarmed in at low altitude to launch torpedoes. These machines were much more formidable than the Royal Navy's Fairey Swordfish: the Heinkels were fast, modern bombers, and each carried two torpedoes. Even so, the first attack was beaten off with no torpedo hits and the loss of one German bomber.

The powerful anti-aircraft defenses of the convoy escorts proved to be very effective throughout the 2nd and 3rd of July, as two more air attacks were broken up. Though two ships were struck, one sinking and the other soon scuttled by the escorts, five or six more bombers were shot down, and Convoy PQ17 continued toward Russia in good order, at full speed. The men on the ships continued to view their mission with confidence and good morale. Though they had taken a few losses, their anti-aircraft guns were getting a few good licks in along the way.

Things looked a lot more frightening to the Admiralty, back in London, some two thousand miles from the action. First Sea Lord Dudley Pound was wrestling with a variety of conflicting pieces of intelligence. Although the British were very good at decoding German communications, the Kriegsmarine had recently changed its codes, and there were some unusual delays in decryption. Clearly, however, Convoy PQ17 had been located, and the Germans were going after it.

The Royal Navy's high command was forced to puzzle together a picture of German operations, but without a detailed understanding of the enemy's intentions. They did know, however, that *Tirpitz* and the heavy cruiser *Hipper* had left Trondheim, and that the pocket battleship *Admiral Scheer* had been ordered to sortie from her base in the far northern port of Narvik. All these developments came as the convoy was rounding North Cape, still as far out to sea as the polar ice would allow it to travel, and beginning the long run due east that would take it to its Russian destination.

The German surface ships boasted guns of 15 inches (*Tirpitz*) and 11 inches (*Scheer*), which meant that in all likelihood they could sink Admiral Hamilton's entire covering force of cruisers and destroyers in a short, sharp engagement. This would then leave the entire convoy as easy prey for the surface ships' guns—and all of the German ships were much faster than any of the merchantmen. To Pound, the potential for disaster was real, and extensive: in a surface attack, the convoy would be a liability, since it would place many tempting targets within range of a raider's big guns.

Of course, Pound could not discern the actual German intentions, and he didn't perceive Hitler's profound reluctance to risk his powerful warships (only a few of which were still afloat) to danger. Moreover, the First Sea Lord was not in face-to-face contact with his commanders on the scene and he seemed to be unaware of the optimism that was emboldening Admiral Hamilton and Commander Broome as they continued to run the gauntlet of German aircraft and U-boats. At this point, only two ships had been lost, and the convoy had passed to the north of Bear Island, a logical halfway point for the dangerous leg of the voyage.

Orders

On July 4 the American ships in the convoy all ran up brand-new oversize flags, in honor of Independence Day; the sight cheered their crews and impressed the British who observed the gesture from their own ships. Later that day, however, the Naval War Staff met in London and arrived at what would prove to be a catastrophic decision, authorized by First Sea Lord Pound, with the full agreement of every member of his staff. Fearing that the German surface ships would strike at any moment, the staff on dry land, far from the action, sent three orders between 9:11 and 9:30 P.M., orders that shocked and appalled Admiral Hamilton and Commander Broome.

All of the orders were prefaced with a "Most Immediate" tag, meaning that they were high priority. The first commanded "Cruiser force to withdraw to the west at high speed." Twelve minutes later came an alarm about the threat from surface ships, with instructions to disperse the convoy, with each ship heading for a Russian port on its own, without benefit of convoy or escort. Shortly thereafter, the unambiguous command "Convoy is to scatter" came over the airways.

This short flurry of communications allowed the German surface fleet to inflict more damage on the Allies than at any other period during the war—and all without firing a shot or even appearing on the horizon! For, unknown to the Admiralty, the mighty ships had already been recalled. Fearing interference from an Allied aircraft carrier, Hitler declined to risk *Tirpitz* in battle. Even more ignominiously, *Scheer* had run aground right off Narvik and was incapable of operating against the convoy.

In the convoy escorts, both Hamilton and Broome were taken aback. They had been brimming with confidence, having beaten off the air attacks with minimal damage, and had yet to suffer a torpedo attack from the U-boats known to be in the vicinity. With Broome's tight screen of destroyers and other anti-submarine vessels, the officers on the scene felt that they had a very good chance of pushing through all the way to Archangel. In the words of one officer aboard an escorting warship, "By simply shifting her anchorage the *Tirpitz* had done what massed U-boats and aircraft failed to do: she had broken the cohesion of the convoy."

The results of the plan were clear to everyone aboard the warships and merchantmen alike: without the tight formation of the convoy, and the presence of the escorts, the cargo ships would be helpless against the obvious threats of German aircraft and U-boats. Emotions verged on rage among the crews and captains of the warships as they were confronted with the confounding change, but they had no choice but to obey the order. As an officer aboard the heavy cruiser *Norfolk* recorded later: "The effect on the ship's company was devastating. . . . We abandoned the convoy. The ship was in a turmoil, everyone was boiling, and the Master at Arms told me he had never known such strong feelings before. . . . It was the blackest day we ever knew—sheer bloody murder."

The cruisers and destroyers turned about, steaming past the lumbering merchantmen even as the cargo ships began to pull away from each other, each ship to make its own way toward Archangel. Admiral Tovey, aboard *Duke of York* and now several hundred miles west of the convoy, cabled a request to London asking that the convoy instead be allowed to reverse course and make for the presence of the battle fleet. The British heavies, augmented further by the U.S. Navy, would certainly be enough to deter the German surface ships from making any attack. But his request was sternly denied; the convoy was to scatter and the ships plot individual courses for Archangel.

No sooner had the escorts steamed over the horizon than the U-boats and torpedo bombers, now augmented by shorter-range but lethally accurate Stuka dive bombers, swept into action. The defenseless merchant ships, easily spotted under the midnight sun, were mercilessly attacked. Twelve ships were sunk in the first twenty-four hours of the disaster. Over the next days, many more would be sent to the bottom. They were easy prey, lacking any significant anti-aircraft gunnery, unprotected by speedy escorts, and trapped as they were by the ice in the north and the landmass of Novaya Zemlya to the east. The scattered ships were picked off wherever they were found, most sinking alone, though four or five were trapped together against the Soviet landmass, where U-boats targeted them like ducks in a shooting gallery.

In the end, only eleven of the thirty-seven ships that had formed up in Iceland actually made it to Russia. The twenty-six vessels that sank carried to the bottom with them more than 400 tanks, 200 airplanes, 3,300 vehicles, and some 100,000 tons of miscellaneous supplies. The disaster caused the cancellation of the arctic convoys, at least during the summer months. As Churchill wrote to Stalin: "It is therefore with the greatest regret that we have reached the conclusion that to run the next convoy, PQ18, would bring no benefit to you, and would only involve dead loss to the common cause."

But it didn't have to be so. A bolder course of action—the course favored by the officers who were actually at sea, with the convoy—would have resulted in much greater success. Already the screening ships had shown how dangerous it was for German aircraft to challenge the anti-aircraft ships, and the slow, obsolete Stukas would have been even more vulnerable than the Heinkels to defensive fire. The U-boats would have challenged the destroyer screen at their peril and likely would have paid a toll in blood if they had pressed home their attacks.

The destruction of Convoy PQ17 has come to be regarded as one of the darkest events in Britain's long maritime history, and much of the blame has fallen on First Sea Lord Dudley Pound. It was his decision and his order that doomed the convoy. While he had legitimate concerns about the German raiders, his choice to err on the side of caution was guaranteed to produce lethal results to the merchant ships under his command. Certainly the best, and perhaps the only, lesson to come out of the debacle was the realization that in matters such as this, it is far better to trust the opinions and judgment of the men on the scene than to try to control naval affairs from an office thousands of miles away, safe and secure on dry land.

Well after the war, Jackie Broome sued a historian who implied that he had abandoned the convoy out of cowardice; the naval officer won a handsome reward in court. It is fitting that he should have the last word on the affair, when he wrote: "What the result would have been had the order to scatter not have been given, no one knows. But with the *Tirpitz* and her consorts then almost regarded as sacred cows, the result could hardly have been worse. The responsibility for what actually did happen must therefore forever rest on the shoulders of the man who gave that order."

DISASTER IN THE DARK

The Battle of Savo Island, August 1942

BY DOUGLAS NILES

Something must be left to chance;
nothing is sure in a sea fight above all.

—Horatio Nelson, 1758–1805

The war in the Pacific shifted tacks irrevocably during the course of three great battles in summer of 1942. First, in May, the Battle of the Coral Sea marked the first time one of Japan's ambitious schemes had been thwarted, when the intended invasion of Port Moresby was turned back before the landing force even came within sight of its objective. Second, in June, the carrier forces of the Imperial Japanese Navy and the United States Navy duked it out in an epic struggle, and Japan suffered one of the most catastrophic defeats in the history of warfare, losing all four of the fleet carriers that she had staked to the fight, while the United States escaped with the loss of but one of three mighty flattops. The momentum of Japan's tide of conquest was permanently blunted.

But it was not until the third great battle that the tide turned, obviously and dramatically: it was at Guadalcanal that the Americans went on the offensive, for the first time seizing territory held by Japan and commencing the long, bloody struggle that would take the U.S. Army and U.S. Navy (and Marine Corps) through the Marianas, the Philippines, and Okinawa, closing in on the Home Islands themselves. Guadalcanal was the start of the long road back, though it was a road with many violent bumps. The first of those bumps lay at the very start of the campaign for Guadalcanal: the Battle of Savo Island.

The progress of the Americans' Pacific War was to be a balancing act between the objectives and plans of the U. S. Army, represented by General Douglas MacArthur, and the U. S. Navy, under Admiral Chester Nimitz. The army advocated a push through New Guinea, to the Philippines—which had great personal symbolism to Mac, since he had been forced to flee the archipelago early in the war and had promised to return—and north to Japan. The navy, naturally enough, advocated an advance through the island groups of the central Pacific, from the Gilberts to the Marshalls to the Marianas, and thence to the Home Islands.

The chain of the Solomon Islands, east of New Guinea and south of the central Pacific, lay directly astride the boundary between these two areas of interest. During the Coral Sea offensive in May, the Japanese had occupied the small island of Tulagi, very near the southern terminus of the Solomons. Shortly afterward, aerial reconnaissance photos showed that the Japanese had put a work crew on the much larger island of Guadalcanal, across a sea channel about twenty miles farther to the south. This crew went right to work, and by July had cleared trees for a landing strip and started on an air base. This base would be the southernmost such installation in all the Japanese empire, and it presented a clear threat to the lines of communication between the United States and Australia.

Both the U.S. army and navy commanders agreed that this base made the Solomons the obvious choice for a place to begin offensive operations against Japan. There was constant friction between the army and the navy in the Pacific, with commanders vying for supplies, reinforcements, and primacy to fight the war in the way they felt was best. Often these disputes, which could become heated, were settled only by intervention at the highest, even Joint Chief, levels. Often the result was a compromise. So after some interservice haggling during June and July, it was decided that the navy and marines would attack Guadalcanal, and the army would take over as the offensive moved up the island chain, with an eventual objective of the massive and heavily fortified base at Rabaul.

The overall commander of the initial Guadalcanal offensives would be Vice Admiral Robert Ghormley. The landings were scheduled for August 7 and would be made by some 19,000 men of the (reinforced) First Marine Division, under General Alexander Vandegrift. The amphibious fleet of transports that would carry the marines, and the escorts that would protect those ships, were under the command of Rear Admiral Richmond Kelly Turner. The landings would be protected and covered by a carrier force, including three flattops, under the command of Admiral Fletcher, veteran of the Coral Sea and Midway battles.

A Good Start

The landings on Guadalcanal went as scheduled and were unopposed by the Japanese, who had mainly a labor force on the island to construct the air base. By midday the marines had advanced beyond the airstrip, which they promptly renamed Henderson Field, after a heroic Marine pilot who had perished at Midway. Across the channel, a smaller force landed at Tulagi, encountering stiff resistance that inflicted some three hundred American casualties. The garrison of the small island was overcome in a little more than a day of sharp combat, with virtually every Japanese soldier fighting to the death—a dark premonition of the kind of war awaiting the United States.

Surprisingly enough, the Japanese had made no preparations to defend their base and seemed totally surprised by the American offensive. This mistake was probably another manifestation of what came to be termed "victory disease," the Japanese high command's complacency as a result of the half year's worth of consistently triumphant campaigns. The empire's generals and admirals developed their own, often very complicated, plans and routinely neglected to consider any plans the enemy might be making to counter those operations.

Even so, reaction to the American landings was not long in developing. Admiral Inouye, in command of the Japanese base at Rabaul, launched air raids on the first afternoon of the campaign. These bombers were escorted by the very long-range Zero fighters, and in a series of attacks on August 7 and 8 they mixed it up with American carrier-based Wildcats in several furious air battles over the landing fleets. Additional Japanese bombers went after the American carriers of Fletcher's task force; these attacks, too, were defeated by the Wildcats of the combat air patrols. No hits were scored on the American carriers.

Many planes were lost by each side, and though little damage was inflicted on the transports, the ships were forced to spend much of both days maneuvering and defending themselves, so much so that unloading operations were badly hampered. As a result, by evening on August 8, nearly all of the marines had been put ashore, but most of their supplies, including rations, ammunition, and the construction equipment needed to complete the airfield and build a proper installation, remained aboard the transports.

On August 7, Inouye also dispatched a task force of seven cruisers and one destroyer, under Vice Admiral Gunichi Mikawa, with orders to attack the American covering force and transports. Mikawa wasted no time in starting down the "Slot"—a long, narrow channel lying between the two roughly parallel island chains that made up the Solomons. This would become a regular naval highway over the course of the next year, gradually changing hands as the Americans slowly moved their way northwest.

Over the next few months, this route would be carefully observed by the legendary "Coastwatchers," mainly planters and natives with allegiance to Australia and, hence, the Allies. They would watch the Japanese ships pass and give precise reports of the type and bearing of the task force. But as of early August, the organization had yet to take root and lacked the means to communicate its sightings to local commanders. Admiral Turner had requested additional surveillance of the Slot during his landings, but this reconnaissance was not carried out; unfortunately, it seems that Turner thought that it was, so he had no idea that a powerful Japanese surface fleet was bearing down on him late on August 8.

The commander of the covering force protecting Turner's transports was a British admiral, Victor Crutchley, who flew his flag in the heavy cruiser HMAS *Australia.* Crutchley had at his disposal a strong force of eight cruisers (six of them heavy cruisers) and fifteen destroyers. However, he and Turner weakened the covering force by spreading his ships out to cover the three possible routes of approach to the landing zone. The channel north of Guadalcanal was wide and deep. To the west, the dormant volcanic cone of a small landmass, Savo Island, rose steeply from the waters, forcing all ships approaching from that direction to go either north or south around it.

Two of Crutchley's destroyers were equipped with radar, and he placed them on picket patterns, one on either side of Savo Island. However, the early shipborne radar was proving to be very unreliable when used near land. This weakness had not yet been perceived by the navy, and in the fighting the radars of both destroyers would contribute nothing to the American knowledge of enemy deployments.

The rest of the covering force would patrol in three groups across the points of access to the landing beaches. The Southern Group included Crutchley's flagship, as well as cruisers HMAS *Canberra* and USS *Chicago,* along with two destroyers; this group was assigned the passage to the south of Savo Island. The Northern Group included three American cruisers, *Vincennes, Astoria,* and *Quincy,* with two more destroyers. These ships, in line, cruised around a square pattern northeast of Savo Island. The Eastern Group included cruisers USS *San Juan* and HMAS *Hobart,* as well as two more destroyers; naturally, it patrolled the eastern end of the channel and would not become involved in the action. The other seven destroyers were brought in close to the landing craft because of worries about Japanese submarines.

The crews of all of these ships were weary because of the oppressive tropical heat and some thirty-six hours of intense operations. As a result, the admiral authorized a Condition II alert level, which allowed half the crews to rest while the other half remained at battle stations.

The Japanese had better intelligence, because Mikawa had launched floatplanes from his cruisers, and they reported back with a fairly accurate description of the Allied ship dispositions. Adding to the Allied confusion, Fletcher decided that he had lost too many fighters during the two days of air battles to continue to maintain a combat air control. As a result, he ordered his carriers to withdraw from the area. Turner, knowing that his transports had lost their air cover, decided that he would have to withdraw as well, though he decided to delay the departure until August 9.

At 4 P.M. on the 8th, Mikawa communicated a plan of attack to his powerful, fast warships: "On the rush-in we will go from south of Savo Island and torpedo the enemy main force in front of Guadalcanal anchorage; after which we will turn toward the Tulagi forward area to shell and torpedo the enemy. We will then withdraw north of Savo Island." Mikawa desired a night battle for several reasons: for one thing, the Japanese navy had drilled extensively in night operations, and their ships were equipped with powerful searchlights and excellent range-finding equipment; for another, he expected that the American carriers would still be nearby, and he wanted to go under cover of darkness to avoid enemy air strikes.

Upon approaching the channel, Mikawa launched some of his floatplanes into the night sky. They were to scout such Allied positions as could be discerned in the darkness and then drop star flares as the Japanese surface ships came onto the scene. These planes were heard by the lookouts on a number of Crutchley's ships, but no one deduced that they were precursors to attack.

Complications

Further hampering Allied defensive preparations, Admiral Turner called a midnight conference to discuss the impact of the departure of Fletcher's carriers. General Vandegrift and Admiral Crutchley reported to Turner's flagship. Crutchley appointed Captain Howard Bode of *Chicago* as temporary commander of the Southern Group and did not inform the rest of his covering force of his absence, which would leave another gaping hole in the command structure of the defending force. Bode, for his part, was awakened from a sound sleep to learn of his temporary appointment and elected not to place his ship in the lead of the patrol, which was the typical position of the command ship. Having made this nondecision, he went back to sleep.

Mikawa flew his flag in the magnificent heavy cruiser *Chokai,* which was followed by four more heavy cruisers: *Aoba, Furutaka, Kako,* and *Kinugasa*. He also had two light cruisers under his command, *Tenryu* and *Yubari,* and one destroyer. Unlike the Allied cruisers, all Japanese cruisers had the ability to launch torpedoes, and they were armed with plenty of the splendid Type 93 "long lance." Mikawa's plan, already communicated to his ships, was to pass to the south of Savo Island as he entered the channel, but on the initial approach his lookouts spotted one of the radar-equipped U.S. destroyers, *Blue.* The Japanese veered away from the destroyer, from which no sailor spotted the impressive line of battle, but then the Japanese caught sight of the other picket destroyer north of Savo Island.

Mikawa reverted to his original plan, slipping undetected by either radar or eyesight between the two American destroyers, passing around the cone-shaped island. Accelerating to a speed of thirty knots, the Japanese strike force raced toward the patrolling cruisers of the Southern Group. Just after 1:30 A.M., August 9, the circling floatplanes dropped flares over the cruisers *Chicago* and *Canberra*. The Australian ship turned to screen the transports from the attacking task force and quickly took about two dozen large-caliber hits and, badly holed, began to sink. *Chicago* took several hits as well. Captain Bode had again been sleeping soundly and seemed sluggish in responding to the emergency. As he arrived on the bridge the cruiser took a damaging hit to her forecastle; afterward, *Chicago* steamed away from the fight for some forty minutes.

Captain Bode never warned the rest of the Allied ships of the presence of the Japanese fleet, and the bulk of Savo Island prevented the ships of the Northern Group from seeing the violence that was occurring not terribly far away.

The destroyer *Patterson* spotted the approach right about the time the star shells went off and broadcast an alarm via radio and signal lamp: "Warning! Strange ships entering harbor!" This alarm, unfortunately, failed to penetrate the ether, leaving the Northern Group still unaware of the danger. *Patterson* then conducted a spirited battle with overwhelmingly powerful Japanese cruisers, taking a few hits herself and blasting away until the speedy attackers had moved out of range.

Defeat in Detail

With two southern cruisers already knocked out of the fight, Mikawa's ships circled Savo Island, operating independently now as each sought targets of opportunity. They split into two separate columns, and as a result when they quickly came upon the Northern Group they were able to attack the Allied ships from two different directions. The Japanese warships sent a barrage of torpedoes and shells into the cruisers patrolling there, disabling and dooming *Vincennes, Quincy,* and *Astoria* in a matter of minutes.

By the time the smoke cleared, the Allies had lost four out of five cruisers engaged—only the *Chicago* would live to fight another day. Mikawa's ships had suffered no torpedo damage and only a few gunfire hits, with casualties of fewer than a hundred men killed. At about 2:15 A.M., he wrestled with the decision as to whether he should close in on the virtually defenseless transports off Tulagi and Guadalcanal, or retire. Unaware that Fletcher had already pulled out his carriers and worried about an American air attack in the morning, he decided to withdraw to the north, following one of the most lopsided victories in Japanese naval history, and without a doubt the most ignominious defeat in the long annals of the United States Navy. A final, tragic postscript to the battle occurred nearly a year later, in Panama. There, upon learning that he was to be censured for his performance in the Battle of Savo Island, Captain Bode shot himself to death.

THE GUNS OF NOVEMBER

Battleships Duel off Guadalcanal, November 1942

BY DOUGLAS NILES

There are no extraordinary men . . . just extraordinary circumstances that ordinary men are forced to deal with.

—Admiral William Frederick Halsey Jr., 1882–1959

The fight over the swampy, mosquito-infested island of Guadalcanal would last for a total of seven months, during which time many basic tenets of the War in the Pacific would evolve. The marines of the First Division established a perimeter and protected the captured airstrip, now called Henderson Field, as the Japanese shuttled in small groups of ground troops and reinforcements. As already described, the Battle of Savo Island at the start of the campaign established the primacy of Japanese night-fighting skill in both gunnery and torpedoes. Following that battle, the channel between Guadalcanal and Tulagi would forever be known as Ironbottom Sound.

By August 20, the marines had made the captured airstrip into a usable base, and fighters and dive bombers flew to the island. The code name for the island was Cactus, and these planes would become known as the Cactus Air Force; their accomplishments would contribute to some of the most glorious chapters of Marine, Navy, and, later, U.S. Army aviation. Long-range Japanese aircraft based at Rabaul and, soon, Bougainville (at the northern end of the Solomons chain) would continue to attack the island, but the United States would never again sacrifice daytime air superiority.

Carrier Battles

The aircraft carriers of both sides also contributed to the ongoing campaign, and both sides paid heavily in blood, aircraft, and ships. Over August 22–25 the Battle of the Eastern Solomons was triggered by a Japanese attempt to reinforce Guadalcanal with 1,500 men. The mission was another nighttime run down the Slot, commanded by Rear Admiral Raizo Tanaka, who was already earning the sobriquet "Tanaka the Tenacious." Two fleet carriers and a light carrier moved to cover the reinforcement.

Though the Japanese had changed their codes after Midway, significant radio traffic tipped the Americans to the movement, and Admiral Ghormley ordered Admiral Fletcher to intercept with the American carrier fleet. By this time, Fletcher had three large carriers: *Enterprise, Saratoga,* and *Wasp*. But the admiral misjudged the timing of the battle and sent *Wasp*'s group away to refuel, so he met the Japanese carrier force with only two flattops. American bombers sank the Japanese light carrier *Ryujo,* but *Enterprise* was heavily damaged in a reciprocal raid. Tanaka accomplished his mission, but the loss of ninety planes and their pilots was another significant blow to the empire's naval air strength.

On the last day of August, *Saratoga* was damaged by a Japanese submarine, leaving only *Wasp* as an operational carrier; then, on September 15, *Wasp* was sent to the bottom by another submarine torpedo attack. On October 11–13, both sides sent additional troop reinforcements to the island. The two fleets met and battled to a draw off Cape Esperance, with both transports delivering their soldiers to the island. After this battle, Admiral Bill Halsey replaced Ghormley as area commander for the U.S. Navy, and Rear Admiral Thomas Kinkaid replaced Fletcher as commander of the carrier task force—which now included *Hornet* and the hastily repaired *Enterprise.*

The next battle was another carrier fight, on October 26–27. This time the Japanese tied their naval operation to their most ambitious ground attack against the Marine perimeter, which was defeated with heavy Japanese casualties. At sea, the Battle of the Santa Cruz Islands was a victory for the Japanese and resulted in more damage to *Enterprise* and the loss of *Hornet*. But *Shokaku,* recently returned to action, was damaged and would be laid up for nine months. Once again, however, the loss of Japanese pilots—some one hundred of them, twice as many as the U.S. Navy's aircraft losses—would have long-term consequences that the Japanese would never reverse.

By this time the routine around Guadalcanal had evolved into a repeating pattern. During the day, under the cover of the Cactus Air Force, the Americans brought ships in, unloaded supplies, and pretty much had freedom of action. At night, however, U.S. ships were withdrawn and the marines hunkered down in trenches and foxholes, while Japanese surface ships cruised the channel and frequently bombarded the airstrip and the Marine positions. The runs down the Slot had become frequent and almost predicable, so much so that they had come to be known as the "Tokyo Express."

By now, too, the network of Coastwatchers had been well established up and down the Solomons chain. These brave scouts, who were relentlessly pursued by Japanese patrols, reported not just ships, but also air raids; they had become a very reliable source of good intelligence for the marines on Guadalcanal and the naval officers in ships around the island. But the initiative had slipped from the Japanese, mostly because they had never reacted to the strength of the American landings with the diligence and numbers necessary to repel them. Whereas the Marines had placed 19,000 men on the island on pretty much the first day, the enemy responded with infusions of 500, 1,000, maybe 2,000 men at a time. Once these troops were on the island, they were poorly supplied and led, often being expended in piecemeal attacks that despite local fury and violence had no chance of actually overrunning the U.S. Marines' position.

A New Strategy

By November 12, the Japanese had perhaps recognized the folly of this operational plan. Tanaka the Tenacious had departed Rabaul with eleven transports, protected by eleven destroyers, and these transports carried a full 13,000 Japanese soldiers, enough to make a significant impact on the American position. Screening this run of the Tokyo Express was an appropriately powerful task force under Admiral Hiroaki Abe. He had two fast battleships (*Hiei, Kirishima*) as well as two cruisers and fourteen destroyers and was under orders to bombard Henderson Field on the night of November 12–13.

On the very same night, Admiral Turner was bringing in another run of transports carrying reinforcements and supplies. The covering force for this transport mission was a fleet of five cruisers and eight destroyers under Rear Admiral Daniel Callaghan.

Having gained intelligence of Abe's approach, Callaghan boldly decided to challenge the heavier force, counting on his radar to give him the advantage of surprise.

Yet once again American shipboard radar did not function as expected. Abe's task force, with the escorts sailing in line abreast to the port and starboard of the two battleships, which were in column formation, entered Ironbottom Sound via the same route Admiral Mikawa had employed during the Battle of Savo Island—that is, to the south of that volcanic cone. Callaghan's ships approached the enemy head-on, in a long column with four destroyers in the lead, followed by five cruisers and trailed by the last four destroyers.

Initial contact was finally obtained at 1:24 A.M. by the radar of a cruiser, *Helena,* in the exact center of Callaghan's column. A few minutes later the lead destroyer, *Cushing,* made visual contact with the approaching enemy; immediately a brutal and confused melee erupted. For only a little more than half an hour the two sides blazed away at each other in darkness shattered only by the flashes of guns. Often, opposing vessels found themselves at virtually point-blank range, and damage was heavy on both sides.

By the time both fleets pulled back, at about 2:15, two U.S. cruisers were sinking and two more were badly crippled; four destroyers also plunged beneath the waves, and three of the remaining four were seriously damaged. Admiral Callaghan, aboard his damaged flagship *San Francisco,* was killed. But the Japanese also lost two of their cruisers, and all the rest of their ships were damaged. Battleship *Hiei* was disabled, unable to steam away from Savo Island, and at first light she was sent to the bottom by a torpedo attack by planes launched from *Enterprise,* on their way to reinforce the Cactus Air Force. Despite the losses, the battle was a clear-cut American victory, since Abe's force was prevented from bombarding Henderson Field and Tanaka's transports were forced to withdraw to the north without debarking their reinforcements.

Three Nights of Battle

The combat of this intense period is sometimes referred to as the First and Second Naval Battles of Guadalcanal, but in reality it was one furious fight that spanned three nights and two days. During the daytime on November 13 both sides launched many air strikes, with fighters wheeling through dogfights in the air over the island and Ironbottom Sound while bombers struck at damaged ships and the marines' ground installations. In the meantime, Halsey was rushing up battleships of his own, two powerful vessels and escorts under the command of Rear Admiral Willis Lee. To date in the war, no Allied battleship had exchanged fire with a Japanese capital ship, and Lee was eager to get *South Dakota* and *Washington* into the fight.

On the night of November 13–14, a task force under Admiral Mikawa's command entered Ironbottom Sound and pummeled Henderson Field, with the main damage coming from two heavy cruisers and their many 8-inch guns. The strike force did not make a fast enough getaway, however, and with the dawn the Cactus Air Force came swarming, sinking one heavy and one light cruiser. The Marine, Navy, and Army fliers also discovered Tanaka's transports as that tenacious admiral again tried to deliver his reinforcements. Intense and relentless air attacks sank seven of the eleven transports, with tremendous loss of life to the soldiers who were being carried to the battlefield.

As the night of November 14 fell, with Admiral Nobutake Kondo now in command, the battleship *Kirishima,* four cruisers, and nine destroyers steamed south at flank speed, with the dual mission of screening Tanaka's remaining transports and, once again, of bombarding Henderson Field. The battleship's heavy batteries, in particular, stood a good chance of inflicting serious damage on the airstrip, and on the planes that were parked in simple revetments all around the field.

As was becoming a pattern, the action again surged and waned all around Savo Island. Admiral Lee intercepted Kondo's force at 11 P.M., and once again Ironbottom Sound was illuminated by the flashes, flares, and searchlights of an intense night battle. *South Dakota* led the charge but quickly suffered numerous hits that knocked out her electrical systems and took her out of the battle. *Washington* came up right behind, however. Even though she was the focus of attack from fourteen Japanese ships, her captain and crew maintained focus and discipline and concentrated return fire on *Kirishima*. The Japanese battleship was battered to a hulk and would soon sink, along with one destroyer; the United States lost two destroyers.

Later that night, Tanaka the Tenacious did succeed in debarking the 4,000 troops from his four remaining transports, and he picked up 5,000 survivors from the sunken ships on his return to Rabaul. But after the naval battles of November, the Imperial Japanese Navy would never again challenge the Americans for control of the waters around Guadalcanal.

THE ENIGMA THAT WASN'T

The Battle of the Atlantic, 1943

BY PAUL A. THOMSEN

Sighted sub, sank same.

—U.S. Navy pilot Donald Francis Mason, in a radio report on January 28, 1942

At the onset of World War II, Adolf Hitler utilized every means at his disposal to bring England to its knees. Although Nazi Germany could not spare troops and supplies from the Russian front to launch an amphibious-based ground campaign against the island nation, Hitler's inner circle of advisers did promise that the precise application of advanced technology and tactics would work just as well. First, German intelligence sent espionage agents. They failed. Next, the Luftwaffe launched daytime and nighttime bombing campaigns, but they too failed to weaken the resolve of the British people.

By late 1940, however, something began to change. U-boats had managed to inflict heavy casualties against Allied convoys with a combination of stealth, ciphered wireless communication, and a few well-placed torpedoes. Even with the United States now at war with Hitler, in 1942 the German U-boat seemed poised to achieve victory in the Battle of the Atlantic. But then, suddenly, the tide turned back against Nazi Germany. As two U-boat captains discovered in June 1943 just north of the Azores, the technology and tactics they had so deftly deployed had, it seems, worked too well.

Nazi Germany's navy in World War II, the Kriegsmarine, developed atypically from most of the German military command structure. As Hitler had been an infantryman, he held a special place in his heart for the army. The Luftwaffe was the play toy of the industrialists, the aviators, and World War I flying ace Hermann Goering. Each German service was quite independent of the others. Hitler feared that if anyone but himself controlled the entire armed forces, that person could become a threat. Eventually this paranoia led to such strange events as Luftwaffe infantry divisions and the SS divisions being effectively a separate army from the Wehrmacht. German intelligence was a battleground for which nearly every sector of the military and police fought. Alternately, the Kriegsmarine were largely considered orphans, partially because of their expense/risk ratio of return and their reputation as mutineers at the end of the last war, and partially because few placed an emphasis on maritime concerns until Germany had achieved hegemony over the continent of Europe. Left to itself, the navy had some room to experiment, innovate, and reconceptualize naval warfare in the twentieth century (albeit on a shoestring budget constrained by the Treaty of Versailles). As a result, in 1939, this think-tank-like environment spawned two competitive and congruent interpretations of Hitler's Plan Z rearmament and enlargement of the navy, including both Alfred Mahan–style big ship surface vessels (comprising battleships, aircraft carriers, cruisers, and destroyers) and a small but vital submarine force, the U-boats.

After the scuttling of the German commerce raider *Admiral*

Graf Spee in the Battle of the River Plate, the U-boat began to emerge as the ideal weapon of Nazi naval warfare. As a submerged vessel, it was virtually undetectable. It could search, acquire, and stalk its chosen prey like a shadowy wraith, waiting for the ideal moment to strike. Once the vessel released its torpedoes at its targets, the captain could then conduct his U-boat away from the unsuspecting victims, set up for a run on another target, and watch as his first target's hull ruptured and sank beneath the waves. If fleet command required special ships or convoys to be attacked or the vessel required supplies, the orders were often transmitted to the U-boats at sea via wireless radio. These signals were then fed through an encryption machine of complex gears, keys, and lights, called Enigma, and a code system that German cryptographers claimed was virtually unbreakable. If fleet command wished, U-boats in a given area could be directed to converge on a specific target and decimate an enemy fleet. Losses could be kept to a minimum while simultaneously maximizing crew combat potential.

For millennia, an empire's ability to project power abroad had been limited only by the speed, armament, and vigilance of her navy, but now the game had changed. In response to the monthly growing U-boat threat, Allied ships were forced to take zigzag courses, run at rapid speeds, and cluster into convoys for mutual protection and assurance that, if a few were lost, at least some freight might arrive at their destination. Crews were also required to be on alert for more than just distant surface vessels. They likewise needed to remain vigilant night and day, constantly scanning the waters for shadows, the telltale signs of a thin telescope watching them amid the rolling waves, or, the sailor's nightmare, thin streaks of white ocean foam hiding torpedoes moving rapidly toward their ship. Even if a torpedo was spotted, there was little cargo vessels could do but try to dodge the fast-moving projectile and try to outrun its unseen source before another attempt could be made. According to historian Commander Jerry Russell, in 1939 an estimated 810 tons of Allied shipping was sent to the ocean's bottom at the cost of nine U-boats, but in 1940, as the crews grew in experience, an estimated 4,407 tons of Allied shipping were neutralized, set against the loss of twenty-two more U-boats and their crews. Between 1939 and 1944, the U-boat fleet grew from 57 to a peak strength of 445 vessels. It was a nearly perfect tool for denying war-torn England the supplies it needed most to resist Nazi Germany.

ULTRA

Since the onset of the war, British intelligence had been detecting, noting, and trying to decrypt the U-boat communications. While codebreakers could identify the signal of a surfaced vessel transmitting commands, the ocean was far too vast and their assets were far too spread out to be able to pinpoint more than a general region of the Atlantic Ocean where they thought the U-boat might be prowling. Similarly, they could listen to the signals sent between Germany and her hunters at sea, but they were consistently having trouble breaking the encryption, which they called ULTRA. They knew that the Enigma machines the U-boats utilized were similar to the devices adopted by other branches of German military. Still, each system had physical variants. Some had an additional coding system known as "plugboards." Some did not. Others had three or four rotors. Each difference gave an added level of complexity to the physicality of the problem. Moreover, German cryptographers utilized different codes for different branches of service, and when they suspected their code system might have been broken, the codes were changed. Trying to deal with so many different types of coding hardware was a truly maddening experience.

In June 1941, British intelligence's cryptographers, based out of Bletchley Park, finally made a breakthrough with ULTRA. They broke the German Hydra code. Now able to read a large number of U-boat-related communiques, they began to warn convoys away from areas signaled as German hunting grounds, until one day, suddenly, ULTRA went silent. The Kriegsmarine, they correctly deduced, had changed something in their code machine and/or encryption methods. Still, they had gained much-needed insight into the established enemy tactics and revealed the daily secrets of the Atlantic U-boats. In December 1941, the United States joined forces with British intelligence and provided American firepower in the form of the U. S. Navy. Before long, convoys were being granted better protection, including a greater number of destroyers, cruiser escorts, and a substantial aviation component of spotter planes and fighter-bomber aircraft. With more ships and a greater number of eyes, the game had become much tougher for Nazi Germany.

While many have believed the final breaking of the ULTRA code in December 1942 spelled doom for Nazi Germany, the U-boat commanders had also been making another crucial mistake. Given the bountiful number of targets coming from North America, the U-boat command had ordered most of their wolf packs to pounce on targets sailing near the Atlantic coast. This required the attack U-boats to resupply and refuel with their tanker/minelayer variant U-boats at regular intervals and at preset points throughout the eastern Atlantic Ocean. The closer the enemy operated to the coast and the more targets they were assigned to hunt and kill, the more fuel they required to maintain operational status. Hence several U-boats would consistently return to a given area for resupply, making their activities in part predictable. One simply had to have enough ships and aircraft with radios in a given area to wait for the next series of calls, then launch aircraft, triangulate their position, and swarm around the signal's point of origin. In 1942 alone, according to Commander Russell, the U-boats had sunk an estimated ten thousand tons of Allied shipping, losing only about eighty-five U-boats in the process. There was no time to waste.

In June 1943, their bloody deeds began to catch up with the U-boats. The U. S. Navy, determining through intelligence that the Germans were utilizing a point just north of the Azores for refueling, had deployed the escort carrier USS *Bogue* with a complement of sixteen fighters and eighteen torpedo bombers and a small task force to patrol the area. When ULTRA intelligence indicated U-boats had been ordered to attack a nearby convoy, the task force turned south to intercept and launch their complement of Avengers. Three U-boats were soon spotted. The task force gave chase and on the following day, after a long game of cat-and-mouse, U-217 was sunk and the remaining two U-boats dispersed. Shortly thereafter, an Avenger spotted another enemy target, U-758. Unlike the others, this U-boat returned fire and, over the next several hours, led the American task force away from the other U-boats. Before finally disappearing from the Americans' sight, the badly wounded vessel, however, had broadcast a distress call for mechanical support. In doing so, they had inadvertently betrayed the location of a previously undiscovered refueling position and U-boat tanker, U-118, to the USS *Bogue*.

Air Cover

On June 12, 1943, several U-118 crewmen were abovedecks when suddenly the *Matrosen-Obergefreiter,* a leading seaman who was on watch, began shouting, "Planes! Planes!" Seconds later, two Avengers from the USS *Bogue* came roaring out of the sun, strafing the vessel from stern to bow with their machine guns. As the

U-boat crew scrambled for the hatch, six more Avengers appeared in the sky. U-118 attempted to submerge, but the damage inflicted in the initial volley was too severe. As the surrounded German vessel broke the water again, her crew began to climb out of the submersible and run toward the deck guns, but they were too late. Suddenly, a bomb released from one of the Avengers detonated on impact with U-118's conning tower and broke the vessel into pieces.

The battle had raged for several days, but the Allies had scored a decisive victory against Nazi Germany's maritime menace. For the first time, Americans and British had gone on the maritime offensive to interdict a submarine's attack while it was still in progress. They had managed to kill one of their quarry and drive off two more U-boats. And they had located and eliminated both a major U-boat refueling point and a prized U-boat tanker. Equally important, they had validated the combined value of operational British-U.S. intelligence and firepower. As a result, the U-boats were forced to retreat from the area, and eventually the region, and hunt in waters closer to occupied Europe.

The German U-boats had come to believe they were unknowable and invisible. As the new Allied tactics of decryption and detection were adopted, the Germans were proven wrong on both counts. Winston Churchill once wrote that "the only thing that ever really frightened me during the war was the U-boat peril." After the decisive Allied victory in the Battle of the Atlantic, it became Adolf Hitler and his U-boat crews who trembled in fear at the sizable forces now amassing to invade the continent his army and Luftwaffe had thought was safely theirs. Technology and innovation had both saved and doomed Nazi Germany's maritime offensive.

THEIR OWN WORST ENEMY

The Battle of the Komandorski Islands, March 26, 1943

BY PAUL A. THOMSEN

In battle, there are not more than two methods of attack—the direct and the indirect; yet these two in combination give rise to an endless series of maneuvers.

—Sun Tzu, 544 BCE–496 BCE

The battle for control of the Aleutian Islands remains one of the most unique campaigns of World War II. The Japanese seizure of the Alaskan islands Attu and Kiska marked the first time a foreign power had held American sovereign territory since the War of 1812. The campaign itself was fought over a piece of nearly valueless real estate and in the most inhospitable of conditions. In such a remote location resupply was vital to victory and had a significant effect on the final results in the Aleutians. But if the U.S. Army had problems at the Battle of the Komandorski Islands, the Japanese proved that their own fleet was their worst enemy.

Since the 1941 attack on Pearl Harbor, the Japanese empire had rapidly expanded to encompass nearly half of the Pacific Rim, but, for all their achievements, the Japanese high command was continuously challenged to keep their seized territory from the United States. By neutralizing the bulk of the American navy in the December 7 attack, Admiral Isoroku Yamamoto had essentially guaranteed his superiors a six-month window of opportunity in which they could project their will as the dominant naval power in the region. The loss of the aircraft carrier *Shoho* and heavy damage to the *Shokaku* at the May 4–8, 1942, Battle of the Coral Sea, however, were clear indicators that the Japanese navy was living on borrowed time. With few alternatives, the Japanese readily embraced a series of audacious plans, including Yamamoto's idea to divide, isolate, and neutralize part of the American fleet at Midway Island and undertake an invasion of American soil at the Aleutian islands of Attu and Kiska, Alaska.

While Yamamoto was preparing to attack Midway Island, on June 3, 1942, the Imperial Japanese Navy struck the unsuspecting Aleutian Islands. The initial Japanese assault force, comprising elements of their Fifth Fleet under the command of Vice Admiral Boshiro Hosogaya, swept through the area like fire, twice raiding the new American airbase at Dutch Harbor, probing the American waters for potential fleet contacts, and shortly thereafter landing a small invasion force on Attu and Kiska. By August, the United States had established an air base on nearby Adak Island to allow bombing runs of Kiska, but by then it was already too late. The enemy refused to be moved from their now-fixed positions. They would have to be forcibly evicted from the island by the American army. The Japanese fleet may have been crippled at Midway on the following day, but, much to the chagrin of the United States, they had managed to entrench themselves in Alaska. As a result,

Alaska was largely considered an army job, to which the navy would offer only token support as they now hunted down the rest of the Japanese fleet.

Outnumbered

On March 26, 1943, a small American fleet under the command of Rear Admiral Charles McMorris sighted a Japanese fleet east of the Russian Komandorski ("Commander") Islands escorting a group of transports making for the Aleutians. At approximately 7:30 A.M., McMorris ordered his fleet to action. The American fleet (composed of the aging light cruiser *Richmond,* the heavy cruiser *Salt Lake City,* and destroyers *Coghlan, Bailey, Dale,* and *Monaghan*) was all that stood between the Aleutian battlefields and the Japanese force. Over the next several minutes, McMorris's lead ships, the *Coghlan* and the *Richmond,* discovered that this enemy fleet, commanded by the returning Vice Admiral Hosogaya, was nearly twice the size of the American force.

By all accounts, McMorris should have recalled his lead ships, come about, and fled the scene, but in the first of many moves that would mystify the Japanese admiral, the American pulled his rear ships into close formation and altered course to intercept the enemy. Admiral McMorris, it seemed, wanted the Japanese transports sunk and was willing to risk the loss of his meager fleet to accomplish the task. Taken aback by the American's boldness, Hosogaya ordered his fleet northward and then northwest. According to American naval historian Samuel Eliot Morison, the Japanese fleet appeared in a single ordered column, which consisted of the heavy cruisers *Nachi* and *Maya,* the light cruiser *Tama,* the destroyers *Wakaba* and *Hatsushimo,* the light cruiser *Abukuma,* the destroyer *Ikazuchi,* the specially armored converted merchant cruisers *Asaka Maru* and *Sakito Maru* (which also contained the bulk of the supplies), and finally the destroyer *Inazuma*. Suddenly the Japanese admiral noticed that the most powerful ship in the American fleet, the *Salt Lake City,* appeared to be lagging behind the main group. Without a second thought, Hosogaya moved to take advantage of this emerging weakness in the American formation. At twenty thousand yards, the *Nachi* opened fire on first the *Richmond* and then the *Salt Lake City*.

Both American ships, unfazed by the incoming salvos, bore down on the Japanese. Once in range, the *Salt Lake City*'s gunners returned fire, scoring two hits on the *Nachi,* but the Japanese fleet's lines likewise would not break and so McMorris was forced to veer off. In his zeal, however, McMorris had allowed Hosogaya's fleet to get too close to his fleet for comfort. Over the next hour, no matter how hard the Americans tried, they could not shake the enemy fleet loose. Repeatedly they endured a relentless volley of near misses from the guns of the heavy cruiser *Maya* as they zigzagged to port and stern between the shells. They also narrowly escaped a full spread of torpedoes fired from the *Nachi*. In the process, the *Salt Lake City* gunners managed to score several direct hits on the *Nachi*.

The *Salt Lake City*'s luck, however, was not infinite. Beginning at around 9:10 A.M., the Japanese gunners on the *Maya* finally acquired the rhythm of their prey's zigzagging ship and began a relentless pummeling of the aged American vessel. For the next two hours, the Japanese heavy cruiser *Maya* attained six successful hits on the American straggler, tearing through deck plates and cutting into the hull of the ship. As McMorris continued to try to shake their pursuers, Hosogaya noticed that the *Salt Lake City* had finally begun to list to one side. The damage inflicted by the Japanese had flooded the American heavy cruiser's engineering section, endangering the boiler fires that propelled the ship. The American fleet's greatest asset had become ready prey for the Japanese.

The Tide Turns

At that moment, the entire battle appeared to be over for the Americans. But then everything came apart for the Japanese fleet. First, the American destroyers *Bailey, Coghlan,* and *Monaghan* turned into the oncoming Japanese fleet. They opened fire as they approached dangerously close to the enemy, scoring a direct hit on one of the *Nachi*'s main guns and causing huge plumes of smoke to billow from her decks. Other successive hits also peppered the main deck of the *Nachi,* throwing shrapnel everywhere and briefly leaving the enemy in disarray.

Admiral Hosogaya, watching both sides erupt in continuous brutal and punishing fire, made the first of many mistakes. Unlike McMorris, the Japanese naval officer was a very cautious fellow. It had taken far longer than Hosogaya had expected for his gunners to hit the enemy heavy cruiser, but with the *Salt Lake City* now within his grasp, he thought he could easily kill the enemy ship. With the heavy cruiser out of the way, he would then devour the remainder of the American force. Yet Hosogaya was also unwilling to risk the loss of even part of his fleet to achieve victory. Over the next and final hour of the Battle of the Komandorski Islands, he struggled to maintain a respectable distance from McMorris's ships and simultaneously be able to continue to strike at the *Salt Lake City.* It was an improbable task made downright impossible by his crew's increasing inability to hit their targets at range. Consequently, over the next half hour, neither the *Maya*'s nor the *Na-*

chi's approximately two hundred shells scored a single hit on the stricken vessel.

Amid this ill-targeted barrage, Admiral McMorris received a call from the commander of the North Pacific Force, Admiral Thomas Kinkaid, stationed on Adak, far to their east. As the weather was now clearing at the Adak base, bombers were being scrambled for the five-hour flight to McMorris's position. Kinkaid also advised McMorris that "a retiring action be considered." Suddenly the entire bridge crew erupted into laughter. By the time air support arrived, they knew, the battle would most assuredly be over. Given the inconsistent behavior of the enemy, McMorris and his crew were also now confident they could exhaust the Japanese. With the superior enemy once again sent reeling by the American fleet's audacity, McMorris now had time to save the *Salt Lake City* and then perhaps sink the Japanese converted merchant ships. He ordered the American fleet to create a chemical smoke screen to hide the wounded ship.

A little after 11 A.M., the Japanese managed to charge at and hit the *Salt Lake City* one final time, but by then Hosogaya was losing his nerve. Fearing the loss of ships to a full spread of torpedoes fired in reprisal for the apparently lucky shot, the Japanese admiral ordered his fleet to make a hard turn and again move away from their prey. Much to Hosogaya's later regret, the expected torpedo attack never came. Worse, he had broken away from his target at precisely the wrong moment. The last shot fired by his men had actually scored a direct hit on the *Salt Lake City* and the sudden upsurge of water in the flooded bowels of the ship had extinguished her engines. Unbeknownst to the Japanese admiral, the old American heavy cruiser was now dead in the water under the smoke screen. It was a mistake he would regret for the rest of his life.

The Japanese and American fleets continued to trade shots a brief time longer, but the David-and-Goliath maritime battle was essentially at an end. When the American destroyers massed to shield the unmoving heavy cruiser and began to move as one on the enemy once more, the Japanese admiral choked, withdrew his forces from the battle, and headed for home. His fuel supply had been dangerously depleted. His ammunition stores were nearly exhausted. He also feared an imminent attack by American bombers, which never materialized. Finally, in retreat, Hosogaya made one last, almost absurd mistake. Upon seeing the splashes in front of his fleet made by the wildly outranged shells from the American fleet, he incorrectly deduced that American bombers had arrived. Orders were rapidly shouted and, seconds later, the entire Japanese fleet filled the sky with anti-aircraft fire to fend off bombers no one saw as they finally gave up and went home.

Although Rear Admiral McMorris's fleet had been decisively outgunned and repeatedly put at the mercy of the Japanese, Vice Admiral Hosogaya's many mistakes and his fleet's poor gunnery skills had handed the Americans a decisive victory. Once the *Salt Lake City* had restarted its engines, the American fleet made for Alaska. After reaching port, Hosogaya was removed from command on charges of cowardice. Conversely, McMorris and his men arrived in Alaska to a heroes' welcome and the undying thanks of the American army. The Japanese never again attempted to reinforce their Alaskan position. The battle for control of the Aleutian Islands ended on August 15, leaving only twenty-eight Japanese prisoners and several thousand bodies.

"YOU SANK MY BATTLESHIP!"

Battle of North Cape, December 26, 1943

BY WILLIAM TERDOSLAVICH

Appraise war in terms of the fundamental factors.
The first of these factors is moral influence.

—Sun Tzu, 544 BCE–496 BCE

The German navy excelled at being an absolute pain in the stern.

Never able to match the Royal Navy's battle fleet in number, the Kriegsmarine could make life miserable for its enemy with the few battleships it had by pursuing two different strategies.

"Commerce raiding" was the first. German battleships would slip into the Atlantic for a few weeks, sinking any Britain-bound freighters they came across. The Royal Navy could counter this by deploying its battleships, carriers, and cruisers in hot pursuit. Such was the fate of the *Graf Spee* and *Bismarck*.

If being aggressive did not work, being passive-aggressive might still pay dividends. The second strategy, "fleet in being," simply required the Germans to sit tight in port, always ready to deploy warships but doing so only on occasion. By simply maintaining the appearance of a threat, Germany would force the Royal Navy to keep its battleships close at hand to counter the threat, thus tying down warships better deployed elsewhere.

The German battleship *Scharnhorst* did both of those missions. While based in occupied France, the *Scharnhorst* did its share of commerce raiding early in the war. Once this strategy became a better mission for U-boats, the German navy redeployed *Scharnhorst* to northern Norway, where it would sit in port with other warships, always threatening to cut the shipping lanes between Britain and the Soviet Union through which Lend-Lease supplies flowed.

To counter this threat from the Nazi capital ships, which were both faster and capable of sinking most merchant ships at a distance, the Royal Navy had to assign at least one battleship and several cruisers to escort every Lend-Lease convoy leaving Britain for the Soviet Union.

Once in a while, that ever-present threat of a German battleship ripping apart a convoy turned into real danger. Such was the last war cruise of the *Scharnhorst.*

A nation builds and uses a navy with a strategy in mind. Britain maintained a large fleet because it had interests all over the globe, and still there were never enough warships to go around. Even though the British fleet was thinly spread, Germany never could hope to match the Royal Navy in sheer number of warships.

Lucky at War

The *Scharnhorst* and her sister ship, *Gneisenau,* were launched in 1936, marking the true rebirth of the Kriegsmarine. The Treaty of

Versailles forbade Germany to have battleships, limiting the navy to warships of less than ten thousand tons' displacement. In 1935, Germany negotiated a new naval treaty with Britain that would allow a new navy to be built up to 35 percent of the size of the Royal Navy, with a rough parity in submarines. This agreement effectively superseded the size restriction in the former treaty and meant Germany could build proper battleships again.

What Germany lacked was the expertise to build these new battleships. Naval architects had to dust off older blueprints from World War I and try to modernize them even as they were pressured to start construction immediately. Thus the *Gneisenau* and *Scharnhorst* were derived from the *Mackensen* class of battle cruisers, never completed in World War I as the German navy switched construction priorities to U-boats. The older World War I ships would have packed eight 13.8-inch guns, but the best that could be mounted on the *Scharnhorst* was nine 11-inch guns. While undergunned, the *Scharnhorst* was blessed with speed, easily reaching thirty-one knots—fast enough to outrun Britain's *King George V*–class battleships.

Through a combination of good gunnery and luck, the *Scharnhorst* began the war on a high note. It sank the British auxiliary cruiser *Rawalpindi* in the North Atlantic and shared credit with the *Gneisenau* for sinking the carrier *Glorious*. *Scharnhorst* also made two Atlantic cruises, sinking a number of merchantmen. Because of maintenance needs, *Scharnhorst* missed out on escorting *Bismarck* on her first—and only—war cruise.

Scharnhorst was at her luckiest during Operation Cerberus in February 1942, when the German navy shifted *Scharnhorst, Gneisenau,* and the cruiser *Prinz Eugen* from Brest through the English Channel to Germany. This brought the warships right under Britain's nose, where they should have been sunk were it not for poor coordination between the Royal Navy and Royal Air

Force. *Scharnhorst* suffered only two mine hits during the Channel Dash.

Gneisenau went into refit shortly thereafter. Naval architects were hoping to upgun her to six 15-inch guns, more akin to the World War I *Yorck*-class battle cruisers, another design similar to the *Mackensen* that never made it off the drawing board. Shortages of war matériel held up the *Gneisenau* refit, leaving *Scharnhorst* available for duty.

In early 1943 Hitler became fed up with maintaining the surface fleet. Sacking Admiral Raeder from the navy's command, he tapped Admiral Karl Dönitz to replace him. Dönitz, who formerly headed the U-boat command, shifted the navy's limited resources to U-boat construction. He convinced Hitler that the surface fleet could still exist as a "fleet in being." So long as the warships could interfere with Lend-Lease convoys sailing by Norway, Britain would have to deploy its battleships and cruisers to escort the merchantmen; this extra task would have the effect of tying down the Royal Navy's most powerful units.

Tucked away in Norway's fjords, *Scharnhorst,* along with the battleship *Tirpitz* and the pocket battleship *Lützow,* rode at anchor. Just by doing nothing, they drove the Royal Navy nuts.

Harsh Lessons Taught by Harsh Teachers

British naval paranoia was not unfounded. The long summer days proved ideal for German efforts to find and sink convoys. This harsh lesson was underscored by the disaster of Soviet-bound convoy PQ-17 in July 1942. The convoy was ordered to disperse upon receiving a report that the *Tirpitz* had sortied into nearby waters. U-boats sank twenty-four of the thirty-seven cargo ships in the ill-fated convoy.

Thus Britain limited the Russia-bound convoys to the winter months, when darkness and foul weather would impede German efforts to find and sink the ships. In the summer of 1943, the Lend-Lease convoys were suspended, much to Soviet annoyance.

That fall, *Scharnhorst* accompanied *Tirpitz* to bombard a weather station in Spitsbergen, an island about five hundred miles north of Norway. It was more a fool's errand than a mission, as the weather station was only knocked out temporarily. *Scharnhorst*'s gunnery was so bad that her captain kept the ship at sea to practice after the mission was done.

That move proved lucky. *Scharnhorst* would be absent from the German base at Altenfjord when British X-craft mini-subs attacked the *Tirpitz,* putting her temporarily out of service. Following the attack, the *Lützow* was ordered back to Germany. That left the *Scharnhorst* as the only battleship that could threaten the Lend-Lease convoys when they resumed in November.

Dönitz would dispatch the *Scharnhorst* to pick off the next convoy. But the commander of that mission would have to know where the convoy was located. And his task force had to be superior to the enemy's escort. That was going to be a challenge, as awful winter weather made for rough seas and low visibility in the Barents Sea, north of Norway.

On December 22, the first in a series of accidents came into play. The Luftwaffe sighted convoy JW-55B, bound for Russia, but without an escort. There would normally be a task force centered on a battleship, in this instance the battleship *Duke of York,* the cruiser *Jamaica,* and four destroyers, all under the command of Admiral Sir Bruce Fraser, commander in chief of the Home Fleet. Fraser was taking his battle group straight north to rendezvous with convoy JW-55B, just as it was ready to cross paths with Britain-bound convoy RA-55A, out of Murmansk, escorted by the cruisers *Sheffield, Belfast,* and *Norfolk,* with a destroyer flotilla trailing.

Dönitz committed *Scharnhorst* to attack convoy JW-55B. The merchantmen would be little more than sheep before a big, bad sea wolf packing 11-inch guns. Five heavy destroyers accompanied *Scharnhorst* as she pulled out of Altenfjord on December 25, course due north, speed twenty-five knots. (Sailors don't get the day off for Christmas when a war is on.) Conditions were appalling—stormy seas punctuated by snow squalls. In these extreme northern latitudes at this time of year, daylight only lasted fifteen minutes, with twilight running about six hours. The rest of the "day" was dark as night.

Commanding the *Scharnhorst* task force was German Rear Admiral Erich Bey. Impetuous by nature, Bey thought that aggressive attack could "make luck" in a fight. He had put this theory to the test at Narvik in 1940, only to see the battleship *Warspite* use his destroyer flotilla for target practice. Bey now found himself promoted to command the *Scharnhorst* task force as his boss, Admiral Oskar Kummetz, was away on sick leave. It can be argued that Bey was not cut out for the job, being a former destroyer captain lacking command experience in larger ships. But the German navy had to make war with the admirals it had, not the admirals it wanted.

While under way around midnight, Bey made a mistake. He radioed to shore for a weather report and any recent information on British movements. The British were very good at radio direction finding—using several radio stations to listen for German radio transmissions, then getting a bearing on their direction. All it takes is two stations in different places to each get a bearing, then drawing lines on the map tracing their course. Where they intersect is the source of the transmission. Do this with three listening posts and you can get a dead accurate fix on the source, hence the term *triangulation*.

In less than four hours, Fraser got a position report on the *Scharnhorst*. Convoy JW-55B was heading east to transit between

Bear Island and North Cape, Norway. Just a hundred miles to the south was the *Scharnhorst* task force, headed north. Cruisers *Sheffield, Norfolk,* and *Belfast* were 150 miles east of the convoy, course due west at eighteen knots. And Fraser's force was just two hundred miles west of the convoy. Unknowingly, Bey had placed his battle group in between two converging columns of British warships. To keep the *Scharnhorst* from finding the convoy, Fraser ordered it to steer northeast to widen the gap with the German warships.

German radio interception failed to pick up any British signals, despite the cruiser force radioing for a position report on the JW-55B convoy and Fraser's order to the same to change course. In fact, German reconnaissance failed to locate any British warship within fifty miles of Bey's task force as of 3 P.M. on the 25th.

It was now 7 A.M. on the 26th, and Bey still had not found his target. He ordered his destroyers to fan out and steam southwest. By spreading out his ships, Bey hoped to increase the likelihood of sighting the British freighters, but this move robbed him of combat power as the dispersed destroyers would no longer be available to fight as a group. Already plunging into heavy seas, the destroyer screen slowed down to ten knots. About ninety minutes later, Bey changed his mind and took the *Scharnhorst* north again, without informing the detached destroyers. *Scharnhorst* was now on a course to cross the path of oncoming ships—namely the *Sheffield, Norfolk,* and *Belfast.*

Within twenty minutes of that course change, *Scharnhorst* showed up as a fat blip on the radar screen of *Belfast,* range 17.5 miles. Rear Admiral R. L. Burnett, commander of the cruiser squadron, maintained course and speed, going for the intercept. Less than an hour later, *Sheffield* spotted *Scharnhorst* at a range of 6.5 miles. Burnett was steering his ships into harm's way. *Scharn-*

horst had thicker armor than the cruisers, and her 11-inch guns outpunched and outranged the 8-inch guns of her British opponents.

The British, however, had their own secret weapon: their attitude. Lord Nelson was the first to put it into words before Trafalgar, and it was tradition ever since: no captain does wrong bringing his guns to bear against the enemy. Burnett was not going to repeat Troubridge's World War I mistake of turning away from a superior foe.

At 9:30 A.M., *Norfolk* opened fire with her 8-inch guns.

The *Norfolk*'s shells splashed around *Scharnhorst*. Bey ordered evasive action, turning the ship away to the southeast, then north again, trying to go around the cruisers to get at JW-55B. Burnett kept his cruiser squadron between the convoy and *Scharnhorst*.

Bey never saw the cruisers that fired on him. He did not know how many ships he faced. *Scharnhorst* could easily damage any one of the cruisers and certainly could have dished out some punishment on all three. Perhaps *Scharnhorst*'s poor gunnery made him reluctant to engage. Bey ordered his detached destroyers to change course to the northeast and close in on his ship. The German tin cans each packed five 5.9-inch guns, pretty close to the guns usually found on a light cruiser. Bey was not giving up on finding the British convoy. It had to be out there somewhere.

Burnett retreated to a point ten miles south of JW-55B's position, ready to screen the freighters from the *Scharnhorst* task force. He had to play for time. Fraser's battle group was closing in on a parallel course farther south in hopes of cutting off *Scharnhorst*'s retreat to Norway should the enemy turn around.

Bey lost his patience again. At noon, he ordered his destroyers (which had not yet rejoined *Scharnhorst*) to change course to the west and start looking for JW-55B. The timing proved unlucky, as *Scharnhorst* now showed up as a fat blip on the radar screen of *Belfast*. Burnett's cruisers were west of the German battle cruiser and closing. Fifteen minutes later, the British cruisers opened fire. Again Bey was taken by surprise, but he returned fire instead of turning away.

A pair of 11-inch shells crashed into *Norfolk,* putting one turret out of action. After twenty minutes, Burnett broke off the action, extending his range to maintain contact. Bey turned *Scharnhorst* south by southeast, speed twenty-eight knots. He could have taken the ship up to its maximum speed and left the cruisers behind in the spray, but he did not. Nor did he turn to meet his attackers, doing to *Sheffield* and *Belfast* what he did to *Norfolk*. Had that happened, Burnett would have been pressed to break contact just to save his ships.

Bad Decisions Are Made with Bad Information

Bey's decision might seem foolish or cowardly, but he was competently acting on the information he had at the time. He had received a report of several small British warships headed his way. The spotting report was a repeat of an earlier sighting, leaving out unconfirmed information, which included a sighting of the *Duke of York*. Bey did not know a British battleship was on its way, and it definitely was more powerful than the *Scharnhorst*.

By 1 P.M. Bey's forgotten destroyer group passed within eight miles of convoy JW-55B. The lousy weather shielded the freighters from the German lookouts. Within ninety minutes, Bey radioed the destroyers to head for home. *Scharnhorst* was still sailing south by southeast, and the destroyers would not be rejoining her. The *Scharnhorst* was alone.

At about 4:15 P.M. a blip appeared on the *Duke of York*'s radar screen, range twenty-two miles, northeast of current position. Even though no one could actually see the *Scharnhorst,* the enemy was "in sight"! The battleship's gunnery radar now began to track the target, while the ship's fire control crew worked out the math problem that would send ten 14-inch shells on a collision course with the enemy. The sighting information was fed to the cruiser *Jamaica,* her fire control department working out the same math problem for her 8-inch guns.

At 4:50 P.M., at a range of fourteen miles, *Jamaica* opened fire. Bey was surprised . . . again! He ordered *Scharnhorst* to turn away from the source of the gunfire, opening fire in return. Some of the shots splashed pretty close to the *Duke of York.*

At this point, *Scharnhorst* was probably running at full speed. The *Duke of York* was about three knots slower and had to elevate her guns to make range. That now meant the shells would follow a higher trajectory, crashing straight down on *Scharnhorst*'s thinner six-inch deck armor instead of plunging into the side of her hull, where her armor was twice as thick.

Sometime during the chase, the *Scharnhorst* stopped firing back. She must have taken some hits. A destroyer squadron attached to Fraser's task force finally caught up. *Savage, Saumarez, Scorpion,* and the Norwegian destroyer *Stord* closed in unmolested by 11-inch shells, exchanging shots with the *Scharnhorst*'s secondary 5.9-inch guns. The destroyers split into two groups to execute a "hammer and anvil" attack with their torpedoes, scoring at least three hits.

The *Duke of York* and *Jamaica* brought their guns to bear at five miles—short range for a battleship. More hits were scored on *Scharnhorst,* with her 5.9-inch guns firing back ineffectively.

It was 6 P.M. Fraser's ships maintained fire and continued firing torpedoes on the stricken German battle cruiser for the next thirty minutes. More hits were inflicted, but no one was keeping score. At 6:45 P.M., *Scharnhorst* rolled over and sank.

Thirty-six survivors were pulled out of the water.

Another 1,800 men went down with the ship.

Her Luck Ran Out

Luck does not last forever, even for a ship as lucky as the *Scharnhorst.* In hindsight, an armchair admiral can count the mistakes. Bey unknowingly overplayed his poor hand against Fraser, who held most of the cards. British radar proved superior to the weaker set operated on the *Scharnhorst.* Royal Navy warships consistently obtained first sightings and got in first shots, even though the enemy was invisible to the lookouts. The Royal Navy's aggressive command culture made its captains willing to take the fight to the enemy, even when outclassed, and to maintain contact, slow them down, and bring more force to bear.

The Royal Navy had a centuries-long tradition of seeking out the enemy and attacking him, always seizing any opportunity to get in the first shot. Captains and admirals who did this best were lionized, admired, and emulated. Those who did this poorly were damned with contempt.

Fraser drove the point home to his officers aboard *Duke of York* after the last shot was fired. "Gentlemen, the battle against the *Scharnhorst* has ended in victory for us. I hope that if any of you are ever called upon to lead a ship against an opponent many times superior, you will command your ship as gallantly as *Scharnhorst* was commanded today."

Convoy JW-55B entered Murmansk harbor the next day, untouched by enemy fire, making a full delivery of much-needed Lend-Lease matériel to the Soviets.

The "fleet in being" strategy now came down to one battleship: the *Tirpitz*. So long as the *Bismarck*'s sister ship existed, so did the possibility that another arctic convoy could be mauled. The British had to do everything possible to sink "the Lone Queen of the North" to end the German threat for good.

DRAWING A LINE IN THE OCEAN

Marshall Islands, January 1944

BY WILLIAM TERDOSLAVICH

That is not to say that we can relax our readiness to defend ourselves. Our armament must be adequate to the needs, but our faith is not primarily in these machines of defense but in ourselves.

—Fleet Admiral Chester Nimitz, 1885–1966

Back when Japan was winning World War II, its fleets ranged far and wide across the Pacific, taking islands and colonies with all the ease of a steamroller flattening a driveway. To protect those gains, Japan relied upon the island chains of the central Pacific—the Gilberts, the Marshalls, the Marianas, and the Carolines—to act as a network of fortresses that could keep the Americans out.

But the Americans just took Tarawa in the Gilberts, albeit imperfectly, suffering high casualties. Little did Japan realize that its defenses were made up of assumptions, not brick or stone. The fortified islands of the Central Pacific would be little more than sand castles, waiting to be washed away by an unstoppable tide of American carriers, battleships, airplanes, and marines.

Gone were the Gilberts. The Marshalls would be next. And the Japanese would try to hold these islands by doubling down on their defensive doctrine.

Every Island Is a Fortress

Before World War II began, conventional wisdom said that amphibious invasions don't work against enemy-held ground. The proof was found at Gallipoli, where a British landing against a Turkish army turned into a bloody stalemate in 1915. Further proof was found at Wake Island in 1941, when the U.S. Marine garrison repulsed a Japanese landing. Japanese amphibious doctrine always stressed the need for unopposed landings, as the alternative just did not work. This fallacy also informed Japanese doctrine on defending against amphibious invasions: just stop the enemy at the water's edge. A garrison usually took up all available space on those tiny central Pacific islands, so there was no way the invaders could outflank them, much less bring overwhelming force to bear. Each invasion could only be a frontal assault.

Then came Tarawa in November 1943. A division of U.S. Marines successfully took the island, despite suffering heavy losses. While this defeat should have raised some doubts among Japanese planners, the orthodoxy held. Each Pacific island was seen as an invincible fortress. Post a hundred aircraft in the right island group and no naval fleet could come within seven hundred miles without being destroyed. Even if the Americans got through, they could not invade an island from its lagoon side—the coral reefs would block any landing craft from getting close to the beach. Japanese machine guns and artillery would make short work of the invaders as they waded to shore. And even if the Americans could do that, their fleet would be too far away from a naval base to be properly supported. The depleted American fleet would be smashed by the quick response of the Japanese navy.

Defense of the Marshalls was entrusted to the Fourth Fleet, Vice Admiral Marasmi Kobayashi commanding. It was not a fleet with ships, but a headquarters tasked with defending the Mandates—the islands in the Central Pacific seized from Germany in World War I, back when Japan was an ally, and subsequently administered under League of Nations order, or mandate. Kobayashi could not defend all thirty-three islands in the group. He would have to pick and choose which ones to hold so that he could deny control of the Marshalls to the invading Americans.

For assets, Kobayashi had the VI Base Force, comprising about 9,000 naval personnel. The Japanese army also provided I Amphibious Brigade, as well as a few miscellaneous battalions to augment the naval garrison. Kobayashi placed his chips on defending the eastern Marshalls, putting a naval guard force each on Wotje, Jaluit, Maloelap, and Mille. (Each "guard force" was about the size of a battalion.) Lagoon defenses were strengthened in light of the experience at Tarawa. A fifth naval guard force was retained on Kwajalein, where Rear Admiral M. Akiyama exercised command of VI Base Force. Backing all this up were about 150 aircraft—greater than the air strength of two Japanese carriers.

The Americans had to take the eastern Marshalls before proceeding westward toward Kwajalein, the administrative center of the group—or so conventional Japanese thinking went. But Admiral Chester Nimitz, in command of the Central Pacific Theater, was not a conventional thinker.

Firing Flintlock

A fleet needs a naval base to support it, basically a safe harbor with facilities for maintenance and repair. The U. S. Navy's nearest base was Pearl Harbor—too far away. But Nimitz figured out how to take a naval base with him using the Fleet Train, a collection of tenders, tankers, cargo ships, and floating dry docks. Working together, these unglamorous ships could keep the battle fleet supplied. They could also patch up any stricken warship well enough for it to steam back to Pearl Harbor, where major repairs could be made.

Once Nimitz took an island group, the Fleet Train would move forward and drop anchor there, always within a thousand miles of the next invasion site.

With the Gilberts firmly in hand, Nimitz was ready to break the rules. The Fleet Train had already dropped anchor, negating the need for support from Hawaii. Nimitz's fleet would be closer to the Marshalls than the Japanese fleet based in Truk, more than a thousand miles away in the Carolines. Thus the operational advantage would go to the U.S. Navy.

Operation Flintlock embodied the indirect approach. In late January, Nimitz unleashed his carriers to raid the eastern Marshalls, destroying Japanese air strength with ease. The Japanese considered their islands to be unsinkable aircraft carriers. But this claim paled when the Americans could put eight hundred aircraft into the skies from a dozen fleet carriers, which could strike anywhere and anytime Nimitz chose.

Troops can't walk on water, so the garrisons on Wotje, Maloelap, Mille, and Jaluit were stuck. No Japanese fleet was sailing to their rescue—General Douglas MacArthur's concurrent drive in New Guinea drew the Japanese navy's focus away from the central Pacific. With the eastern Marshalls bypassed, Nimitz used his marines to take the ungarrisoned island of Majuro, thus gaining a lagoon big enough to be turned into a temporary naval base that could support the next invasion. Nimitz was now free to attack Kwajalein, where the Japanese least expected him.

Kwajalein Atoll, a ring of small islands enclosing a coral-fringed lagoon, was defended by about 9,000 personnel, not all of them infantry. At the northern edge of the ring were the conjoined islands of Roi and Namur, each measuring about five hundred yards square. One had an airfield; the other had the support buildings. About 345 Japanese naval troops plus 2,150 air personnel, 350 laborers, and another 700 assorted troops held these two islands. Thirty miles away on the south edge of the ring was Kwajalein Island, which also had an airfield and a bunch of support buildings, housing about 5,000 Japanese personnel, of which only 1,800 or so were combat troops. Prepared defenses were few to none. There wasn't any time to fabricate them, either.

On January 31, 1944, U.S. marines and army troops began landing on smaller adjoining islands to set up artillery fire bases to support the main landings. The next day, 14,000 men of the Fourth Marine Division slammed into Roi and Namur, outnumbering the defenders by four to one. Only two regiments were used, each tasked with clearing one island.

Roi was easier to take. The entire island was just a big airfield. Resistance was futile—and uncoordinated. With no higher headquarters to call the shots, Japanese defenders fought alone or in small groups, always to the last man. Even after Roi was declared secure at 6 P.M., marines still had to put up with sporadic potshots from the few survivors who did not get the memo. Skittish marines, in their first battle ever, fired at any sound in the dark. "Mopping up" became the mission of the next day.

The story was different on Namur. The island was thick with palm trees and administrative buildings, as well as some dugouts and pillboxes. Preparatory bombardment turned all of it into an undifferentiated mass of wood chunks and rubble, which surviving Japanese defenders used for improvised cover. Marines advancing into the mess had only small arms to work with until M4 Sherman tanks came up to deliver direct fire with their 75mm main guns. While the remaining Japanese fought bitterly to the last man, it was often in small groups, lacking overall command or even a preset plan to go by.

The American advance on Namur stalled when a marine stuffed a satchel charge into a bunker containing torpedo warheads. The blast killed 20 and wounded 100. But even this self-inflicted setback proved temporary, as reserves were committed to maintain the pace. By nightfall, the marines held three-quarters of Namur. By 2 P.M. the next day, marines backed by tanks overran the last quarter of the island.

If Roi-Namur was a good example of using a sledgehammer to crack a walnut, Kwajalein was like dropping a boxcar to crush a cockroach. Shortly after 6 A.M. on February 1, three battleships, three cruisers, and eight destroyers opened fire to "soften the defenses." Four batteries of artillery from nearby islands, plus B-24 bombers flying in from the Gilberts, dropped tons of exploding metal on the hapless island, adding to the carnage. As one well-quoted observer said, it was as if someone had taken Kwajalein up to twenty thousand feet and just dropped it.

The U.S. Army's Seventh Infantry Division would be landing there, fresh from retaking the Alaskan islands of Kiska and Attu from the Japanese. At 10:15 A.M., two battalions of the division waded ashore at Kwajalein's narrow western end. The island was shaped like a banana, about a half mile wide by two and a half miles long. The division ground its way up one-third of Kwajalein's length that first day, applying massive firepower to overcome any resistance.

The Japanese might have had a chance to defend Kwajalein to the same extent as Tarawa—if they had had time to prepare. They were not expecting the Americans to drop in so soon, bypassing their main line of resistance farther east. Planned defenses were arrayed against the ocean side of the island, not its lagoon side. There were no large artillery pieces to bring the beaches under fire, no concrete bunkers with overhead cover to protect any defenders. The only option was to fight to the last man.

During the first night, what Japanese defenders remained used the darkness to infiltrate the American lines, taking potshots at soldiers and lobbing grenades. A rumor spread among Japanese troops that the Americans had a secret weapon that detected metal at night, killing anyone who left a foxhole or a trench. But taking off their helmets or removing the bayonets from their rifles did nothing to protect Japanese soldiers from the overwhelming firepower the Americans could bring to bear on any "tactical inconvenience."

Nothing slowed the Seventh Infantry as it chewed its way up the middle third of Kwajalein the next day. But open ground gave way to thick stands of palm trees interlaced with bunkers. It became the bloody chore of the 184th Infantry Regiment to clear out this assigned sector, one strongpoint at a time. The going was slow. Seawater had shorted out the telephones on the rear ends of the M4 Shermans, leaving squad leaders without the means to tell the tank commanders inside which targets to take out.

The location of the front line became unclear. American attackers and Japanese defenders became intermingled, which required divisional commander Major General Charles Corlett to reorganize units to resume the slow, grinding drive to Kwajalein's northward tip. By the time the island was secured at day's end on February 4, divisional losses amounted to 173 killed and 793 wounded, while the Japanese defenders had more than 4,800 killed.

The army had the tougher job of taking a larger island with more defenders. This reality did not impress the corps commander, Marine Corps Major General Holland "Howlin' Mad" Smith. He rated the Seventh Division's performance as slow and lackluster. This anti-army bias would make Smith increasingly difficult to work with in future campaigns.

Taking Islands with a Catchpole

With Kwajalein in his pocket, Nimitz could afford to be aggressive. Rather than wait until May to invade Eniwetok, he moved on it immediately with his reserves—the U.S. Army's 106th Infantry Regiment and the Twenty-second Marine Regiment, now formed up together as Tactical Group 1, Marine Corps Brigadier General Thomas Watson commanding. D-Day was set for February 17, which would also see a massive carrier raid on Truk to keep the Japanese fleet pinned there. (The raid destroyed 260 Japanese aircraft and sank twenty-four transports and another nine warships.)

Eniwetok is a ring-shaped atoll located about 350 miles northwest of Roi-Namur. Operation Catchpole had three objectives: taking Engebi Island, at the ring's twelve o'clock position; Parry Island, located at roughly four o'clock; and Eniwetok Island, at roughly five o'clock. The lagoon is roughly twenty-five miles in diameter, making Eniwetok a fine anchorage to support the next drive westward toward the Marianas.

Defending the island was a force of about 2,500 men, including the bulk of the Japanese army's I Amphibious Brigade, Major General Yoshima Nishida commanding. This was more than double the garrison estimated by U.S. intelligence. Nishida planned on orienting his defenses toward the lagoon side. He was counting on the Americans halting operations long enough to rest, regroup, and reorganize before attacking Eniwetok. Ample material was delivered to construct the bunkers and pillboxes needed to encase the artillery and machine guns to defend at the water's edge. About twenty-eight contact mines were also anchored in the lagoon, but that was as far as the defensive work got when the 8,000-strong American force hit the beaches.

Despite the incoming attackers, Nishida's men still managed to dig an interconnected network of foxholes and trenches, hidden from aerial photography by dense treetops. Nishida's order to his men was simple: hunker down.

D-Day saw the Americans taking smaller, nearby islands to position the artillery that would be providing fire support for the next day's main effort against Engebi, which also had an airfield. After massive prep fire on the morning of February 18, two battalions of marines hit the beach at about 8:45 A.M. Calling in air strikes and artillery to neutralize Japanese foxholes and trenches, the marines chewed their way across the island, taking possession by 3 P.M. The 800-man garrison was mostly wiped out, yet more mopping up was needed to kill off the few survivors still resisting. Captured documents then revealed the details of Nishida's dispositions.

The Americans increased their prep fire for the next target, Eniwetok Island, on February 19. Two battalions of the 106th Regiment landed but were slowed by a stiff Japanese defense behind a high embankment just beyond the beach. Clearing this line, the army's advance was again stalled by mortar and machine-gun fire from hidden Japanese positions. Watson then committed the reserves—an unused battalion of marines from the Twenty-second Regiment. The marines chewed their way straight ahead to the other end of Eniwetok Island, then turned right to line up with an army battalion to grind across the island to the other side. Not quite reaching the end, both units had to spend an uncomfortable night filled with Japanese sniping and potshots. A banzai charge aimed at the Marine battalion's headquarters was beaten off. No major counterattacks came after this, as the remainder of the operation consisted of "mopping up." By the 21st, Eniwetok Island was American-owned.

Parry Island, site of Nishida's headquarters, came next on February 22, as two battalions of the Twenty-second Marines hit the wrong beach. Battleships delivered direct fire as close as fifteen hundred yards from shore. Nishida's remaining 1,300 men were reduced to a small pocket of resisters along the island's southern edge, wiped out shortly after sunrise the next day.

For the loss of 2,500 garrison troops and another 1,000 or so laborers, Japan killed about 350 Americans and wounded about 850. But the loss of Eniwetok removed an important node in Japan's web of air bases in the central Pacific. Now there was no base that could allow Japanese aircraft to stage farther eastward or mount any strike against Nimitz's fleet.

No Great Loss?

Taken together, the losses of the Gilberts and the Marshalls were serious, but not grave. Japanese planners were hoping that the defenders would inflict bloody losses and slow down the Americans long enough for more formidable defenses to be erected in the Carolines and Marianas.

There was a cumulative downside for Japan. With every island garrison fighting to the last man, there were no experienced survivors who could help develop a counterstrategy to stop the Americans. Commanders on the scene did transmit real-time reports describing American technique versus the Japanese defense, but this yielded a limited analytical dividend.

Nishida was the first general to show some smarts by planning a defense from the lagoon side of the atoll, but he lacked the time needed to construct adequate defenses. The Americans were learning from their mistakes, building a new amphibious attack doctrine that fused their advantages in carrier-borne aviation, ship-to-shore bombardment, amphibious operations, and logistics. This technique would shatter every "impregnable" island defense Japan erected. The Japanese would later call these invasions "Storm Landings." The name was apt.

The Americans made their luck. They used 54,000 assault troops, 297 ships, with 12 fleet carriers and 8 escort carriers launching 800 planes to take a major island group defended by about 12,000 Japanese troops and 150 planes. The Japanese had plenty of raw courage, yet that could not make up for lack of numbers and firepower. Defensive command belonged to the Japanese navy, which did not have the army's talent for reading ground and orienting a proper defense against the invaders. And the fleet needed to drive away the invaders was too busy elsewhere to help.

How could Japan hope to win against overwhelming odds? It was like suffering defeat by default.

And this was only the beginning.

With every invasion, the American sledgehammer could only get bigger.

OVERLORD AT SEA

Operation Neptune, June 1944

BY DOUGLAS NILES

Military intelligence *is a contradiction in terms.*

—Groucho Marx, 1890–1977

Operation Overlord, the great invasion of France on June 6, 1944, would open the path to a direct and decisive land campaign between the Anglo-American army and the German Wehrmacht. Not only did the attacking forces have the liberation of France as an initial objective, but through France they would obtain a route into the German nation itself, and perhaps even open the road to Berlin—which, of course, was a primary Russian objective as well. The landing in France would be the key event, making or breaking the campaign of the war in the west. It would bring the British and Americans into the war at full strength and provide at least the potential to counterbalance the growing power of Stalin's Red Army, which by 1944 was steadily closing in on the German Reich from the east.

Of course, British and American forces were already battling the Germans in Italy, but that mountainous, narrow peninsula was ideal defensive terrain, and the going was very slow indeed. Despite a great amphibious landing near Naples in September 1943, the Allies had yet to advance as far as Rome. Indeed, it would take them until May 1944 to even close in on the Italian capital, which was barely more than a hundred miles from the initial landing beaches.

The decision to make a cross-channel invasion, so obvious in retrospect that it seems almost inevitable, was not a slam dunk, however. No less a personage than British prime minister Winston Churchill fought vigorously against the plan, and for a long time he felt certain that it could result only in a catastrophic defeat or, at best, a return to the stalemate of trench warfare as experienced in World War I. Throughout 1942 and 1943, Churchill relentlessly sounded his warnings of disaster. He continued to advocate for a second offensive out of the Mediterranean, through Greece or Yugoslavia—both of which were remarkably impractical routes toward the German homeland, every bit as mountainous as Italy and even farther from the German heartland. In his reluctance to approve the invasion, he was seconded by many of the British General Staff, including Field Marshal Alan Brooke, chief of the Imperial General Staff and the most important military adviser to the prime minister.

If the British were too reluctant to invade the continent, it is also clear that the Americans were far too hasty in their initial efforts to push the plan. Originally the Yanks wanted to storm the French beaches in 1942, which would almost certainly have resulted in unmitigated disaster. The U.S. Army only accepted the alternative of French North Africa when the British refused to endorse the plan. Even as the plans for that far less ambitious operation took shape, the Americans continued to express the desire to make the landings on French shores in 1943. Again British cautions—and perhaps the growing American experience of combat with the German army—persuaded them to delay for one more year. In 1943 the focus of ground warfare between the Anglo-Americans and the Germans would remain in the Mediterranean, but by 1944 the U.S. Army had the largest force in play and would no longer accept any delay in implementing the cross-channel assault.

By then the Anglo-American armies had gained valuable experience in working together, and more specifically, in making amphibious assaults—widely regarded as the most complex of military operations. The first big landing in North Africa, in Operation Torch (November 1942), had involved attacking Vichy French forces instead of Germans. Even against this very light opposition, many challenges had been discovered. After clearing the Axis armies from the African continent, the Allies crossed the Mediterranean to land on Sicily (Operation Husky, July 1943) before making the jump to the Italian mainland a few months later. All three of these campaigns had necessitated an amphibious assault on an enemy-held shore, and the lessons learned by American and British commanders would all be applied to Overlord, which would be the greatest invasion of them all—indeed, it would be the most massive amphibious assault in all of recorded history.

Naturally, Overlord would require a huge naval complement, an operation in its own right. It could never even be attempted without complete control of the sea, which by then the English and Americans had obtained—though they still had to worry about German submarines. Once the U-boat threat had been handled, the naval forces would be responsible for transporting the assaulting troops, landing them on the beaches, and protecting them and their support shipping from interference by enemy forces. Befitting its separate order of battle and sphere of responsibilities, the naval complement of Operation Overlord would be termed Operation Neptune.

The commander in chief for Operation Neptune was Admiral Sir Bertram Ramsay. He first rose to prominence in his role as Flag Officer Dover, when he had presided over the evacuation of British and Allied forces from the beaches at Dunkirk in May 1940. There was a certain symmetry in the assignment of Ramsay: the man who had been responsible for allowing hundreds of thousands of troops to escape the Nazi onslaught would now take charge of shipping an army, including many of the same men, back to the continental shores. But there was more than poetic justice in the choice, since Admiral Ramsay had also been in overall command of the naval component of Operation Torch, and he had shared fleet command for Operation Husky. When it came to large amphibious assaults, there was no more experienced commanding officer in the European Theater.

Of course, the naval forces were responsible mainly for safely transporting the troops from England to the shores of France. In this, Ramsay and the rest of the Royal and American naval commanders would be implementing a plan formed by the highest-ranking ground forces commanders in the theater.

Several important generals had risen to the tops of their respective national command staffs during the earlier campaigns. Leader of them all would be General Dwight D. Eisenhower, who would command from his Supreme Headquarters, Allied Expeditionary Force, and who would be known as SHAEF, or by his nickname of "Ike," for the duration of the war. Eisenhower had a keen mind for strategy, but perhaps more important, he was a diplomatic enough leader to hopefully maintain the delicate balance of egos and reputations between his British and American subordinates.

British Field Marshal Bernard Law Montgomery had established his reputation by defeating German Field Marshal Erwin Rommel at the Battle of El Alamein in Egypt. He had been present at the final victory in Africa and had commanded the British forces during the Sicilian campaign. Personally vain and acerbic, "Monty" had a well-earned reputation as a diligent and careful planner. He would be in overall command of the land forces going ashore on D-Day and was intensely involved in all aspects of planning for the attack. Two other generals, American Omar Bradley and British Miles Dempsey, would be in tactical command of their own forces on the beaches and beyond.

The Unexpected Choice

As early as the summer of 1943, the site for the landings was chosen, and it was a bit of a surprise. The obvious choice would have been Pas-de-Calais, which lay across the narrowest stretch of the English Channel and was relatively close to Belgium, the Netherlands, and Germany itself. The Calais area also offered several significant ports in the immediate vicinity and a fairly short route to the real prize, the huge Belgian port of Antwerp. It was widely acknowledged that a large port capacity, quickly seized, would be crucial to maintaining the supply line and reinforcing buildup required for the massive land campaign.

But Pas-de-Calais was as glaringly apparent an objective to the Germans as it was to the Allies, and it was known to be well defended with a large number of first-rate Wehrmacht and SS formations. Simply because it looked like such a likely destination, it was discarded from the plan—though it was not forgotten by the planners. Indeed, a vast ruse would be established to try to convince the Germans that Calais was the real objective. Dummy tanks and trucks were created in southeast England and a network of radio stations broadcast signals as if they were large military formations. The entire organization was termed First United States Army Group. The FUSAG did not in fact exist, but it had a famous commander: the news was leaked out that General George S. Patton, who was not to be involved in the D-Day landings, was commander in chief of the fictional army group. The ruse turned out to be so successful that even weeks after D-Day Hitler refused to allow all of his French-based troops to be sent to Normandy, for he remained convinced that Calais would soon be the site of the "real" invasion.

Instead of Pas-de-Calais, however, the Allies chose a place farther west, the Normandy coast east of the Cotentin Peninsula and west of the port of Le Havre. The original landings called for a three-division front across some thirty miles of beaches. Here Montgomery raised an objection, stating that the force was too weak to guarantee success. As a result, the landings were expanded to a five-division front, across fifty miles of beaches. Three airborne divisions would also be employed, with the total assault placing well over 100,000 men ashore by the end of the first day of the attack.

The naval missions in support of the invasion were many, and complicated. Fortunately, by this point in the war, all of the major German surface warships had been sunk or trapped, damaged, in their ports. However, the Third Reich had developed a series of small torpedo boats, called E-boats, that were bigger and longer-ranged than the American PT boats of Pacific War fame. Operating under cover of darkness, these boats were capable of inflicting a lot of damage, especially against unarmored transports and cargo ships. This fact was proven when one of the practice landings along the English coast, part of the preparation for D-Day, was disrupted by an E-boat attack with horrific casualties among the many troop-laden transports and landing craft. (This disaster was such a catastrophe that even the fact that it occurred remained classified for many years after the war.)

German U-boats, too, were always a threat to Allied shipping. Furthermore, much of the English Channel and the entire coast of France were heavily mined, and the beaches themselves were defended by obstacles that could tear the bottoms out of landing craft and other shipping that dared to approach close to shore. The threats of torpedo boats, U-boats, and mines were all challenges that Operation Neptune would have to meet and overcome.

The first mission of the invading fleet would be to protect the vulnerable transports from interference by German defenders, which required substantial anti-submarine forces on both sides of the crossing path, as well as vigorous minesweeping in the path of the armada itself. The second mission would be the heavy gun bombardment of the beaches themselves, in order to soften up the positions that would be attacked by ground troops. Ships ranging from destroyers all the way up to battleships would perform this task. The third mission was the actual transport of the assault troops; for this, the U.S. Navy had a variety of landing craft and ships. Many of these were flat-bottomed vessels capable of sliding right up onto the beach. They ranged from the Landing Craft, Infantry, with the bow dropping as a ramp, to ships that could beach themselves and disgorge tanks and other vehicles from their gaping bow-hatches. Others were transports that would anchor in deep water, off the beaches, and lower their troops via net or ladder into boats and landing craft for the ultimate assault. Finally, the ships of the invasion fleet would have to provide supplies, reinforcements, and hospital beds, since the troops on the beaches would have no rear-echelon depots or medical facilities until they could move well inland.

An Engineering Miracle

One of the things that made the Normandy coast counterintuitive as a site for the landings was the lack of a major port in the immediate area. It was Winston Churchill himself who came up with the idea that allowed this challenge to be overcome: he suggested that the Allies create artificial harbors off the landing beaches, using a combination of old ships—termed "Gooseberries"—that would sail into position and then be scuttled, as breakwaters. Afterward, hundreds of massive caissons, formed of concrete and steel, would be dropped into place around the wrecks, creating a solid breakwater right off the beaches. Large piers, designed to rise and fall with the tide, would facilitate unloading in these artificial harbors; the harbors themselves would be called "Mulberries." In the event, two harbors were created. One, on the American beaches, was destroyed by a storm not long after the landings; the other would serve as a key link in the supply chain throughout the Normandy campaign and beyond.

The timing of the landings had to be very carefully chosen and would limit the options to three consecutive days in each lunar month. It was decided that the ships (and the transport planes carrying the airborne troops) needed moonlight after midnight to make their approaches to the continent. In addition, the troops needed to land about halfway through a rising tide—if the water was too low, they would be exposed to a wide, unprotected swath of sand; but if the tide was too high, the landing craft would be fully exposed to the vast array of underwater obstacles lining every beach. The timing at Normandy was further complicated by the fact that, over the fifty-mile stretch of beaches, the high tide varied by as much as an hour and a half from one end to the other of the assault zone.

Delays

The invasion was originally scheduled for May 1944, but there were not enough landing craft on hand by that date, so the target was moved to June. British and American factories continued to produce these precious craft as quickly as possible, while additional boats were called back from the Pacific Theater over the objections of Americans Admiral Ernest King and General Douglas MacArthur, both of whom rather myopically viewed the European Theater as a minor sideshow to the real event: the war with Japan.

With enough landing craft finally on hand, the month of June was a go. Possible dates in that month were the 5th, 6th, or 7th; a failure to land during this window would push the invasion back to July and almost certainly result in loss of the element of surprise. The final decision, the order to go, would come from General Eisenhower.

Under Ramsay's command was mustered a force of nearly 7,000 vessels, a fleet Churchill described as "the greatest armada that ever left our shores." The forces came from eight different navies in total and included more than 4,000 transport and landing craft, 1,200 warships, and 1,500 supporting ships and merchant vessels. More than 100,000 combat troops would be transported to the beaches by sea.

The whole nautical operation was choreographed almost like a dance. Ships would leave from ports in Northern Ireland, Scotland, and all around southern and western England at precisely determined times, steaming in carefully specified orders. Experience had shown that ships needed to be reverse-loaded—the most important equipment should be the last placed on the ships, so it could be the first pulled onto shore. A screen of minesweepers would precede the whole invasion fleet across the channel, and a path more than fifty miles wide would be cleared, and patrolled, throughout the operation.

Both flanks of that route would be sealed by vigorous anti-submarine patrols, from aircraft, destroyers, and smaller ships. A steady stream of air cover would circle above the ships, fighter planes making sure that enemy air forces had no chance to interfere. Strike forces of fast destroyers and corvettes would remain on the alert, ready to race to confront any reports of interference from German torpedo boats. Every ship, every boat, had a place to be, a mission to perform, and a roster of equipment and personnel that had to be ready on board.

The initial order was given for an invasion on June 5. Ships of the bombardment force departed from Northern Ireland on June 3, and some of the assault troops also boarded their transports from West Country ports on that same day. Many of the front-rank troops would embark from the British channel ports, including Portland, Poole, Portsmouth, Shoreham, and Newhaven; they would not board ships until the evening before the invasion. By Sunday, June 4, however, the channel was being swept by one of the violent and frequent storms that have always plagued that watery crossing. The weather forecast indicated that June 5 would be even worse, so Ike made the difficult decision to push the invasion back by a day. Muttering, disgruntled, and seasick, many of the unhappy troops were forced to return to port.

Meteorology was a young science in 1944, but the Allies had the advantage of weather stations on Greenland and Iceland and aboard ships in the North Atlantic. The weather forecasters cautiously predicted a brief period of good weather on June 6, before the storms would return. General Eisenhower, in one of the most portentous decisions of any military commander ever, authorized the invasion for June 6. Ironically, the weather actually went a long way toward ensuring surprise, as the Germans—who did not have access to the data from the North Atlantic—predicted that the weather would be too bad to allow an invasion on the 6th. The German field commander in charge of the defense of France, Field Marshal Erwin Rommel, even extended a visit to spend time with his wife in Germany for an extra day because of his mistaken belief that the weather would be too bad for a landing. He would spend June 6 racing back to his headquarters instead of commanding his troops in the field.

Strategic and Tactical Surprise

As it happened, the Germans along the invasion beaches—and indeed, throughout France—were taken completely by surprise. An hour or so before dawn, the battleships opened up with their big guns from many miles offshore, and a punishing barrage of 14-inch shells assaulted the French shoreline. Smaller ships moved in closer, adding 8- and 6-inch ordnance to the barrage. Many of the local defenders discovered the attack only when the bombardment ships opened up. A stunning array of high-explosive shells plummeted onto the beaches and the fortified positions behind them. Just after dawn, the landing craft surged toward the beaches, while the bombardment was lifted to avoid danger to friendly troops.

The big naval guns had inflicted some damage but did not silence the defenders. In many places, most notably on the American objective known as Omaha Beach, German artillery did an awful amount of damage, with many landing craft suffering hits and blowing up a mile or more from shore. Waves tossed and sometimes capsized other boats, while whole companies of amphibious tanks, "swimming" by virtue of a canvas enclosure that was supposed to keep out the sea, were swamped and sank to the bottom, carrying nearly all hands with them. Casualties were heavy all along the front, and most especially at "Bloody Omaha." But the troops made it ashore everywhere, and even on Omaha they had secured a solid foothold by the end of the day.

In the meantime, the flanks of the great armada were guarded so effectively that not a single U-boat or E-boat was able to slip through the cordon to make an attack. The complicated dance of Operation Neptune proved to be a resounding success, as Mulberries were built; the troops, tanks, and trucks poured ashore; and the Anglo-Allied expeditionary force was in mainland Europe to stay.

HELLCATS OVER THE PHILIPPINE SEA

The Marianas Turkey Shoot, June 1944

BY DOUGLAS NILES

In no other profession are the penalties for employing untrained personnel so appalling or so irrevocable as in the military.

—General Douglas MacArthur, 1880–1964

The Grumman Aircraft Corporation had been supplying sturdy, reliable aircraft to the U. S. Navy since the 1920s. Their F4F Wildcat, which entered service in the mid-1930s, was a good example of the Grumman ideal: squat and wide-bodied, it had a circular cowl around a radial engine and .50-caliber machine guns in the wings. The wings could be folded up, allowing for more of them to be stored in an aircraft carrier's hangar. Though the Wildcat was not as fast or maneuverable as the Japanese Zero, it could absorb significantly more punishment than its lightweight opponent. The Wildcat proved itself more or less equal to the Zero in dogfights over the Coral Sea, Midway, and the Solomon Islands.

Yet even before the attack on Pearl Harbor, Grumman had been working on the successor to the Wildcat. Originally planned with a 1,700-horsepower engine, the Hellcat was upgraded to 2,000 horsepower based on combat experience with the Zero and analysis of one of the Japanese fighters that had been shot down over the Aleutian Islands and was recovered, nearly intact, on American territory. The F6F Hellcat entered service late in 1943, and by 1944, when the Americans were producing a new fleet carrier almost every month, all of the frontline carrier fighter squadrons were flying Hellcats. Some described the F6F as the Wildcat's "big brother," and at first glance the resemblance is readily apparent. Yet the Hellcat was a whole order of magnitude more advanced than the Wildcat. The Hellcat would be able to take off and climb to an altitude of twenty thousand feet in about seven minutes, which was a huge advantage in fast-paced carrier operations.

After the decisive clashes at Coral Sea, Midway, and the Solomons in 1942, the year of 1943 passed without a major carrier battle between the Japanese and American navies. The Japanese did manage to launch a few more aircraft carriers, including the huge, modern *Taiho,* but they could not match the production of American shipyards. Also, given limitations on fuel for training, and the horrific losses of the 1942 battles, the Japanese had to operate with a shortage of trained pilots and an inadequate instruction regimen for new fliers. Some of their pilots went into battle with only about twenty hours of experience in a cockpit.

Still Powerful

Nevertheless, by early summer of 1944, the Japanese navy was able to muster a force of nine aircraft carriers, five large and four small. With a total complement of some 450 planes, this was the largest naval aviation force the empire had ever put together. Though the Zero was still the mainstay, there was a new dive bomber type, the Yokosuka D4Y1, designated by the Americans as "Judy." This machine had an astonishing range of nearly two thousand miles and a speed of better than 300 mph. Furthermore, many Zeros were now being modified to serve as dive bombers, equipped with a 550-pound bomb slung under the fuselage. Naturally, once that bomb was dropped, the Zero could function in its intended design role as a fighter.

The United States, by contrast, provided extensive training for its new pilots, and still produced enough planes and the men to fly them to see that all of the new carriers coming off the rails were manned with skilled, fully staffed aircrews. The whole array of carrier-based aircraft had advanced to a new generation from the planes that had flown at Midway. In addition to the Hellcat, a new dive bomber, the Curtiss SB2C Helldiver, had taken over the dive-bombing role from the venerable Douglas Dauntless. It was bigger and faster than the SBD, though it was not initially popular with pilots because of its size. The torpedo bomber was now the TBF Avenger, which had proven much more durable than the old Devastators. Both the Avenger and the Helldiver carried their ordnance inside a belly hatch, which served to reduce drag during flight.

A new series of fleet carriers, the *Essex* class, now formed the backbone of the aircraft carrier force. Only *Enterprise* still survived from the carriers that had begun the war, but six new large, fast flattops had joined the fleet. A class of light carriers, a little smaller than the *Essex* ships but fast enough to fit right into the speedy battle fleets, augmented the flight decks of what was now known as Task Force 58.

By summer of 1944, the War in the Pacific had moved relentlessly closer to the Japanese Home Islands. General MacArthur's U.S. Army forces had advanced across the island of New Guinea and proceeded westward along the north shore of that vast, jungle-covered landmass; they were poised to make the next great leap, into the Philippines, before the end of the year. The Gilbert and Marshall island groups had been seized by U.S. marines making amphibious assaults. The lessons learned from the high casualties during the first of these, at Tarawa, continued to be applied and refined. These operations against enemy-held shores were inherently dangerous, but never during the entire war were the marines defeated once they set foot on an enemy shore.

An Expected Offensive

By June, the Americans were ready to strike at the key island group in the central Pacific, a trio of landmasses that the Japanese regarded as a crucial component of their interior defensive perimeter. The Marianas Islands included Saipan and Tinian, which had long been Japanese territory, and Guam, which had been a U.S. territory before the war and had been taken by the Japanese shortly after Pearl Harbor. Admiral Nimitz, commander in chief of the United States Pacific Fleet, reasoned correctly that the Japanese would not let the Marianas go without a major naval challenge.

Indeed, Vice Admiral Jisaburo Ozawa had been appointed as overall commander of Japan's main battle fleets, including the carrier strike force that had been restored to at least numerical strength, and the First Mobile Fleet, including a number of fast, modern battleships. These included the *Yamato* and *Musashi,* each with batteries of massive 18.1-inch guns—the largest shipborne cannons in the world, on the largest battleships ever to sail the seas. In addition, the Imperial Japanese fleet included seven more fast, modern battleships. Two of them, *Hyugo* and *Ise,* had been modified into hybrid battleship-carriers. The aft gun turrets had been removed and replaced with a flight deck and a small hangar, enough that each could carry fourteen aircraft.

Ozawa moved out in May, initially with a plan to lure the American carriers into the west-central Pacific, where his fleet could be augmented by numerous land-based aircraft on nearby islands. It was not long before Japanese scout planes, always a reliable part of the naval air component, discovered the American fleet approaching the Marianas. Still west of the Philippines, Ozawa's fleet was spotted by U.S. submarines around May 16, and the contact was reported back to the U.S. Navy headquarters in Hawaii.

By then preparations for the Marianas campaign were well under way. The landing forces, as at Guadalcanal, were under the command of Admiral Richmond Turner; now he had more than 500 ships at his disposal, and they carried some 125,000 soldiers, sailors, and marines. The American commander of the ships at sea that formed the massive Task Force 58 was Admiral Raymond Spruance, the hero of Midway; his main battle fleet, organized into five battle groups, was led by Admiral Marc Mitscher. At his disposal he now had all seven heavy and the eight light carriers, for a total of fifteen modern flattops. These were split between four of the battle groups, with each group centered around three or four carriers. The fifth battle group included Mitscher's fast battleships and many other modern, powerful surface ships.

Aware of Ozawa's position and approach, Mitscher knew he had a little time before he needed to screen the Marianas invasion fleet. He first made a series of raids against the land-based aircraft on the Marianas islands, which numbered better than two hundred planes under the command of Admiral Kakuji Kakuda. The islands formed, essentially, unsinkable aircraft carriers, and these planes were an important part of the defensive plans. However, over two days, massed squadrons of Hellcats flew against the Japanese air bases, destroying pretty much every one of the Marianas-based planes. Whether for reasons of shock or shame, Admiral Kakuda never informed Admiral Ozawa of this devastating loss, so that when the Japanese carriers arrived on the scene a week or two later, Ozawa assumed he would be going into battle with a total of 650 planes and didn't know that nearly a third of that total had already been wiped out.

The Japanese were still some distance away, so Spruance ordered seven of Mitscher's carriers—two of the four carrier battle groups—to detach from Task Force 58 and rush 650 miles to the north, where they staged raids against Iwo Jima and Chichi Jima, small island bases much closer to the Japanese Home Islands than the Marianas were. These two bases were also effectively neutralized before the detached carrier groups steamed back south to rejoin the task force.

The Japanese battle fleet had escaped from the surveillance of the submarine pickets, and Spruance was tempted to send his carriers on a search-and-destroy mission. However, the careful admiral—one of the most logical and thoughtful men ever to hold such a command—didn't want to take the risk of the enemy fleet outflanking him and falling on Turner's amphibious fleet, so he decided to keep his carriers in the vicinity of the Marianas and let the Japanese come to him. He ordered Mitscher to take up position about 150 miles west of Saipan, straddling the route that must be taken if the Japanese fleet approached. And like Nimitz, Spruance was certain that the Japanese navy would not let the Marianas Islands fall without a decisive fight.

"The Fate of the Empire"

By the time Ozawa was again spotted by submarines, Mitscher was well positioned to protect the Marianas, as the Japanese fleet approached him across the Philippine Sea. Sensing the stakes of the impending battle, both commanding admirals broadcast inspirational messages from their headquarters to the ships at sea. For Tokyo, Admiral Soemu Toyoda invoked the memory of Admiral Togo just before the Japanese fleet destroyed the Czar's Russian fleet at the Battle of Tsushima, when he said, "The fate of the empire rests on this one battle. Every man is expected to do his utmost." From Pearl Harbor, Admiral Nimitz declared to Spruance: "On the eve of possible fleet action, you and the officers and men under your command have the confidence of the naval service and the country. We count on you to make the victory decisive."

By this time, U.S. radar was much more effective, with a long-range capacity and accuracy that was far better than had existed in 1942. But the spotter seaplanes that had long been a feature of the cruiser force had been discarded because they had proven to represent a significant fire risk. Thus Mitscher did not have the long-range "eyes" that his counterpart could and would routinely employ. The one other advantage Ozawa had was the range of his planes, which was about a hundred miles farther than U.S. naval air groups. Thus when Ozawa's scout planes discovered the U.S. carriers on the morning of June 19, he made good use of this advantage, launching two large strikes at extreme range.

Mitscher's radar detected these fleets far away from his carriers, and he posted a strong force of new Hellcat fighters about fifty miles west of the carriers, using the radar reports to place his fighters at the perfect position and altitude for interception. After launching his fighters, Mitscher sent his dive bombers and torpedo bombers, unladen by ordnance, into the air to circle out of harm's way and keep his flight decks clear for fighter operations. They would spend the day strafing the Japanese air bases on the nearby islands, effectively putting them out of action (though the Japanese planes, as noted, had already been destroyed).

Even before the air battle commenced, Ozawa suffered a grievous loss as the newest, largest carrier, *Taiho,* was torpedoed by an American submarine, *Albacore,* before 9 A.M. The sub's skipper was disappointed to see the carrier continue on, apparently unaffected by the impact; however, a combination of gasoline fumes and sparks combusted an hour later and the mighty, modern ship exploded and sank. Shortly after noon, *Shokaku*—one of the Pearl Harbor strike force—was also sunk by an American submarine, this time the *Cavalla,* which put three torpedoes into that venerable flattop.

Mitscher's Hellcats pounced on each wave of approaching Japanese aircraft when they reached the point about fifty miles away from the U.S. carriers. The Hellcat proved itself extremely capable in these air battles, able to maneuver on an equal basis to the Zero, every bit as fast as the Japanese fighters, and a whole heck of a lot tougher. The Grummans had armored cockpits and self-sealing gas tanks, whereas the Zeros had proven themselves to be real tinderboxes.

Over the course of a day's aerial combat, the Japanese lost some 340 planes (in addition to the two carriers) at a cost to the U.S. of some 30 lost fighters. The battle in the air was so lopsided that it quickly came to be known as the "Great Marianas Turkey Shoot." By nightfall, a shaken Ozawa had recovered his surviving planes and turned away from the American fleet. He was down to a little more than a hundred combat-ready planes and knew he couldn't stand up to another major aerial engagement with the American fleet. His aircrews had reported sinking as many as four American aircraft carriers, and a battleship, but in reality the only significant hit had been a bomb that struck the battleship *South Dakota,* doing minimal damage.

Mitscher chased after the Japanese fleet at flank speed through the night and the next day but was not able to establish contact with the Japanese ships until late in the day of June 20. He was hampered during the battle by the fact that the wind was steadily blowing out of the east. Since carriers needed to turn into the wind to launch or recover planes, every time a carrier conducted flight operations it had to come about and steam away from the enemy fleet.

Still, the pursuit eventually closed, and by late afternoon Mitscher had located his target—the fattest array of enemy warships that had ever presented itself to a powerful American task force. Knowing that the late hour meant that his airmen would be returning after dark, the American admiral nevertheless ordered a strong strike. More than two hundred planes flew westward, finding and sinking several Japanese carriers and other vessels. It wasn't the decisive blow that the Americans had wanted, but the light air opposition encountered over the enemy fleet was pretty clear evidence that Japan's naval air arm had been badly decimated. In that battle the U.S. Navy lost twenty planes, while the toll for the Japanese was a further sixty-five machines, leaving Ozawa's remaining carriers all but empty of aircraft.

The American fliers, making their way back to their carriers in darkness, encountered many challenges. The range was great, and some engines sputtered out as fuel tanks ran dry. The Helldivers in particular were burdened by inadequate range, and they began to splash with distressing frequency. Altogether about eighty planes of all types ditched or crash-landed in the ocean. Those who were still in the air were greeted by an astonishing sight as they finally returned to Task Force 58: ignoring the risk from enemy submarines, Mitscher had ordered every light in the fleet illuminated. That blessed brilliance brought home the majority of his strike force and forever made him a legend in the eyes of navy pilots.

Ozawa's fleet made its escape throughout that night. Mitscher pursued as long as he dared, while detaching many destroyers to pick up downed fliers, some fifty of whom were saved by those destroyers, as well as by submarines. At daybreak, knowing he was still responsible for the protection of Turner's landing force, he turned back to screen the landings, comfortable in the assessment that Japanese naval aviation had been delivered a blow from which it would never recover.

The Battle of the Philippine Sea was one of the most decisive victories in the history of naval warfare. Rather unfairly, Admiral Nimitz expressed some disappointment that the bag of enemy ships had not been greater. In truth, from this point on Japan's once-vaunted carrier force was fit only to serve as a decoy. Though it would perform this task very well one more time during the war, it was finished as an offensive weapon. If the Battle of Midway had marked the point where the modern U. S. Navy had come of age, the Battle of the Philippine Sea was the event that put it firmly in the category of military mastery.

AFTER THE TURKEY SHOOT

Invasion of the Marianas, June–August 1944

BY WILLIAM TERDOSLAVICH

We have met the enemy and they are ours.

—Oliver Hazard Perry, 1785–1819

To Japan, an island was a dirt hole in the middle of the Pacific Ocean into which it poured men and matériel to produce an indestructible fortress.

To the Americans, an island was just a bloody speed bump with an airfield on it.

The loss of the Gilberts and the Marshalls was cause for concern among the Japanese admirals and generals running the Pacific War. These island groups were important, but not essential for defending the empire. Perhaps their loss would tally as a Pyrrhic victory for the Americans. Kill enough of them and surely they would give up. But it was not working out that way. Admiral Chester Nimitz was just getting started.

The Gilberts and the Marshalls fell in corps-size operations supported by hundreds of warships and naval aircraft. Now Nimitz was going to double down on the Marianas. Operation Forager called for launching two corps-size attacks to take Tinian and Saipan from the Japanese, and retake Guam. Committed to the operation were 535 ships and 166,000 men.

For Japan, the Marianas were not expendable.

Yankee Ingenuity Meets Samurai Stubbornness

Japan activated its Fourth Fleet as a headquarters unit responsible for the defense of the Marianas and placed Vice Admiral Chuichi Nagumo in charge. Nagumo, who led the carrier strike at Pearl Harbor, had languished in disgrace since losing big at Midway.

The Japanese army would also restructure, forming the Thirty-first Army to control three divisions and an assortment of independent brigades and regiments to "do the job right"—all under the command of Lieutenant General Hideyoshi Obata. Technically, Obata was under Nagumo's command. Both men agreed that the senior officer on each island would be in charge of its defense, just to avoid the interservice feuds that usually stymied cooperation.

The true defense of the Marianas was in the hands of Vice Admiral Jisaburo Ozawa's First Mobile Fleet, which possessed the bulk of Japan's remaining aircraft carriers. It was this force that would defeat the American Fifth Fleet, then destroy the transports of the American invasion force like a wolf taking on a flock of sheep.

By now, the central Pacific drive was hitting its stride. Vice Admiral Raymond Spruance had two corps of marines and army troops to work with, backed by 15 fleet carriers and 14 escort carriers launching close to 900 aircraft; 14 battleships, 25 cruisers, and 152 destroyers. Fire support would be abundant and on call, with a battleship tasked to every division, a cruiser ready for every regiment, and a destroyer handy for every battalion. Task Force 58—consisting of the fast carriers under the command of Vice Admiral Marc Mitscher—raided Truk, then doubled back to the Marianas. Pre-invasion raiding was now standard, as the carriers formed a portable air force that could operate anywhere in the Pacific, usually overwhelming Japanese land-based air by a factor of three or four to one.

Unlike the smaller atolls of the central Pacific, the U.S. Army and Marine divisions would be fighting for large rocky islands, sometimes punctuated by large, central mountain peaks. The Americans would have some space to maneuver, while the Japanese would have the room to defend in depth, if they chose. Saipan would be the first to suffer American attack, putting these geographic factors into play.

Welcome to Saipan. Now Die.

Measuring about forty-seven square miles in area, Saipan is shaped like a pork chop with a bite taken out of its lower right side. It has a broad base in the south, with a rocky, mountainous spine rising halfway up the island running northward to its tapered tip. Mount Tipo Pale overlooks the invasion beach, backed by the 1,500-foot Mount Tapochau in the center of the island. About 25,000 Japanese civilians lived on Saipan, which until 1944 was a sleepy administrative center deep in the backwater of Japan's Pacific defense perimeter.

The Japanese army's Forty-third Division was responsible for defending Saipan at the water's edge, with three battalions entrenched near the beach and the other six held back for counterattack, supported by a tank regiment. A "mixed brigade" of infantry, plus two detached battalions, rounded off the army's commitment.

The navy's V Base Force was also present, its roughly 3,000 troops bringing up Japan's total defensive strength to about 28,000 men—the equivalent of two divisions. The defenses would have been stiffer were it not for American subs sinking transports laden with troops, artillery, and building supplies.

About 66,000 Americans were going to slam into Saipan under the banner of the V Amphibious Corps, Lieutenant General Holland "Howlin' Mad" Smith commanding. His Second and Fourth Marine divisions would land side by side against Saipan's southwestern edge. Having previously fought at Tarawa, Second Marine was tasked with driving straight inland to seize Mount Tipo Pale and Mount Tapochau. To the south, the Fourth Marine Division would first secure a beachhead two thousand yards deep, then drive forward to seize Aslito Airfield, thence to the farther shore on Saipan's southeast coast.

As General Obata was away at this moment, command of Saipan's defense devolved upon Lieutenant General Yoshitsuga Saito. He saw Saipan's craggy features as a natural fort that could be used to defend the island in depth but had no time to capitalize on this insight. At the water's edge Saito had to defend, but he expected the marines to strike from the east at Magicienne Bay (the "bite" taken out of the pork chop), instead of the southwest. Saito's artillery officers, however, planned for all contingencies, positioning their guns mostly in the island's center to be able to hit all shore points with indirect fire.

On June 15, 1944, those guns opened fire on the incoming marines aboard the first of over 700 LVT amphibious tractors hitting the reef line. Near misses sprayed shrapnel and direct hits blew them up. About twenty of the tractors were lost in the first wave, but despite Japanese positional advantage, the beach was taken and held by the first wave of eight battalions. A fake Marine landing to

Saipan's northwest was supposed to gull Saito into committing his troops early, but he did not take the bait.

By nightfall about 20,000 marines—about a third of the invasion force—were holding ground, but it took 2,000 casualties to pay for it. Japanese artillery fire was competent and accurate, but lacked the means to mass fire on smaller targets, American-style. The marines were not moving in quickly, so there might be a chance for a Japanese night counterattack to drive them into the sea.

Saito would lead that attack, using the Ninth Tank Regiment, supported by the troops of the 136th Infantry Regiment and the Yokosuka First Special Naval Landing Force, Japan's equivalent of marines. But in truth, only thirty-six of the regiment's forty-eight tanks were handy, with barely a thousand infantry to support them. American naval gunfire disrupted the units staging for the attack, separating Saito from his staff. With the hours of darkness slipping past, an officer on the spot launched the tank attack anyway, without telling the infantry commander. The tanks charged downhill toward the marines, holding the town of Charan Koa, but the thrust bogged down in the swamp east of the town. Bazookas, M4 Shermans, and offshore 5-inch guns held the line, shredding the tanks and the follow-on infantry alike.

Saipan triggered the commitment of Japan's First Mobile Fleet, under Vice Admiral Jisaburo Ozawa, to destroy Spruance's Fifth Fleet, in conformance with Japanese strategic planning. Spruance calmly dispatched Mitscher's Task Force 58, resulting in the "Great Marianas Turkey Shoot." The American carriers defeated the Japanese fleet, removing the threat to the transports now unloading at Saipan.

Spruance prudently ordered his corps reserve to be landed—the hard-luck Twenty-seventh Infantry Division, Major General Ralph Smith commanding. This unit was also the reserve for the

Guam landing, so that operation had to be postponed. The First Mobile Fleet's attack to the west did not compel the American transports to "bug out." More than eleven thousand tons of supplies were landed on Saipan. Saito could see for himself that nothing was going to stop his enemy from taking the island.

By June 22, the two Marine divisions turned north to advance toward Marpi Point while the Twenty-seventh Infantry went south to mop up. But the marines had to cover too much ground, so the hapless infantry unit was ordered to head north into a patch of low ground the Americans nicknamed "Death Valley," because it was flanked on both sides by higher ground. There their advance stalled.

Now the differences between the U.S. Army and the Marine Corps became painfully clear. The marines always charged hell for leather toward the farther shore of every island, eager to cut the enemy position in half. Executing that doctrine, however, meant suffering heavier casualties to take an island in less time. The army did things the other way around, massing firepower to overcome resistance and taking the objectives at a slower pace, thus suffering fewer casualties.

Common sense for the army did not make sense to Howlin' Mad Smith. Ever since Makin Island, Smith saw the army's performance as deficient, and that went double for the Twenty-seventh Infantry Division. With the blessing of Fifth Fleet higher-ups, Smith sacked Major General Ralph Smith for his division's lack of drive at the so-called Death Valley. The division gained no ground until the marines took Mount Tapochau, outflanking the Japanese position. Nevertheless, interservice relations would take a major hit from Howlin' Mad Smith's hissy fit. And this could only complicate a campaign where army-navy cooperation was vital.

Despite the staunch defense, the Japanese were down to 1,200 able-bodied men and three tanks by June 25, ten days after the invasion began. Radio reports from the beleaguered garrison spoke of being surrounded by fire whenever a unit dared move—even at night. Maneuvering became impossible. But there was no talk of surrender. Radioing directly to Tokyo, Saito apologized for not doing better, given the lack of air superiority. "Praying good luck for the emperor, we all cry 'Banzai!'"

On June 30, the Americans finally broke through the Death Valley salient. Any wounded Japanese in the field hospital who could still walk retreated north, while the more gravely wounded were given hand grenades and ordered to die rather than surrender. They obeyed.

By July 5, the Japanese barely held the northern sector of Saipan around Marpi Point. Japanese culture now dictated strategy. To atone for the failure to hold Saipan, Saito and Nagumo committed suicide. For the troops, atonement would come in the form of a last-ditch attack. On 4 A.M. on July 7, a mixed force of 3,000 Japanese soldiers and civilians gathered along the shoreline to charge the American line to their south, toward the town of Tanapag.

The human wave crashed into the 105th Infantry Regiment, 27th Infantry Division. "If you shot one, five would take his place," recalled Major Edward McCarthy, commanding the Second Battalion. He managed to pull the remnants of his command into Tanapag village, holding out until relieved by a tank platoon the next day. Not so lucky was Lieutenant Colonel William J. O'Brien, commanding the First Battalion, who was last seen alive manning a .50-caliber machine gun. About 650 GIs were killed or wounded as their lines were overrun. Next came the artillery positions of the Fourteenth Marine Regiment, where the gunners fired over open sites on the assaulting mob. That was not enough to stop the charge, as marines and Japanese alike died by the guns.

Despite the damage done, the Japanese had shot their bolt. There would be no more banzai charges on Saipan. By July 9, the island was declared secured by naval amphibious force commander Vice Admiral Richmond Kelly Turner. But that did not mean the battle was over. A few Japanese diehards did not get the memo and were still sniping at marines.

The battle's final drama took place at Marpi Point, where the majority of Japanese civilians and a few troops still clung on. Despite assurances from the Americans that no one would be harmed if they surrendered, the remaining Japanese men, women, and children jumped off the cliffs to their deaths, into the surf hundreds of feet below. Battle-hardened marines saw the war veer from horror to insanity.

Winning Saipan took twenty-four days of close combat. American casualties approached 16,000 while Japanese losses were close to 20,000 killed.

Taking Back What Is Ours

The early commitment of the Twenty-seventh Infantry to Saipan robbed the Americans of their designated reserve for Guam. Replacing that division was the Seventy-seventh Infantry Division, based in Hawaii as the theater reserve. This division was assigned to III Amphibious Corps, Lieutenant General Roy Geiger of the U.S. Marine Corps commanding. Also assigned to III AC was the Marine Third Division (veterans of Bougainville) and the First Marine Provisional Brigade, formed from the Raider battalion of the Fourth Marine Division and the veteran Twenty-second Marine Regiment, fresh from the Marshalls. Geiger's naval counterpart would be Rear Admiral Richard L. "Close In" Conolly, who liked to bring his ships close to shore to deliver hellacious fire support. Conolly was planning to deliver thirteen days of preinvasion bombardment.

Defending Guam would be the Japanese Twenty-ninth Infantry Division, along with the Forty-eighth and Tenth Independent Mixed Brigades and the Fifty-fourth Naval Guard Force, all commanded by Lieutenant General Takeshi Takashina.

Guam is shaped like a guppy, with its head to the south and its tail to the north. About where the top fin would be was the narrow Orote Peninsula, jutting out like a narrow finger westward from the island. Takashina oriented his defense against Tumon Bay, on Guam's west shore, about two-thirds up the length of the island. That was the site of Japan's invasion that had taken the island a few years ago.

Geiger was going to break a few rules to do the unexpected. He committed the Third Marine Division to hit the beaches north of the Orote Peninsula, just west of Agana town and well south of Tumon Bay. Five miles farther south, on a similarly narrow beach, First Marine Provisional Brigade, backstopped by the army's Seventy-seventh Division, would land. Each force would be one-half of a claw that would cut off the Orote Peninsula from the rest of the island. The First Marine Provisional Brigade would then clear out the peninsula while the Third Marine Division and the Seventy-seventh Infantry fought their way north, side by side. But Geiger's plan was risky. The terrain between the two landing beaches was rough. A stubborn defense here could stop the two claws from closing, perhaps raising the risk that the Japanese could defeat one of the divisions in detail before it could join with its mate.

The navy committed 274 ships to land the 54,000-man force on July 21. The pre-invasion bombardment had little effect, as Japanese artillery raked the incoming waves of LVTs. With so many of the amphibious tractors knocked out, bottlenecks developed. The Seventy-seventh Infantry had to wade to shore from the reef line, all the while under fire. Artillery could not displace forward.

Ammo could not be landed fast enough. At one point, roughly one-fifth of the landing force was busy manhandling supplies from ship to shore instead of fighting the enemy.

The Japanese fought by their book, their futile attacks failing to stop the marines anywhere. The two offensive claws closed over the Orote Peninsula. The army and Marine divisions turned inland and began their bloody advance, opposed by uncoordinated Japanese "banzai charges" that were quickly destroyed by massive firepower. By August 11, Guam was American again. III Amphibious Corps suffered 8,000 casualties, among them 1,796 dead. Japanese losses were 11,000 killed and 10,000 more who "quit the war" to hide in the jungle, many holding out until 1945. A few more diehards refused to surrender for the next several decades. Japanese culture considered surrender worse than death.

Meanwhile, III Amphibious Corps began preparations for taking the Palaus.

Tinian: The Perfect Landing

American attention now turned to Tinian, located just three miles south of Saipan. The island, roughly the size and shape of Manhattan, was pretty flat, offering a mix of farms and cane fields but few suitable beaches for landing. The good beach was near Tinian town, on the island's lower west side. A frontal assault there was ruled out as "another Tarawa" by Howlin' Mad Smith, so planners began eyeing two small, narrow beaches on the island's upper west side. This entry point was a very tight bottleneck through which the Fourth Marine Division would pass, but it was close to Ushi Point Airfield, at Tinian's northern tip.

The defense consisted of 9,000 men, divided between the Fiftieth Infantry Regiment, Colonel Keishi Ogata commanding, along with another army battalion and the navy's Fifty-fourth Naval Guard Force. Another by-the-book officer, Ogata would also try to defend at the water's edge, focusing on Tinian town and the generous adjoining beach.

The invasion began on July 24. Long-range artillery on Saipan pounded southern Tinian, which only reinforced Ogata's thinking that Tinian town would be the likely landing site.

To fake out Ogata, the battleship *Colorado* peeled off from the invasion fleet, leading columns of landing craft holding the Second Marine Division. Japanese 6-inch naval guns opened fire, hitting the battleship twenty-eight times in fifteen minutes, causing about 285 casualties. The Americans turned tail and headed away. Ogata radioed the good news to Tokyo: American invasion repulsed!

And that was when the Fourth Marine Division motored ashore at those two north Tinian beaches, relying on 500 LVTs and 130 DUKWs (amphibious trucks) to push inland.

Guadalcanal veteran Major General Clifton B. Cates commanded the Fourth Marine Division. Good planning by his staff turned the landing site's liability into an asset. The LVTs and DUKWs drove inland to deliver supplies and reinforcements on north Tinian's plateau. Seabees built several exit ramps near the landing beaches so that returning vehicles did not have to fight traffic to get back to sea. Tanks, halftracks, and anti-tank guns were brought ashore early to reinforce the marines for the expected night attacks. American losses so far amounted to 15 killed, 225 wounded.

Ogata had erred, but he was quick to make up for it. Playing to his advantage on night attack, he launched well-coordinated thrusts against the Marine line, supported by a half-dozen tanks. But Cates had all 15,000 men of his division onshore, giving no ground as the Japanese broke themselves against stout defenses.

The next day, the Second Marine Division hit the same two narrow beaches, again speeding inland. Tinian's open terrain allowed the Americans to bring tanks and halftracks into play. Artillery was thick. As one of the few Japanese fighters captured on the island put it, "You couldn't drop a stick without bringing down artillery." The two Marine divisions pressed on grimly side by side, reaching Tinian's southern tip by August 1. American losses amounted to 2,355 casualties. Ogata's 9,000-strong command was wiped out.

What Happened Next . . .

For Japan, the loss of the Marianas was grave—the islands were the linchpin of the empire's "Inner Defense Line." The need to protect the islands was important enough to commit the fleet, which was defeated. Three island garrisons fought to the last man. Prime Minister Tojo was forced to resign due to these failures. And now the Americans had finally secured a base close enough to Japan to handle long-range B-29 heavy bombers, which would soon begin the airborne destruction of the Home Islands.

The price was not a cheap one for the Americans. About 26,000 out of a total force of 166,000 were killed or wounded taking the islands. The mass suicide of civilians on Saipan convinced Nimitz that taking the Japanese Home Islands was going to be a grim and bloody enterprise.

The fallout over the relief of Major General Ralph Smith by the Marines' Howlin' Mad Smith put a bad strain on army-navy comity. While Spruance and Turner thought the move was justified, Nimitz did not. After Saipan, Nimitz promoted Smith to command Fleet Marine Force, an administrative billet. Never again would Smith command troops in battle. But more important for Nimitz, never again would Smith deal with the army.

The loss of the Marianas also changed Japanese thinking on island defense. Turning the enemy back at the water's edge just did not work in the face of overwhelming naval gunfire and airpower. Japanese planners rated the support fire of one American battleship as equal to five of their own divisions, and the Americans always used a dozen or more battleships to deliver pre-invasion bombardment and follow-on fire support.

The Americans were also just too damn fast. "[E]verywhere you attacked before the defense was ready. You came more quickly than expected," said Admiral Kichisaburo Nomura in a postwar interview.

With no hope of matching American airpower or seapower, Japanese planners had to find another way to defend against these storm landings. While the Americans gained more experience with each landing, Japanese defenders were getting wiped out every time, leaving their radio reports the only means of transmitting their experience.

The Japanese would find their answer at Peleliu. And it was not what the marines expected.

HALSEY LEAVES THE BACK DOOR OPEN

The Battle of Leyte Gulf, October 1944

BY DOUGLAS NILES

Never interrupt your enemy when he is making a mistake.

—Napoleon Bonaparte, 1769–1821

When Douglas MacArthur was questioned about his plans after his ignominious retreat from the Philippines in spring of 1942, the ever-dramatic general responded with a single memorable phrase: "I shall return." By October 1944, he was finally ready to make good on his pledge. He selected for the initial landings the island of Leyte, near the middle of the archipelago, easily approachable from the east. In fact, the operation was put together with remarkable speed, after being moved up some two months from its originally intended date.

By this point in the war, the U.S. Army and Navy had worked out a very accomplished system of cooperation, allowing the ground forces to "island-hop" across the ocean in great strides, bypassing some of the strongest Japanese bases such as Truk and Rabaul. By the end of the war, the more than 100,000 Japanese soldiers in Rabaul, for example, would essentially be reduced to the level of subsistence farming, as their military relevance had long since faded to inconsequence.

The land campaign in the Philippines would be an army affair, with a landing force even greater than the one employed by Admiral Turner in the Marianas. As with all amphibious operations, a strong naval component was necessary. In the case of the landings at Leyte, this would include the largest fleets to participate in the Pacific War to date. The resulting action was the Battle of Leyte Gulf, which is widely recognized as the largest naval battle in the history of the world.

The U. S. Navy, for the duration of the war, would function under a unique command arrangement. While the ships and the officers and men at sea would remain the same (and, in fact, many of them would remain away from port for a year and a half or more during the climactic phase of the war), the command staff would rotate. Admiral Spruance, victor of the Philippine Sea, was recalled to Pearl Harbor to commence planning for the next stage of the war, which would be the campaigns against Iwo Jima and Okinawa. His Fifth Fleet was renamed Third Fleet, and Admiral Bill Halsey was placed in command. Admiral Marc Mitscher remained in command of the five-group fast battle fleet, but what had been Task Force 58 under Spruance became Task Force 38 under Halsey.

As recounted, the Japanese navy had suffered a catastrophic blow to its naval air arm in the Battle of the Philippine Sea, in June 1944. The airplanes that had struck so many lethal blows from the decks of their carriers had been virtually annihilated, and Japan now lacked the fuel, the manufacturing capacity, the resources, and the time to replace them. In the meantime, the Americans kept launching more carriers, churning out hundreds of new airplanes every month, and thoroughly training whole new corps of pilots to fly them.

But the Japanese navy's high command knew that the moment of decision was at hand. Already U.S. submarine operations had drastically reduced the capacity of Japan's merchant fleet. If the Philippines joined the Marianas in American hands, the U.S. military would have a massive barrier right across the very heart of the Japanese empire. With all of Japan's important resources, most notably oil reserves and refining facilities, located in the south, and the Home Islands located to the north, the Americans would have effectively severed the country from its essential base of supply.

The result was the Sho ("Victory") plan, a desperate gamble conceived with the certain knowledge that failure would lead to almost inevitable defeat. At its most basic level, it involved employing the Imperial Japanese Navy's remaining aircraft carriers, which had only about 110 aircraft and the aircrews left to fly from them, as a decoy. These carriers would form the Northern Force and again be commanded by Admiral Ozawa, still smarting from the debacle in the Philippine Sea. His objective was to sortie southward from Japan when the attack commenced, allow himself and his carriers to be discovered, then retire northward at speed, drawing the main U.S. battle fleet after him.

In the meantime, the powerful Center Force, under Admiral Takeo Kurita, was to move northward from bases in Borneo and Malaya, traversing the South China Sea before passing through the San Bernardino Strait from west to east. The strait was the main sea passage through the central Philippines. Kurita would have under his command two super-battleships, *Yamato* and *Musashi,* as well as three more battleships, twelve cruisers, and fifteen destroyers.

Another, almost equally powerful surface fleet, the Southern Force, under Admiral Shoji Nishimura, was to pass through the

Surigao Strait, south of Leyte and north of Mindanao. Nishimura would sail with two battleships, four cruisers, and eight destroyers. These two powerful fleets, with two of the greatest battleships in the world, were then to trap the American landing force between them and annihilate the transports and their escorts in a great surface battle while the American carriers and battleships of Task Force 38 were off chasing Ozawa's decoy fleet. As with most Japanese battle plans, this one was exceptionally complicated. Unlike most of the previous plans, however, it would come shockingly close to success.

To counter the Japanese, the Americans had assembled a vast collection of shipping, including two massive amphibious forces to make and supply the landings; a gunnery support group under Rear Admiral J. B. Oldendorf to support the landings; and an air support group under Rear Admiral Thomas Sprague to cover the landings. Oldendorf's force was built around six older battleships, most of them refloated or repaired after the Pearl Harbor attack. Sprague was in command of sixteen escort aircraft carriers (so-called jeep carriers) and twenty destroyer and destroyer escorts to screen them. The one potential flaw in the American plan involved a divided command, in that Admiral Halsey's Third Fleet would remain under Nimitz's, not MacArthur's, command. Halsey was assigned a duel role in the battle: he was to screen the landing force, as Spruance had done so well in the Marianas, but if the chance to destroy the enemy's main battle fleet presented itself, he was to take advantage of the opportunity. (It should be noted that the Americans were not aware of just how depleted the Japanese carrier air groups were after the Marianas Turkey Shoot.)

The troops of the first wave waded onto the shores of Leyte on October 20, but the Japanese had guessed the objective based on earlier American reconnaissance and had put the Sho plan into effect as of October 17. The three huge fleets, Ozawa's decoy carriers in the north and Kurita's and Nishimura's powerful surface fleets coming from the west, moved into action.

The Battle Begins

The first action occurred in the Sibuyan Sea, a small and sheltered body of water in the center of the Philippine archipelago. Two U.S. submarines, *Dace* and *Darter,* were on station there; they spotted Kurita's mighty battleship fleet as the Japanese ships came through the Palawan Passage, leading from the South China Sea into the Sibuyan Sea. After flashing word of the movement to Admiral Halsey, the two bold subs—which would achieve fame as a pair of the most legendary boats in the American fleet—sank two Japanese heavy cruisers and damaged a third.

Throughout the 23rd and 24th, Kurita continued westward, now harassed by the bombers and torpedo planes of Task Force 38. Over the course of the two days, the mighty *Musashi* was battered into wreckage and finally sunk. The Japanese admiral, late in the day on the 24th, abruptly turned about and steamed westward at high speed, on a course that would take him back to the South China Sea. Admiral Halsey assumed that the Japanese surface ships were retreating.

Also on the 24th, Japanese land-based planes from Philippine air bases found and attacked Task Force 38. Most of these aircraft were lost in these attacks, but the survivors pressed through with fanatical courage, sinking the light carrier *Princeton* and badly damaging a heavy cruiser. After dark, the determined Kurita changed course again, steaming eastward through the Sibuyan Sea and making for the San Bernardino Strait, north of Leyte, as called for by Operation Sho. This change of course went undiscovered by American ships and planes.

To the south, Nishimura was sticking to his part of the plan, bringing his ships in two groups, his own battleship force and a trailing force commanded by Vice Admiral Kiyohide Shima and built around a couple of heavy cruisers, through the Bohol Sea (another of the small seas protected by the Philippine Islands) toward the Surigao Strait. This passage was just to the south of Leyte, and if he had made it through he would have been very close to Kinkaid's landing forces.

But Nishimura's ships were spotted by American aerial reconnaissance flights and then shadowed into the Surigao Strait by PT boats. Admiral Kinkaid ordered Admiral Oldendorf, commanding the six old battleships of the bombardment force, to steam south and wait for the Japanese ships at the end of the strait, blocking them from passing into the Philippine Sea. During the night of October 24–25, two squadrons of destroyers—including several Australian ships—closed in to make torpedo attacks against the Japanese surface ships, hitting one of Nishimura's battleships, *Fuso,* as well as four destroyers. Nishimura steamed on, unaware of the damage for some thirty minutes, until the stricken battleship exploded, broke into two sections, and sank.

By the time the Japanese admiral, his flag flying from battleship *Yamashiro,* emerged from the strait, Admiral Oldendorf had his own battle line in perfect position to cross the Japanese T. As if in revenge for the attack on Pearl Harbor, the old American battlewagons erupted with broadside after broadside, smashing into the enemy flagship with lethal accuracy. In a matter of minutes *Yamashiro* came to a stop, disabled, and it wasn't long before she sank, carrying Admiral Nishimura and most of her crew into the depths with her.

Of the doomed admiral's command, only the badly damaged heavy cruiser *Mogami* survived (though she would be sunk by aircraft the following day), accompanied by a single, battered destroyer.

Admiral Shima, bringing his cruisers up behind Nishimura, was able to fire a few harmless torpedoes in the night, but then he retired in the face of the six American battleships. Oldendorf gave brief chase but, mindful of his charges in the landing fleet, returned to his covering duties as Shima's cruisers slunk away.

Thus far, the Battle of Leyte Gulf had encompassed two separate actions: the Battle of the Sibuyan Sea and the Battle of the Surigao Strait. Both of them had been resounding victories. In the meanwhile, Admiral Halsey, with the powerful carriers and battleships of Task Force 38, had been steaming off the San Bernardino Strait, without sighting a single enemy ship. The ever-aggressive admiral was particularly eager to discover the Japanese carriers.

Admiral Ozawa, steaming toward the Philippines with those same carriers, was just as eager to be found. After all, it's hard to fulfill a role as a decoy if the enemy never notices you! But American air reconnaissance remained less effective than its Japanese counterpart, and Ozawa had to bring his fleet to within two hundred miles of Task Force 38 before, finally, his ships were discovered.

Not a Menace?

Here, finally, Halsey's dual role became a complication, with tragic overtones. Task Force 38 included some fifteen modern aircraft carriers with full complements of aircraft and aircrews, as well as all of the fast, modern battleships in the U.S. Navy order of battle. Ozawa had six flattops in his fleet, with only about a hundred planes (though, as noted, the Americans didn't know how understrength were these air groups). Furthermore, Halsey's latest reports had indicated that Kurita's powerful surface fleet, battered by aircraft and submarines in the Battle of the Sibuyan Sea, was retiring westward.

It is perhaps inevitable that Halsey turned north to pursue the Japanese aircraft carriers, the ships that had been his focus and goal from the very morning of December 7, 1941. What is less understandable is that Halsey took his entire fleet with him, when he could easily have left a screening force of several battleships to protect the San Bernardino Strait. And what is very hard to understand, or forgive, is that after leaving the strait unguarded, he failed to communicate this fact to anyone else in the U.S. Navy!

Halsey eventually sent a communication to King and Nimitz in which he stated:

> *Searches by my carrier planes revealed the presence of the Northern carrier force on the afternoon of 24 October, which completed the picture of all enemy naval forces. As it seemed childish to me to guard statically San Bernardino Strait, I concentrated Task Force 38 during the night and steamed north to attack the Northern Force at dawn. I believed that the Center Force had been so heavily damaged in the Sibuyan Sea that it could no longer be considered a serious menace to the Seventh Fleet.*
>
> —As quoted in E. B. Potter, *Bull Halsey* (1985), p. 307

Instead, he took off like a dog after a meaty bone, which is exactly what the Japanese wanted him to do. His departure left the strait unscouted by so much as a PT boat, so when Kurita, with most of his ships—including the *Yamato*—intact, sailed into the open sea, not only did he do it unopposed, he was undetected as well. Scarcely able to believe his luck, he nevertheless followed up on the Sho plan, turning his fleet southward off the island of Samar, seeking the American amphibious fleet.

One of the supporting fleets for the Leyte landings was the escort carrier force under Rear Admiral Clifton Sprague. On the morning of October 25, he was with six of those carriers—which were much smaller and slower even than the light carriers accompanying the battle fleet—as well as three destroyers and four destroyer escorts (the latter being essentially small, light destroyers). The biggest guns on his ships were 5-inch bore. He had squadrons of planes on the escort carriers, but their primary ordnance was the fragmentation bomb, desirable for bombing enemy troops but almost harmless against the armored deck of a warship.

Sprague and his men were stunned by the appearance on the northern horizon of first the pagoda-shaped masts and then the long, low hulls of massive Japanese warships. Four battleships, six heavy cruisers, and ten destroyers bore down upon him and began showering his "tin cans" with shells ranging up to *Yamato*'s massive 18.1-inch bore. Broadcasting a desperate call for help to anyone who would listen, Sprague turned tail and churned away with all the speed his little fleet could muster. In an amazing running battle, with incredible courage displayed especially by the officers and men aboard the little destroyers and destroyer escorts, the American ships twisted and turned. The jeep carriers fled, while their bombers plastered the enemy warships with their loud but ineffective missiles, and the destroyers boldly sallied against the huge Japanese ships, firing torpedoes and popping away with their 5-inch batteries.

It is difficult to understand how any of Sprague's ships survived. One of the carriers, *Gambier Bay,* went down early in the fight, and two destroyers and one destroyer escort also sank, all with heavy loss of life. But the rest of the ships held on, while more ground attack bombers—from other escort carrier groups in the area—joined in the fight. Kurita apparently thought the air attacks were coming from Mitscher's carriers, and he had also received word that Nishimura's force had been annihilated in the Surigao Strait. Whatever his reasoning, and while he had the rest of Sprague's group dead to rights, in his sights and well within range of his guns, Kurita decided to retire.

Center Force turned about and returned to the San Bernardino Strait, which was still unscreened by American ships. As Kurita made his escape, more land-based Japanese aircraft joined in the attack on the escort carriers. For the first time in the war, a number of Japanese pilots were observed to fly their airplanes directly into American ships—the first instance of apparently planned kamikaze attacks. These were lethal enough to sink another escort carrier, the *St. Lo*.

Halsey, meanwhile, finally caught up with Ozawa in the morning of October 25. The admiral had been infuriated by a message from Nimitz, asking his whereabouts in light of the battle off Samar. He took out his frustrations against the Japanese carriers, sinking all of them, before turning about and steaming back toward Leyte at flank speed.

Despite the grievous error Halsey made in leaving the strait unprotected, the Battle of Leyte Gulf was a smashing American success, essentially finishing off the Imperial Japanese Navy as an organized fighting force. Some 282 ships were involved in the action, including 216 American, 2 Australian, and 64 Japanese. The Japanese lost 29 ships and more than 10,000 men killed; the United States suffered 6 sunk and nearly 3,000 men killed. Halsey's mistake was profound, especially since he had neglected to inform Kinkaid, MacArthur, or Nimitz of his maneuver, but in the end it was mitigated by Kurita's countering error, in his timid failure to complete the annihilation of the targets he had before him in clear sight.

THE FORGOTTEN BATTLE

Peleliu, September–November 1944

BY WILLIAM TERDOSLAVICH

If you entrench yourself behind strong fortifications, you compel the enemy to seek a solution elsewhere.

—Karl von Clausewitz, 1780–1831

The only way to halt an unstoppable force is to create an unmovable object. This was the Japanese approach to the defense of Peleliu, a battle largely overlooked by many historians of the Pacific War. The Japanese still lost the battle, but how they lost was a nightmare that would be compounded in island battles yet to come. For the Americans, it was a bitter victory more often forgotten than remembered.

The Japanese Losing Streak

By the summer of 1944, Japan had lost every major island battle in the central Pacific. Tarawa was a near-run thing, but Roi-Namur, Kwajalein, Eniwetok, Saipan, Guam, and Tinian were all overwhelming defeats. About one percent of the defending force in each battle was captured—the rest died fighting. Lack of retreating survivors made it difficult for lessons learned to be passed on to the next island garrison. Detailed reports radioed during each battle provided the only hints.

Imperial General Headquarters formed an analytical team to sift through these reports, looking for clues that would help win the next battle. Americans always committed land forces at odds of around three to one, backed by overwhelming naval firepower and carrier-borne airpower. The lesson the Americans took away from the bloody marginal victory of Tarawa was: never send an infantryman into harm's way when you can instead drop lots of bombs or fire plenty of shells.

Japanese doctrine called for defense at the water's edge to stop the invaders. If that failed, launch a night counterattack (the banzai charge) to throw the Americans into the sea. It never worked. Massive American firepower destroyed defense positions and shredded infantry attacks day or night, leaving suicide as the only recourse for survivors.

The only way the Japanese could deal with American strength was to make it useless. To this end, the Imperial headquarters issued its new doctrine, "Defense Guidance on Islands," that August. The advice was not cheerful. Assume worst-case conditions—plan to defend without air or naval support. Expect your positions to be hit by ten thousand to twenty thousand tons' worth of incoming fire and ordnance. Making a limited defense of the beach might disrupt the incoming assault, but it would be foolish to depend on this tactic to win. Expect the enemy to choose landing sites that are closest to airfields, which they can quickly put to use. Forget about banzai charges—they are futile in the face of massive enemy firepower. Better to save manpower by defending in depth rather than counterattacking en masse.

"Decisive Engagement" now became "Endurance Battle," according to the new doctrine. Defense in depth required soldiers to construct "Fukkaku positions," basically networks of tunnels connecting numerous firing positions. These positions were a mix of bunkers and cave entrances where emplaced guns could lay down mutually supporting fires to halt the attacker. Fukkaku positions turned time into a Japanese weapon. Stout defenses would slow the enemy attack from a run to a crawl, inflicting massive casualties for every yard taken. Islands that once fell in days would now take weeks, or months, perhaps replicating the casualties inflicted at Tarawa. If this was done often enough, the Americans just might quit the war before getting to Japan.

On to the Palaus

Also known as the Western Carolines, the Palaus are equidistant from New Guinea, the Marianas, and Mindanao, the southernmost large island in the Philippine archipelago. By holding the Palaus, Japan guarded its oil shipment route between the Netherlands East Indies (now Indonesia) and the Home Islands. The Palaus became more important once the Japanese abandoned their main naval base at Truk in the Eastern Carolines. Earlier in April, the Imperial Japanese General Headquarters reached into the "elite" Kwantung Army in Manchuria, dispatching the veteran Fourteenth Division to defend the Palaus. Unlike reinforcements bound for the Marianas, the Fourteenth Division made the trip unscathed by American submarines. Once the American attack on the Marianas became apparent, the Japanese defenders in the Palaus got more time to dig in.

Lieutenant General Sadae Inoue had 25,000 men to defend Angaur in the south, then Peleliu, Koror (the administrative center), and Babelthuap, the largest island in the chain. Farther off to the northeast were Yap and Ulithi. Inoue tried to defend everything, and in the end defended nothing. He expected the main American effort to hit Babelthuap (also known as Palau Island), valuable for its paved airfield. There he concentrated his defenses. To Angaur he sent a battalion. Another garrison was placed on Yap. But the second-biggest bet was placed on Peleliu, where Inoue committed his division's Second Infantry Regiment, plus two battalions of the Fifteenth Regiment, Colonel Kunio Nakagawa commanding. Inoue also dispatched his assistant, Major General Kenjiro Murai, to serve as Nakagawa's "tactical assistant," but his real mission was to yell back at the navy if any admiral tried to pull rank and alter the division's defensive mission.

Peleliu is shaped like a lobster claw, measuring two miles wide by six miles long. Off its northern shore was a narrow causeway connected to the smaller island of Ngesebus, where an airfield was being constructed. A finished airfield graced Peleliu's southern flatland, at the base of the lobster claw. The narrow half of the claw is a spit of land flanked by a mangrove swamp. The Umurbrogol, a nasty tangle of brush-covered hills, ridges, canyons, and caves, dominated the thicker half of the claw. Nakagawa's tactical eye was drawn to this natural fortress. More than five hundred caves were carved out of the Umurbrogol's living rock. Every firing position could draw support fire from a neighboring strongpoint.

Nakagawa did not neglect the beaches. He figured the Americans would go for the airfield at Peleliu's southern end, so he posted one battalion on the southwestern beach as his "welcoming committee." The coral ridges were turned into emplacements for machine guns and 47mm anti-tank guns. A company of light tanks would deliver a counterattack once the Americans made it to shore—assuming they were not already mauled by defensive gunfire and the anti-boat mines placed 150 yards from the shore.

Knowing the marines' penchant for speedy advance, Nakagawa ordered his troops to engage in passive infiltration: Let the green wave wash over their positions. Once the marines were past, pop up and open fire on their rear to slow their attack. (The marines just kept going, leaving the scut work of clearing bypassed defenders to the next wave.)

To stop the Sherman tanks and amphibious tractors, Nakagawa would rely on "human bullets"—soldiers carrying explosives who would run up to the armored vehicles and blow themselves up. They were to be used sparingly, only when they had a chance to kill a tank.

Nakagawa had no reason to let the Americans waltz in unscathed. But stopping them at the beach was not important. He was banking on his positions in the Umurbrogol to deliver success.

Is This Trip Necessary?

General MacArthur was planning to move north to the Philippines in the last quarter of 1944, once he was done in New Guinea. Securing the Palaus would gain a major airfield to support the invasion with long-range bombers. But Third Fleet commander Admiral William Halsey encountered light resistance as he raided the Philippines, leading him to downgrade his estimate of enemy strength. So why not skip the Palaus? Halsey was by practice a "fighting admiral," not well regarded by Nimitz when it came to strategy. MacArthur still wanted the Palaus for their support value. The invasion fleet had already been dispatched. Nimitz did not change plans. After all, order followed by counterorder yielded disorder.

Dubbed "Operation Stalemate," the invasion plan for Peleliu called for three days of naval bombardment, followed by the landing of the First Marine Division, minus one battalion held back as a division reserve. Paired with the marines would be the army's Eighty-first Infantry Division (Wildcats), tasked with taking Angaur. Together, these divisions constituted III Amphibious Corps, Marine Lieutenant General Roy Geiger commanding. Yap and Ulithi would be taken by the XXIV Corps.

The invasion followed the basic doctrinal script: U.S. Navy carriers would raid various islands in the region to destroy Japanese air units and deceive the enemy as to where the next blow would land. The carriers would then double back to support the naval bombardment of Peleliu. The Eighty-first Division was sent to take out Angaur. Babelthuap would be skipped, leaving the Japanese garrison there to "wither on the vine." For the navy, the prize would be Ulithi atoll to the north of the Palaus—a massive anchorage that could act as a forward base with the support of the navy's Fleet Train. The atoll lay undefended. The First Marines would then hit Peleliu, aggressively pushing in to seize the airfield, reach the farther shore, then turn north to mop up the Japanese—just like on all those other islands. Major General William Rupertus, who commanded the First Marine Division, said the landing would be rough but expected to take Peleliu in two to three days.

But that's not how it turned out.

Where Did That Ridge Come From?

The First Marine Division, veteran of Guadalcanal and Cape Gloucester, hit the beaches of southwestern Peleliu on September 15. The shore bombardment was not as heavy as other assaults, but it had to do. Landing on the left was the First Marine Regiment, tasked with seizing the base of the Umurbrogol as well as supporting the Fifth Marine Regiment's center drive to take the airfield. The Seventh Marine Regiment landed to the right. Local strongpoints to the left and right of the landing beaches hampered but did not stop the Big Green Wave from hitting shore. But the cost was high. King Company, Third Battalion, First Marines saw its strength chopped from 230 men to just 18 as it struggled unsupported against a fortified promontory on the extreme left. Incoming LVTs and DUKWs were getting blown up here and there by the deadly flanking fire.

Geiger was not going to watch the invasion from the bridge of the command ship *Mount McKinley*. Battle reports were coming in garbled. Regiments were not gaining ground. He went to the ship's access ladder and hailed a landing craft like it was a taxi and ordered the coxswain to take him to shore. He could see things were not going well. About twenty-four LVTs and many DUKWs were burning in the shallows and on the beach. Geiger could hear the Japanese firing from the Umurbrogol. Where did that high ground come from? It wasn't on the map. None of the aerial photographs showed it, as the ground was well covered by brush. Geiger then worked his way inland, pausing to raise his head above a dirt mound to get a look at the airfield. He nearly got his head blown off by an incoming round. Peleliu was not going to be easy.

Assistant divisional commander Brigadier General Oliver "O.P." Smith was already on the beach but lacked sufficient sealift to land the reserve battalion or the divisional headquarters by day's end. The marines still made it to shore with all eight battalions of infantry, several batteries of 105mm and 75mm howitzers, and the tank battalion. But that cost 200 dead and another 900 wounded to gain a beachhead three thousand yards long by five hundred yards deep. This was not as bad as Tarawa or Saipan, but worse than Guam or Tinian.

Taking the airfield was the job of the division's Fifth Regiment.

Its three battalions, plus one from the First Regiment, advanced across the runways, all within view of the three-hundred-foot high Umurbrogol. Japanese forward observers called in artillery fire while raking the open ground with machine guns. "Through the haze I saw Marines stumble and pitch forward as they got hit," recalled Eugene Sledge, who survived to chronicle his ordeal in his memoir, *With the Old Breed*.

"The farther we went, the worse it got. The noise and concussion pressed in on my ears like a vise," Sledge wrote. "To be shelled by mass artillery and mortars is absolutely terrifying, but to be shelled in the open is a terror compounded beyond the belief of anyone who hasn't experienced it."

Not the sharpest knife in the drawer, Rupertus applied the Marines' "speed at all costs" doctrine to Peleliu, only to run up against the Umurbrogol. Rather than going around the problem, he committed the division's First Regiment, under Colonel Lewis "Chesty" Puller, to attack. And attack. And attack. And attack.

Rumors of the debacle ran through the division. Sledge recalls hearing the bitter scuttlebutt from a buddy who heard it from another: "[T]hey got them poor boys makin' frontal attacks with fixed bayonets on that damn ridge, and they can't even see the Nips that are shootin' at 'em. . . . There just ain't no sense in that. They can't go nowhere like that. It's slaughter."

After six days of seeing the same mistake repeated, Geiger overruled Rupertus. The First Marine Regiment would come out of the line, to be replaced by a regiment from the Eighty-first Infantry. Rupertus was too stubborn to admit failure, sincerely believing that any regiment in his division was superior to the entire Eighty-first. But that pride nearly destroyed the First Marine Regiment, which suffered losses close to 60 percent trying to storm "Bloody Nose Ridge."

"What once had been companies in the 1st Marines looked like platoons; platoons looked like squads. I saw few officers," wrote Sledge. "I couldn't help wondering if the same fate awaited the 5th Marines in those fateful ridges."

In the first week of fighting, First Marine Division seized the airfield, all the ground to the south and east of the Umurbrogol, and a foothold on that dismal high ground—in effect, all the tactically important ground on the island. Geiger had to secure the rest, but that could not be done by frontal assault. Using his amphibious assets, he shifted units to pick at the Japanese defense from a different angle. On September 26, the Fifth Marine Regiment landed on Ngesebus Island (recently reinforced with a Japanese battalion from nearby Babelthuap), then drove south into the high ground.

The Umurbrogol was slowly reduced, one bunker, one cave at a time. But it was a confusing ordeal. Japanese defenders held fire until sighting a target and then fired briefly for effect before going back under cover. Again, Sledge recalled the experience: "If we moved past a certain point, the Japanese opened up suddenly with rifle, machine-gun, mortar and artillery fire. It was like a sudden storm breaking. More often than not we had to pull back, and not a man in the company had seen a live enemy anywhere." The defenders had no hope of reinforcement. The marines were not retreating. The killing would go on, with the battlefield acquiring its own nicknames for certain features—"Death Valley," "Five Sisters," "Wild Cat Bowl," "the Horseshoe," "Boyd Ridge," "Knobs."

Geiger pulled out the only tank battalion, reasoning that the armor would not be able to move across the rough terrain. That robbed the marines of much-needed direct fire support. Instead, the marines would rely on their own close air support, provided by the F4-U Corsairs of Eleventh Marine Air Group operating off of Peleliu's captured runways. Some pilots didn't even bother raising their landing gear, flying low over Bloody Nose Ridge to drop napalm canisters close to the front lines. They didn't arm their loads to detonate. Marine small arms fire did that instead.

There was not enough dirt on rocky Peleliu to dig a hole. The unburied dead rotted quickly under the hot sun. With no water, unwashed marines began to smell as bad as they looked. And with no way to dig latrines, the Umurbrogol became one giant cesspool. All that worsened in the 100-degree heat and 100 percent humidity, which also claimed its share of casualties from heat exhaustion.

Rock pile. Junkyard. Sauna. Garbage dump. Open sewer. Cemetery. Peleliu. "At every breath one inhaled hot, humid air filled with countless repulsive odors. I felt as if my lungs would never be cleansed of those foul vapors," Sledge wrote. "The stench varied only from foul to unbearable."

On October 12, Geiger declared the island "secured," though the news was greeted with much derision by marines on the front line. By October 15, when the Eighty-first Infantry exchanged places with the two remaining regiments of the reduced First Marine Division, the Japanese position in the Umurbrogol already measured 400 yards by 500 yards. It would take the soldiers another six weeks of close-in fighting to wipe it out. By November 24, Nakagawa and Murai committed suicide in their underground headquarters. "Our sword is broken. We have run out of spears," read Nakagawa's last message to Tokyo.

If You Are Going to Die, Die Hard

Peleliu was the big game-changer in Japanese defensive thinking. The same tactics would be repeated at Iwo Jima and Okinawa. The same defensive technique would also be applied to the defense of Kyushu, one of Japan's four large Home Islands, should the Americans invade.

Peleliu did not play any supporting role for MacArthur's "return" to the Philippines on October 20. None of its hard lessons were passed on to the marines slated to assault Iwo Jima. Halsey's hint to bypass the Palaus gave the battle the cast of irrelevance before the first shot was fired. Apologists groped for a reason that would redeem the whole bloody mess. Taking the island isolated more than 250,000 Japanese in various garrisons throughout the Carolines. One of Japan's best infantry divisions was destroyed. The United States got a valuable air base. The First Marine Division sharpened itself to extraordinary competence, which would come in handy in Okinawa.

But was this worth close to 10,000 casualties, among them 1,200 dead? It was calculated that the United States had to expend close to 1,600 rounds of ammo in every caliber just to kill one Japanese soldier. That effort had to be repeated 15,000 times to kill off the Japanese garrison.

No one lacked courage at Peleliu. The victors certainly took pride in their accomplishment, finding honor in sacrifice. The battle hardly got any press at home, pushed off page one by events in Europe. Not all agree today that this battle needed to be fought. It might have shrunk to a scholar's obscure footnote were it not for Sledge's memoir. Writing fifty years later, Sledge claimed that the battle "left a bitter taste" with its veterans. "I shall always harbor a deep sense of bitterness and grief over the suffering and loss of so many fine Marines on Peleliu for no good reason."

SINK THE *TIRPITZ*!

Norway, 1942–1944

BY WILLIAM TERDOSLAVICH

Wars may be fought with weapons, but they are won by men. It is the spirit of men who follow and of the man who leads that gains the victory.

—George S. Patton, 1885–1946

The *Bismarck* was bad enough. For six days, the Royal Navy scoured the North Atlantic, very eager to eliminate the German battleship as payback for sinking the *Hood* and mauling the *Prince of Wales*. It was no contest when the better part of the Home Fleet ran down the *Bismarck,* smashing it to pieces with torpedoes and shells. The German battleship died hard and mean.

And to make sure this never happened again, the Royal Navy had to sink the *Tirpitz*!

You mean there was another *Bismarck*? Yes!

Separated at Birth

Bismarck and *Tirpitz* were destined to be the first true battleships of the Kriegsmarine when it placed orders for both ships in 1935–36. The design called for eight 15-inch guns in four turrets on a hull displacing thirty-five thousand tons. Final weight came in around forty-two thousand tons.

These ships were the last word in German naval design—from twenty years before World War II. Thanks to the naval prohibitions of the Treaty of Versailles, Germany lost the services of an entire generation of experienced naval architects. Engineers had to blow the dust off the blueprints for most recent battleship made in World War I, the *Baden* class, then update them as best as they could to create the *Bismarck* and *Tirpitz.* There were parts they just didn't get right.

Bismarck and *Tirpitz* could reach twenty-nine knots—about a half knot faster than the British *King George V*–class battleship—but only by using 27 percent more power. That implied an inefficient power plant for the German dreadnoughts. *Tirpitz*'s armor belt was 12.6 inches thick, compared to 14 to 15 inches of armor for the *KGV.* And the British managed to mount ten 14-inch guns with longer range into a warship weighing 5,000 tons less than the *Bismarck* and *Tirpitz.*

The British had a very good look at *Tirpitz*'s World War I predecessor, the *Baden,* shortly after the Great War ended. British naval design incorporated that knowledge, yet it didn't seem to make much of a difference. *Bismarck* sank the *Hood* and mauled the *Prince of Wales* (very similar to the *King George V* class). The British Admiralty took *Tirpitz* very seriously, assuming that it would take two *King George V*–class dreadnoughts and an aircraft carrier to even the odds in a naval fight. That was a lot of steel to keep handy in home waters, just to deter one enemy battleship.

Join the Navy and See . . . Norway?

None of that information was known—or feared—when *Tirpitz* was finally launched on April 1, 1939. It was April Fool's Day, and the battleship was no joke. Construction was not completed until February 1941, followed shortly afterward by sea trials. After the demise of the *Bismarck,* and given the shortage of fuel oil, German dictator Adolf Hitler thought it unwise to base the *Tirpitz* on the French Atlantic coast. Instead *Tirpitz* was shifted to Trondheim, Norway. The Royal Air Force greeted the arrival of the battleship with a bombing raid on the night of January 28–29, 1942, the first of many raids to come.

Tirpitz was ideally placed to cut off British convoys transporting Lend-Lease aid to the Soviet Union. With the *Tirpitz* in Norwegian waters, every convoy bound for Murmansk had to be escorted by at least one British aircraft carrier and one battleship, plus an assortment of cruisers and destroyers.

One sortie by the *Tirpitz* in March 1942 nearly resulted in blows when the ship came within ninety miles of a task force consisting of the battleships *King George V, Duke of York,* the battle cruiser *Renown,* and the carrier *Victorious.* Bad weather shielded the *Tirpitz* from any sighting by British aircraft but masked the two convoys that passed within a few miles of the battleship. *Victorious* did launch air strikes against *Tirpitz* once the weather cleared, but scored no hits. But the experience made the German navy gun-shy. Now the *Tirpitz* became dependent on the Luftwaffe. Sighting the British fleet first ensured avoidance of nasty surprises like the one that sank the *Bismarck.*

The existence of the *Tirpitz,* coupled with the *Bismarck's* reputation, began to drive British naval planning. A commando raid on St. Nazaire, France, destroyed the only drydock big enough to handle the German battleship, much needed to support any foray into the Atlantic. As the British fought enemy capabilities, German intent saw no future Atlantic missions for the *Tirpitz.* Three more air raids on Trondheim failed to hit the battleship. Even the rumor that *Tirpitz* was at sea with a pocket battleship and a cruiser for escort was enough to get Murmansk-bound convoy PQ-17 to scatter. U-boat wolf packs picked off the sheep-like freighters with ruthless ease.

Send in Special Forces

Commerce raiding was out. The *Tirpitz* settled down as part of a new strategy: the fleet in being. Germany used this trick in World War I, keeping their warships in port, merely existing as a threat that had to be matched by a vigilant Royal Navy. This tactic tied down enemy warships so they couldn't be used elsewhere. Only now the Germans would keep their small surface fleet in Norway's fjords. The narrow waters, lined by mountains and cliffs, prevented strike aircraft from making torpedo runs at anchored warships. There would be no Taranto at Trondheim. High-level bombing never worked, as the British flew at night and were lucky to hit targets as big as cities. The odds of hitting a warship were pretty lousy. Norway's geography, and not the German navy, would be the *Tirpitz*'s best protector.

Fighting fair with fleets and bombers certainly wasn't getting Britain anywhere. Killing the *Tirpitz* required the British to resort to so-called dirty tricks, also known as using special forces. This concept didn't have a name yet, but the scheme was simple: infiltrate a small group of highly trained, specially equipped men. Their inferior number should defeat the greater force, provided they can sneak in and move quickly to complete their single mission. In the case of the *Tirpitz,* that meant sneaking in by sea.

On October 26, 1942, the fishing boat *Arthur* appeared inconspicuously off the coast of Norway near Trondheim. Her skipper, Leif Larsen of the Norwegian resistance, was going to place six British frogmen into the frigid waters, each trio riding a modified torpedo called a "chariot." The concept was very close to the "pigs" used by Italian frogmen to vex British transports and warships in Gibraltar and Alexandria—just ride the torpedo underwater to the target, attach the warhead to the side of the ship, set the timed fuse, and get the hell out. The resulting explosion should sink the warship.

The *Arthur* towed both chariots underwater to the launch site. The scheme actually survived inspection by German guards at the head of Trondheim fjord, who boarded the *Arthur* and noticed nothing funny about a couple of heavy-duty lines running overboard. But simple deception could not keep the weather from turning foul. Rough seas caused both lines to snap, losing both chariots just five miles shy of reaching the *Tirpitz*. Larsen put the *Arthur* to shore, and all but one of his crew managed to evade capture and escape to Sweden after landing.

Tirpitz shifted base to Altenfjord, much farther north and much closer to the route taken by Russia-bound convoys. In September 1943, while operating with the battle cruiser *Scharnhorst, Tirpitz* finally got to fire its guns in battle. But the two ships were just ordered to destroy a weather station up north in Spitzbergen, about five hundred miles north of Norway. It was *Tirpitz*'s finest hour, even though the weather station was back on the air in a couple of weeks.

The British went back to scheming. If chariots could not do the job, the X-craft could! Ready for duty shortly after the Spitzbergen raid, X-craft were midget submarines that each carried a crew of four. They were not built for comfort. The skipper on each boat could easily reach out and touch all of his crew members while on station. An air lock allowed a single diver to exit the X-craft to operate the hydraulic shears needed to cut through steel anti-torpedo nets. Each X-craft measured fifty-three feet long, displaced three hundred tons, and could dive down to three hundred feet. On batteries, it could do about eight knots. Armament was a pair of explosive charges in formfitting pallets attached to either side of the mini-sub. Each charge contained two tons of amatol, a high explosive.

The X-craft scheme began in August 1942, when the Royal Navy began screening volunteers for the "dangerous mission." Six mini-subs were built, with crews trained throughout 1943. Two sets of crews would be needed. One would man the craft and keep it trim and operational while it was towed by a larger oceangoing sub. Upon reaching the vicinity of Altenfjord, the under way crew would swap places with the attack crew, who would then cast off and proceed to the target. Six X-craft left Scotland on September 11, 1943, bound for Altenfjord. Two were lost during the passage.

The *Tirpitz* was not going to be an easy target. Each warship at anchor was guarded by anti-torpedo nets and patrol boats, as well as guards on deck instructed to scan the waters for any sign of periscopes or bubbles—telltale signs of mini-subs or frogmen. The challenge for the Germans was keeping alert in the face of numbing routine. When nothing happens for a long time, guards get sloppy.

Four X-craft cast off their towlines at 8 P.M. on September 20. They made their way to lie-up stations about ten miles from the *Tirpitz,* beginning their final approaches shortly after midnight on September 22. It still took hours to cover the final leg, with the

X-craft arriving at their targets shortly after sunup. Pressing the approach was very problematic. *X-6* had a leaky periscope, was listing 15 degrees, and suffered an electrical fire, and the crew was totally fried from being up for thirty-six hours, punctuated by fits of brief sleep in the cold, wet compartment. Lieutenant Donald Cameron polled his crew—press on or quit? They opted to complete the mission, even though it was quite likely they would not make it back to rendezvous with their mother ship, the good sub *Truculent.*

Meanwhile, aboard *X-7,* Lieutenant Godfrey Place had to dive deep to avoid a patrol boat. His mini-sub ran afoul of a loose section of anti-torpedo net, wasted an hour shifting ballast to break free, suffering a screwed-up gyroscope and trim pump, and fouled again on a stray cable. He pressed on as well.

Neither skipper knew the other was nearby. They both were detected nonetheless. *X-6* suffered a compass failure, had to surface to take a bearing, got spotted and shot at by guards, submerged, and released its two charges near *Tirpitz*'s hull, right around the forward turret. Cameron ordered *X-6* to resurface as the boat was taking on water. The crew cleared the mini-sub as it sank and were picked up by a guard boat.

It was already 7 A.M. The crew on *Tirpitz* was slow to go to battle stations. Watertight doors slammed shut. The captain ordered all preparations made for getting under way. That was when *X-7* was spotted broaching the surface.

The *Tirpitz* was swung on her cable away from where *X-6* was spotted. Place steered *X-7* toward the battleship's hull, hitting it. He ordered one charge cast off, again near *Tirpitz*'s forward turret. He then turned *X-7* to run aft another two hundred feet, then cast off the second charge. *X-7* ran afoul of the anti-torpedo net again and remained stuck until about 8:15 A.M., when all four charges went off.

The explosion lifted the 42,000-ton *Tirpitz* six feet out of the water. The battleship splashed down, a total mess, listing five degrees to port. Damage was extensive to the lighting system, the electrical system, all three turbines, the anti-aircraft gun control, the hydrophone station, one generator room, the port rudder, the range-finder, and two of the four gun turrets. In hindsight, results would have been more impressive had the mini-subs attached their two-ton charges directly to *Tirpitz*'s hull. Instead, the charges were dropped alongside the ship, sinking to a depth of 100 to 150 feet. Had the *Tirpitz* sunk, the loss would have been beyond salvage.

The damage to *Tirpitz* was a major mission kill. It would take six months of repairs to make her seaworthy again. British losses were near total. *X-7* was fatally stricken when the amatol charges went off, with Place and one other crewman surviving. A third X-craft went missing. The fourth was assigned a secondary target—either the *Scharnhorst* or the *Lützow*—but did not drop charges for fear of tipping off the attack on the *Tirpitz,* the main target. It managed to make it back to its mother ship.

The Lone Queen of the North

After the X-craft attack, *Tirpitz* underwent repairs in place. *Lützow* was ordered to return to Germany. *Scharnhorst* attempted to intercept a Murmansk convoy in late 1943 and was sunk in the Battle of the North Cape. That left the *Tirpitz* as "the Lone Queen of the North," a single battleship to carry on the fleet-in-being strategy.

The Royal Navy was not giving up. On April 2, 1944, the fleet carriers *Victorious* and *Furious,* along with escort carriers *Emperor, Searcher, Pursuer,* and *Fencer,* launched two air strikes, each with twenty-one Barracuda dive bombers escorted by forty fighters, targeting *Tirpitz*.

The surprise was complete. *Tirpitz* was readying for her sea trials after six months of extensive repairs. Crews were slow manning the smoke generators and firing the anti-aircraft guns. It was all over in one mad minute. The fighters strafed *Tirpitz*'s deck while the dive bombers pounded their lone target. An hour later, the same nightmare repeated itself, only now the smoke screen was thicker and the anti-aircraft fire was better.

The Royal Navy lost only four aircraft. They scored fourteen hits on the *Tirpitz* and one damaging near-miss. But many of the bombs were dropped from too low an altitude, striking the armored deck with insufficient force to break through. The *Tirpitz* was put out of action for only three months.

The Lone Queen of the North was attracting many unwanted suitors. The Royal Navy tried repeating the strike six times, with many of the missions called off because of bad weather. One final attempt in July put two more bomb hits into the *Tirpitz*. A 1,600-pound bomb managed to penetrate eight decks before exploding, but the blast turned into a fizzle, as the bomb had only been half filled with explosives.

Who You Gonna Call? Dam Busters!

Altenfjord was too far away for the Lancasters of R F Bomber Command to strike. But that was not going to stop hem. If they flew to Yagodnik in the Soviet Union's far north, t y could refuel and re-arm, hitting Altenfjord on the return leg Britain. Tapped for the mission were 9 Squadron and 617 S adron—the latter well known as "the Dam Busters." Only ow each Lancaster carried a single 12,000-pound Tallboy b . On September 15, twenty-eight Lancasters overflew the T itz. A growing smoke cloud enshrouded the ship. Each bor ardier aimed as best he could. The *Tirpitz* may have been lucky many times, but the RAF only had to be lucky once. And once was good enough, as a single Tallboy slammed into the *Tirpitz*'s forecastle, penetrating the ship's deck armor. It exploded, peeling back the deck.

Tirpitz, though stricken, could still make eight knots, even if she could never again undertake another high seas cruise. German navy chief Admiral Karl Dönitz ordered the *Tirpitz* moved two hundred miles south, to Tromso. There the ship would be anchored to become a floating artillery battery. Engineers would construct a sand bed to keep the ship from capsizing should it take another hit. About thirty fighters were based at a nearby airfield to provide air cover.

Tromso was just close enough for the RAF to try again, only now the Lancasters were going to need some modification. The dorsal gun turrets came off. The armor was stripped. Extra fuel tanks were fitted. The engines were upgraded to the more powerful Rolls-Royce Merlin 24. New precision bomb sights were installed.

At 3 A.M. on November 12, the twenty-nine Lancasters of 9 and 617 Squadrons took off from Lossiemouth, Scotland, bound for Tromso. Each bomber was two tons over takeoff weight, each brimming with fuel and a 12,000-pound Tallboy bomb, each bomb tipped with an armor-piercing cap. Daylight bombing was not an RAF preference and the crews fully expected to be shot down by the German fighters.

Five hours later, the Lancasters droned in at fourteen thousand feet from the landward side, trying to catch the *Tirpitz* by surprise. The day was clear. Eight German fighters took off from Bardufoss airfield, twenty miles away from Tromso, all flying intercept courses. The ground crews by the *Tirpitz* fired up the smoke generators, hoping once again to obscure the target from the bombardiers. Just as the smoke thickened, one of the 12,000-

pound Tallboys struck the *Tirpitz* amidships. A second Tallboy hit aft. Two massive explosions tore apart the machinery and boilers below. A hundred-foot gash opened along the ship's side, letting in the water, causing a 30-degree list. A third bomb hit, wiping out the gun turrets. Shock waves from near misses tore at the hull. Finally, the aft magazine exploded.

As the bombers turned for home, the *Tirpitz* turned turtle, trapping more than a thousand crew belowdecks. Survivors knocked on the hull plates to alert relief workers, who then used cutting torches to get them out. About eighty sailors were rescued this way. Other knocks and clangs were heard, but one by one the taps weakened, then ceased.

The *Tirpitz* was finally dead.

Losing the Hard Way

If the mission of the *Tirpitz* was to sink British warships and merchantmen, then it failed miserably. As a ghostly threat, though, it succeeded beyond expectations. Britain could not shift any forces to the Pacific so long as Germany had a few warships that could tangle with the Russia-bound Lend-Lease convoys. That forced Britain to keep some battleships and carriers in home waters to match the threat. By the time the *Tirpitz* was eliminated, the U.S. Navy had pretty much won the naval war against Japan, making moot the need for the Royal Navy in the Pacific.

It was a cheap and hollow victory for the *Tirpitz,* which served a fleet that was destined to lose its war.

IRRESISTIBLE FORCE, IMMOVABLE OBSTACLE

Iwo Jima, February 1945

BY ROLAND J. GREEN

The battle of Iwo Island has been won. The United States Marines, by their individual and collective courage, have conquered a base which is as necessary to us in our continuing forward movement toward final victory as it was vital to the enemy in staving off ultimate defeat. . . . Among the Americans who served on Iwo Island, uncommon valor was a common virtue.

—Fleet Admiral Chester Nimitz, 1885–1966

Iwo Jima is one of the Ogasawara Islands (also known as the Bonins), named for the sixteenth-century Japanese seafarer who discovered them. Like its neighbors, it is of volcanic origin. Its highest point, Mount Suribachi, is modestly active—it erupted with hot water and fumes in 1984. The Japanese annexed it in 1861. By 1914 the Japanese navy had built a radio station; by 1940, an airfield.

A modest civilian population of small farmers, fishermen, and sulfur miners shared the seven and a half square miles of volcanic rock with the garrison. Meanwhile, the Japanese navy's garrison grew to 7,000 in mid-1944, running two airfields, starting a third, emplacing coast-defense guns up to 6 inches, and preparing defenses for the beaches on either side of the southern half of the island.

When the United States invaded the Mariana Islands, Guam, Saipan, and Tinian, Iwo Jima ceased to be a backwater. The invasions breached the main Japanese defensive perimeter and gave the United States bases from which their new VHB (Very Heavy Bomber), the B-29, could reach the Japanese Home Islands.

If the Iwo Jima campaign had a catalyst, it was the B-29. This magnificent high-performance aircraft had gone into battle before all the bugs were out of it. The engines failed or caught fire, and the host of advanced subsystems needed delicate handling; as a result attempts to operate B-29s from China were just this side of a fiasco. The Marianas, on the other hand, offered plenty of room for building modern airfields with men and materials brought in conveniently by sea, to a place that the Japanese army could not overrun, as they did the Chinese airfields that same summer of 1944.

B-29 raids from the Marianas started in November 1944 and promptly ran into trouble that took several forms: bad weather over Japan, the continued unreliability of the B-29, and Iwo Jima. The island had fighters that its radar stations could vector onto the bombers, both coming and going. It could refuel bombers attacking the B-29 bases, and B-29s did not grow on bushes. And in American hands, the island could be a refuge for B-29s limping across the long miles of ocean with mechanical failures or battle damage.

These issues confirmed the need for what the American planners had begun work on almost as soon as the Marianas fell—the seizure of Iwo Jima. Their work had begun about the same time that the island's defenses began to grow rapidly under the formidable Lieutenant General Tadamichi Kuribayashi. He had arrived with orders to turn Iwo Jima into a fortress. He started by conscripting able-bodied civilians into the garrison, shipped the rest back to Japan, and went on from there. In the course of obeying those orders, he turned the island into what may have been the most heavily fortified area of comparable size in the history of warfare.

Contrary to legend, Kuribayashi did not have many "crack troops" under his command. But he had about 22,000 hard workers, from navy base personnel, gunners, and ground crew to enough army conscripts (many middle-aged) to make up an improvised division.

At the Water's Edge

After the fall of Saipan, Imperial General Headquarters issued orders to abandon the "defeat them at the water's edge" tactics that had sacrificed so many Japanese lives to American firepower. Kuribayashi was already laying in defense in depth, although he was a cavalry officer, a breed not known for their mastery of positional warfare. Possibly his five years in North America as a language student and attaché had something to do with it; he had assessed American war potential and been opposed to Japan fighting the United States.

He set up three complexes of fortified positions, one around Mount Suribachi in the south and two arranged in successive lines across the northern part of island. The best estimate is fifteen hundred individual fortified positions, ranging from massive blockhouses and caves filled with heavy mortars, rocket launchers, and artillery down to individual sniper positions. Each complex was interconnected by a maze of tunnels, sometimes offering four or five different entrances and exits to a given position.

Kuribayashi's men dug about thirteen miles of tunnels. He planned to connect the Suribachi complex to the first northern complex, with tunnels dug right under the airfields, but ran out of time and materials. The men also had to rotate in short shifts—as little as twenty minutes in some places where the sulfur fumes and geothermal heat were particularly bad. But the volcanic rock was soft enough to be worked with pickaxes, and in the end the Japanese were able to bring fire on almost every part of the island where an enemy might stand.

It also took a lot of hard work to prepare an amphibious landing force consisting of three U.S. Marine divisions (the Third, Fourth, and Fifth), with their landing craft, transports, and fire-support vessels. Additional support would come from the Seventh Air Force, flying from the Marianas, and the fast carriers of Task Force 58.

For seventy-four continuous days before D-Day, the United States hit Iwo Jima with air or sea bombardment. They also tried to interdict the flow of reinforcements and supplies to Iwo Jima. The island had no harbor, so cargo ships ran to Chichi Jima, 150 miles north, and unloaded into barges for the final island-hopping leg to Iwo.

The Americans used planes, submarines, and an occasional sweep by surface ships. They sank a good deal of shipping, but not enough to starve either Iwo's garrison or its weapons. And while the fighter sweeps and bombing raids put the airfields out of action, they barely dented the defensive positions. Two-thousand-pound bombs might have helped, but the still-active European Theater had priority on those superior bunker busters.

Even the Arsenal of Democracy could not supply everybody with everything.

On February 16, 1945, the final bombardment began. Shells, bombs, rockets, and bullets saturated the island but had comparatively little effect until the third day, February 18. Then the beach defenses opened up on a group of landing craft converted into gunboats, covering the underwater demolition teams as they scouted for mines and underwater obstacles. Apparently the Japanese thought this was the spearhead of the landing.

The gunboats took heavy damage and casualties. The now-exposed beach defenses took worse, when everything from battleships down to the surviving gunboats, plus air strikes, descended on them. It's been estimated that the last day's bombardment did far more damage than the other two days' together.

Should the bombardment have been longer? The senior marine on the spot, Lieutenant General Holland M. ("Howlin' Mad") Smith, gave an adamant "yes" in his memoirs. Ten days was his idea of enough bombardment. But the plan couldn't have been changed at the last minute; ships and ammunition were needed in the Philippines, and then they had to be available for Okinawa, scheduled for April 1. The bombardment plan could have been extended in advance, but probably only at the price of delaying the Okinawa invasion. And what then, with Okinawa more heavily fortified than ever and more kamikazes ready to swarm over the invasion fleet?

It's not clear that more bombardment at Iwo was a realistic option. What does look dubious in retrospect was the rigid timetable of invasions, dictated by the strong American desire to get hands around the throats of the Japanese on their home soil.

Tragically, Iwo Jima would do nothing to weaken that impulse.

February 19 dawned overcast and cool, with light winds and nearly calm seas. By now amphibious operations in the Pacific were down to a fine art, although there were always improvements to be made. At Iwo, one improvement was a first wave of armored amphibious tractors (Landing Vehicles, Tracked, or LVTs) mounting 75mm howitzers.

Then came conventional LVTs, holding marines. Following were the LCVPs, wooden barges holding more marines. Finally landing craft and landing ships, loaded with vehicles, construction equipment, and artillery, with assorted small craft to guide these vessels through the waves to the right beach.

Nearly everybody landed where they were supposed to. In doing so, they created what is now called a "target-rich environment," and the Japanese opened up. It didn't help that the ashy sand reduced marines with eighty-pound loads to a creeping pace, and terraces above the beach made progress slow for wheeled and even tracked vehicles as they struggled to reach level ground. The marines slogged, rather than stormed, ashore.

The Fifth Division on the left pushed straight across the island, then turned north. The Fourth Division on the right wheeled toward the north as quickly as the Japanese allowed.

Grinding Attrition

The Fourth's approach was not very fast, as the Japanese were using every weapon in their arsenal. The most common were light mortars and machine guns; the most horrifying were huge mortars and rocket launchers. When one of their five- or six-hundred-pound projectiles hit even a dispersed platoon, it reduced the unit not merely to bodies but to body parts.

Marines died by the score, including Guadalcanal Medal of Honor winner John Basilone, killed on the first airfield by a mortar fragment. But new heroes were also emerging, such as Tony Stein, who won the Medal of Honor for cleaning out Japanese strongpoints with a .30-caliber machine gun salvaged from a wrecked navy plane on Guam.

As afternoon came, so did deteriorating weather. Surf built up on the beaches, tossing landing craft ashore or slamming them together. Beach parties were too shorthanded to do unloading and rescue work at the same time. And wrecked boats and bogged-down vehicles so encumbered the beach that it was hard to find any place to land reinforcements.

Enter the Seabees, navy construction battalions, who had quite literally bulldozed their way across the Pacific. The advance parties of three battalions went straight to work, hauling landing craft out of the way or pushing them back into the sea, bulldozing rough roads up the terraces and through the ashes, and rescuing bogged-down vehicles. The landing-craft drivers also benefitted from two LSTs (Landing Ship, Tank) fitted out to provide them with hot meals and dry bunks.

The marines ashore didn't make quite as much progress. In fact, they halted where they were at nightfall, dug the best foxholes they could in the treacherous, flowing sands, and settled down to wait for a banzai charge.

It didn't come, because Kuribayashi had forbidden what he considered unsound tactics. Those charges simply exposed soldiers to superior American firepower, allowing them to die for the emperor but not to do much damage in the process. His men were to fight from cover, using firepower instead of spiritual strength, and move in the open only when the situation justified the risk.

It is ironic that such a civilized man as Kuribayashi had to lead his men in what was not technically a banzai charge, but something even worse—a campaign of mutual slaughter.

D + 1

By the next day the pattern of the ensuing battle began to emerge. With less opposition to its immediate front, the Fifth Division assigned its Twenty-eighth Marines to reduce the Suribachi complex. It did this quickly enough that by D + 4 (February 23), the regimental commanding officer decided to send a patrol to the top of Suribachi, to spy out the land.

Forty men scrambled up the mountain, meeting more opposition from the terrain than from the Japanese. They had a small flag with them, and at the summit raised it on a piece of pipe salvaged from a rainwater catchment system.

It is not true that nobody could see this first flag. The men at the foot of the mountain and in boats close offshore saw and cheered. This reaction gave the battalion commander an idea. Why not a bigger flag, one that everybody could see?

A Marine lieutenant (who must have been very sound of wind and limb) ran down to an LST that he knew had an extra battle ensign, salvaged from a navy dump at Pearl Harbor. He got the flag and ran back to Suribachi, where another marine carried it to the summit. The patrol found another, longer piece of pipe for a flagpole.

Then the old flag was lowered and six men of the patrol started to raise the new one. At that moment photographer Joe Rosenthal arrived, with just enough breath and presence of mind to point his camera and shoot.

The rest is history. So, by the end of the battle, were three of the six flag-raisers. Pharmacist's Mate John Bradley was badly wounded, but won the Navy Cross and survived to become the father of the author of *Flags of Our Fathers*. Ira Hayes drank himself to death. René Gagnon died in 1979.

Of the forty men in the patrol, only four left Iwo Jima alive and unwounded.

By the time the Twenty-eighth Marines finished mopping up Suribachi and rejoined their parent Fifth Division, the situation on Iwo had changed, and somewhat for the better. Two regiments of the floating reserve, the Third Division, came ashore and moved up the center of the island. The fighting was still intense and brutal, but the combination of riflemen providing covering fire while assault squads went in close with satchel charges and flamethrowers was taking its toll on Japanese positions. And as each position fell it made a gap in the interlocking Japanese fields of fire.

It was still a foolish marine who turned his back on any patch of ground that hadn't been blasted, flamed, or grenaded recently. At night, infiltrators made the hours hideous with grenades and knives, and any marine who moved around at night was likely to be taken for one of those unwelcome visitors.

One Marine officer had fantastic luck. He took a breather on a sand heap that concealed a 75mm howitzer. When the howitzer opened fire—fortunately not at him—he scrounged reinforcements and dumped grenades through the firing slit.

Grenades in fact played a large and lethal role on both sides. Marines could throw them at night infiltrators without revealing their position. The Japanese could do the same. One Marine private became one of the few men in history to smother two enemy grenades with his own body and lived to wear the Medal of Honor.

Heavier weapons were also joining the marines—105mm and 155mm howitzers, 4.5-inch rocket launchers on trucks, and a steadily increasing number of Sherman tanks. At first coordinating tanks and infantry had been difficult because of delays in fueling the tanks, then the tanks had to advance across ground often well sown with anti-tank mines and commanded by Japanese anti-tank guns (including some tanks buried with only their turrets aboveground).

Eventually the tank infantry tactics were reduced to starting with an armored bulldozer clearing the ground. After that came a tank with a bulldozer blade, clearing while shooting. Then came regular and flamethrowing tanks, firing the infantry in while the infantry kept a watchful eye out for mines, tank traps, and desperate Japanese with grenades and pole charges.

Overhead, fighter-bombers and torpedo bombers from a dozen escort carriers provided close air support, a Marine specialty directed by some of the best forward air controllers in the American armed forces. Task Force 58 had moved on after kamikazes damaged a fleet carrier and sank an escort carrier sunk to shortly after D-Day, pounding airfields in Japan itself to prevent further trouble from that quarter.

The fire-support vessels and their shore fire-control parties stayed. Each ship had an assigned sector to provide with fire support, and if a ship had to withdraw another took its place. The indispensable destroyers cruised close enough to shore by day to use their automatic anti-aircraft weapons, and at night fired star shells regularly to rob the Japanese of the cloak of darkness for either attack or movement.

All forms of fire support became more accurate when the Seabees had the new airfield ready to take light spotting planes. In fact, by early March the waist of the island looked like a combination of airfield, construction site, Marine camp, and vehicle park.

Payoff, the First B-29

As the marines worked their way toward the key points in the Japanese second line, on March 4 the airstrip landed its first distressed B-29. *Dinah Might* had a malfunctioning fuel-transfer pump and nearly ran out of runway coming in. With mortar shells bursting too close for comfort, the crew repaired the pump, getting airborne by the skin of their teeth.

The key to the second Japanese line was a trio of hills—382, 362A, and 362B. They were all heavily fortified even by the standards of Iwo Jima—a supporting position on one hill became known as the Meat Grinder. The marines saved themselves some trouble by taking a leaf from the Japanese's book and launching a night attack, which carried one of the hills.

By now most Marine regiments were down to 50 percent combat effectiveness. Sergeants commanded companies. Corporals or privates first class commanded platoons. Shore parties had long since been fed into the rifle units. The individual marine was ragged, gaunt, red-eyed from smoke and lack of sleep, often wearing a bandage, and almost too tired and footsore to care that he was actually winning.

While the fighting for the high ground went on, the flank divisions were working their way toward Kitano Point, at the northern tip of the island. An ambitious patrol bypassed its defenders to reach the sea. They filled a canteen with seawater and sent it back to corps headquarters with a tag, "For evaluation, not consumption."

This turning movement reduced the Japanese to a few pockets of still-intense resistance. One called the Gorge gave the Japanese the ability to fire down on intruding marines. Another was Kuribayashi's own command bunker, now filled not with his staff but with miscellaneous refugees from shattered units.

On February 23, Kuribayashi sent a last radio message, mourning his dead—unusual for a Japanese general. The bulk of the fighting ended by February 26 with the last banzai attacks at the end of the island.

Iwo Jima was declared secured on March 16, and the 147th Infantry Regiment took over mopping-up operations, while the marines filed down to the boats and army and air force personnel filed up from them. On March 26, the newcomers had to face a well-organized attack, possibly led by Kuribayashi himself. He either committed seppuku or was killed in that attack, his body never to be found.

The new American garrison took 800 prisoners and killed 1,600 more Japanese. The last Japanese holdouts finally turned themselves in during 1946.

A Truly Pyrrhic Victory

The Battle of Iwo Jima makes one think of putting two weasels in a cage and letting them fight it out. One weasel is noticeably larger and stronger, but both are equally determined. Also, people outside the cage keep poking the smaller weasel with sharp sticks.

The Americans won, but at the price of nearly 7,000 dead, severely wounded, or missing in action, primarily marines and navy. There were an additional 21,000 wounded plus about 2,500 combat fatigue cases. The Japanese lost 21,000 dead and about 1,000 prisoners.

The Americans did achieve their main objective—a forward base for supporting the B-29 campaign. More than 2,200 B-29s in some sort of trouble landed on Iwo Jima before the war ended. While not all of them would have ditched without the island refuge, one has to consider that each one that did had a crew of eleven men. It is not impossible that by permitting emergency fields on Iwo and air-sea rescue from it, every marine who died there saved two of his countrymen.

The planned P-51 escort missions also started in April, and continued until June, when Okinawan fields became available. The B-29s did more than burn Japanese cities; they also laid mines that sank or crippled three-quarters of the Japanese merchant marine that American submarines and tactical aircraft had left afloat. The Japanese edged steadily closer to starvation, and the vaunted Kwangtung Army could never have been shipped from Manchuria to Kyushu in time and in sufficient troop strength.

What was in every American planner's and soldier's mind, however, was the fear that an invasion of Japan would meet the same kind of resistance as on Iwo and Okinawa. It was an appalling prospect—and built the case for not only ongoing B-29 raids but also Hiroshima and Nagasaki.

Admiral Nimitz's words about Iwo, "Uncommon valor was a common virtue," apply to both sides. But the valor of the Japanese may well have served their country badly.

DIVINE AND DEADLY WIND

Kamikazes at Okinawa, April 1945

BY DOUGLAS NILES

If only we might fall like Cherry blossoms in the spring—so pure and radiant.

—Haiku by a kamikaze pilot in the Seven Lives Unit, 1945

Despite a string of uninterrupted defeats at sea and on land, and in spite of the fact that her ally Italy had surrendered in 1943 and Nazi Germany was on the ropes, with the front lines closing in on Berlin, by April 1945 the empire of Japan showed no sign of being ready to quit the war. Her forces had been annihilated in the Marianas, overwhelmed in the Philippines, and ground into dust on the volcanic sands of Iwo Jima. Her aircraft had been shot down far faster than they could be replaced, and virtually all of her once-proud navy had been sent to the bottom of the sea. Yet the emperor and his military commanders were determined to fight on: in the Japanese mind-set, surrender was simply not an option.

For the attacking Americans, war weariness was becoming a

reality. Japan was beaten! Why didn't she just quit already? Lacking any real answer to that question, the United States Army, Navy, and Marines simply knew they had to go to work again, taking another island away from their determined foe, continuing the relentless advance that, everyone assumed, would end only when American boots trod at will across the length and breadth of the Japanese homeland.

Before them lay another objective, part of the Ryukyu Islands chain that, while not considered the Home Islands, had been Japanese territory for a very long time. The 450,000 people who lived on Okinawa considered themselves part of the empire, and the territory was administered as part of the homeland. There was every reason to believe that they would fight, and die, as tenaciously as the Japanese had already proven themselves willing to do.

The invasion of Okinawa would, in fact, turn out to be the climactic battle of the Pacific War, though at the time (since the atomic bomb remained a highly classified secret) it was viewed by most as a precursor to the fights that would occur when the main Home Islands of Kyushu and Honshu were eventually invaded. And if it was a look into the future, it was a very horrific future indeed. All through the war the Japanese soldiers, sailors, and airmen had shown what the Westerners viewed as a fanatical willingness to die for their emperor, most notably displayed in their utter unwillingness to surrender, even in a hopeless position. Now, with the enemy at the nation's very doorstep, this fanaticism had increasingly been displayed in suicide attacks by fliers who dived their planes, often laden with extra explosives, into enemy ships. Drawing on Japan's historical legend of a typhoon that had disrupted a Mongol invasion fleet some seven hundred years earlier, these suicide fliers were called Kamikaze, or "Divine Wind."

The operation would be the biggest offensive of the Pacific

War, an amphibious invasion that only Operation Overlord would exceed in scale. Operation Iceberg, as it was termed, aimed to put 180,000 combat troops onto the island. Two Marine divisions and four army divisions would make up the Tenth United States Army, under the command of Lieutenant General Simon Bolivar Buckner.

Admiral Raymond Spruance was again in charge of the naval component, which was designated the Fifth Fleet. Admiral Richmond Turner, by now the acknowledged master of amphibious assaults, would command the landing fleet, while Admiral Marc Mitscher retained command of Task Force 58, including not just the American aircraft carriers and fast battleships, but a new task group of British ships under Vice Admiral H. B. Rawlings. His Majesty would be sending four more aircraft carriers and one battleship to the party. The British ships were as fast and modern as the Americans. The key difference was that English aircraft carriers had steel-plated (armored) flight decks, while the American decks were made of teak. As a result, the U.S. carriers could operate larger air groups, but the armored decks would prove significant in the coming campaign.

The task of supporting the assault against Okinawa was complicated by the lack of any land-based airpower in range (with the exception of some long-range army bombers), so the fleet would have to provide all of the fighter cover and tactical attack planes in the fight. The Japanese, conversely, had a number of air bases on Okinawa, and the island was in range of their fighters based to the south, on Formosa, and to the north, on the home island of Kyushu. Based on the experiences in invading Luzon (the main Philippines island) and Iwo Jima, in which the Japanese had displayed a growing willingness to make suicide attacks, a large number of kamikazes were expected to take to the air around Okinawa.

On the island itself, the Japanese had posted the Thirty-second Army, with some 130,000 men under the command of Lieutenant General Mitsuru Ushijima. Following the model that had proven so lethal on Iwo Jima, Ushijima decided not to defend the landing beaches themselves. Instead he constructed a strong network of trenches, tunnels, and fortifications, most notably throughout the southern end of the long, narrow island.

The invasion was scheduled for Easter Sunday, April 1, but as had become the typical pattern, first efforts would be made to disrupt the enemy's ability to send aircraft from peripheral bases to interfere with the operation. During the last two weeks of March, Mitscher's carriers moved north and relentlessly pounded the Japanese air bases and aircraft on the island of Kyushu. Kamikazes came after them in waves, Japanese suicide pilots flying into the control towers and flight decks of a number of carriers. *Franklin* was so badly damaged that she had to be towed away from the area and was in great danger of sinking or exploding, though in the end she survived. *Yorktown* and *Wasp* (both *Essex*-class replacements of the original carriers lost earlier in the war) also suffered damage from the planes of the Divine Wind. Nearly a thousand Americans were killed in these attacks, but the Japanese air bases were effectively neutralized.

The British carrier group concentrated on bases south of Okinawa, most notably in the Sakishima island group, which lay between the objective and the large island of Formosa (now Taiwan). The British carriers were subjected to kamikaze attacks as well, but here the armored flight decks proved their worth: a suicide attacker crashing into a British carrier typically wouldn't penetrate the deck, so the wreckage could just be pushed over the side and the carrier could resume operations. Land-based bombers from Luzon also hammered Japanese air bases on Formosa and flew as far as the main island of Honshu to strike at industrial targets.

In the final week of March, army units of the Seventy-seventh Division were landed on some of the outlying islands off the Okinawan coast. Capture of the island of Kerama, in particular, resulted in Allied possession of a secure and sheltered anchorage, which would prove invaluable through the coming campaign as a refueling and seaplane base. Capture of Kerama also resulted in the discovery of small boats, armed with two depth charges apiece, that would have been used for suicide nautical attacks against the invading fleet.

April 1

The landings began right on schedule, just after dawn on April 1. Eight waves, one after the other, of assault craft put the troops onshore, landing them against virtually no opposition from Japanese ground troops. Some 60,000 troops were landed on the first day and moved inland far enough to secure two air bases before nightfall. By the second day the attackers had pushed all the way across the narrow island to the eastern shore. The marines, who landed to the left, turned north and moved out, while the army corps, on the right, turned south. For four days progress was steady; the marines would meet little resistance to the north and would clear that large section of the island by April 20. The U.S. Army offensive, however, quickly ran into the extensive network of defensive positions, anchored by three successive and well-fortified lines; these were the trenches where the land campaign on Okinawa would gain its bloody reputation.

At sea, the Imperial Japanese Navy decided on one last, valiant mission for its remaining powerful ship. It would be a forlorn hope: the battleship *Yamato* took on only enough fuel for a one-way trip and departed the Inland Sea with the intention of fighting her way to the beaches and breaking up the landing. On April 6, she steamed southward, the focal point of Operation Ten-Go.

On April 7, while *Yamato* had been spotted by American submarines, the Japanese unleashed their first kamikaze attack of the campaign, and the largest such raid to date. About 350 suicide pilots, and another 350 regular dive bombers, swarmed against the Fifth Fleet. They sank six ships and damaged another twenty-four; about 300 of the dive bombers survived to fight another day. That same day, however, Mitscher's air groups swarmed against *Yamato.* Over the course of four hours of pounding, the super-battleship suffered hits from an estimated fourteen bombs and fourteen torpedoes. She sank before the end of the day, marking the effective end of the Japanese surface fleet as a fighting force. Her guns claimed some fifteen American bombers.

It turned out to be a curiously bungled mission, in the end. If the battleship had reached the fleet, her big guns—with an astounding range of more than forty thousand yards—could have inflicted incalculable damage. If the Japanese high command had employed their remaining aircraft to give air cover to *Yamato* for that one day, she very well could have completed her mission. As it was, she was effectively wasted.

Beginning on April 12 and continuing through the rest of the campaign until the island was finally cleared on June 21, nine more waves of kamikazes attacked the ships of the Fifth Fleet, a maddening onslaught that was virtually impossible to effectively defeat. Over the course of these attacks, the suicide bombers would eventually sink twenty-one ships, wreck forty-three more beyond the possibility of repair, and knock out another two dozen for at least a month or more.

The Kamikazes' Success

The tactic of the suicide attack was one that went a long way toward convincing the Americans that the Japanese were simply operating under an entirely different value system than the Western world. Unlike the war in Europe, the war against Japan had always had a strong element of racial alienation, on both sides. Now it was clear to everyone that it truly was a duel to the death.

THE WORST PLACE TO LAND

Inchon, September 15, 1950

BY WILLIAM TERDOSLAVICH

Never forget that no military leader has ever become great without audacity. If the leader is filled with high ambition and if he pursues his aims with audacity and strength of will, he will reach them in spite of all obstacles.

—Karl von Clausewitz, 1780–1831

It looked like a bad idea on paper. Land a division on an unfriendly shore fronted by a seawall, in a port afflicted with thirty-foot tides that would prevent reinforcement for twelve hours, and hope that the landing site is not well defended. That's Inchon.

This is the battle the North Koreans should have won with a little effort. Instead, it turned into a decisive defeat with serious strategic consequences, for the North Koreans as well as the Americans.

When All Is Lost, Risk It All

The Korean War started in late June 1950, when seven North Korean divisions and an armored brigade rushed over the border to conquer South Korea. Taking a cue from Mao Zedong's communist victory in the Chinese civil war, North Korean leader Kim Il Sung thought he could do the same—use force to reunify his country under the Red Banner. With Soviet dictator Joseph Stalin's blessing, Kim attempted what he thought was possible.

And why not? American occupation forces had already withdrawn, leaving about a half-dozen poorly trained South Korean divisions with no armor or artillery. This may seem foolish to do in the middle of a cold war, but American planners did not want South Korean strongman Syngman Rhee invading North Korea.

The South Korean capital of Seoul, located close to the border, fell quickly. General Douglas MacArthur, in charge of the Far East Command, flew over from Tokyo to assess the situation. South Korean soldiers were retreating with their arms. The rear areas were not filled with any wounded. No one was putting up a fight. If nothing was done soon, there would be no more South Korea left to fight for.

In New York, the United Nations Security Council voted for armed intervention to save South Korea. The Soviet ambassador was absent over a tiff about seating Communist China, so no veto could be cast. President Harry Truman committed U.S. ground troops to the defense of South Korea but did it without a declaration of war.

MacArthur had to do what he could with what he had. The army possessed ten divisions in its order of battle, all understrength and equipped with worn-out, leftover weapons from World War II. Four of these divisions were occupying Japan. These would have to do.

Eighth Army commander Lieutenant General Walton Walker was put in charge of the defense of South Korea. The cagey commander drew his defensive line along the Naktong River, with the port of Pusan in the rear to funnel reinforcements and supplies forward. With four U.S. divisions, a provisional brigade of marines, and whatever Republic of Korea (ROK) divisions were left, Walker held his ground. It was like playing chess for keeps, as Walker shifted units around his perimeter, defending one trouble spot after another.

MacArthur had a plan up his sleeve, an idea that had been brewing since July. Why not land a corps behind enemy lines, outflanking the North Korean army along the Naktong? That move would threaten communist supply lines, forcing the North Koreans to fall back, thus saving Eighth Army.

There were six ports along the west coast of the Korean Peninsula that could fit the bill. Taejon was too far south to be of much effect. Hitting North Korea from the sea was too far north. But Inchon looked promising. The route inland led to Kimpo Airfield and Seoul. Inchon was the worst place to land, so the enemy would never expect it.

Or would they?

Anybody Can See That!

August 1950 found Kim Il Sung focused on breaking the enemy line along the Naktong to push the American running dogs into the sea. The Americans were good at retreating. They had won World War II, but you wouldn't know it looking at this bunch. North Korean units were down to half strength from battle losses. Each breakthrough by these units moved no faster than a foot march, and each breach was sealed by Americans riding to battle in trucks or on tanks. Kim did not pay attention to this. The Great Leader did not count American equipment as a factor that worked against him. Communism was sure to win.

Chinese dictator Mao Zedong had reason to doubt his ally's zeal. The People's Republic of China was not in the war yet. Mao had his eye on Taiwan and was readying forces to invade. But Mao did not want his North Korean ally to suffer any setback that would force him to abandon the Taiwan project.

Mao assigned General Lei Yingfu of the general staff to deduce what the Americans might do next. He started by analyzing MacArthur. During World War II, MacArthur's campaigns in New Guinea and the Philippines saw more than twenty amphibious landings, so Lei assumed this tactic would be used again. Many of these landings were done to bypass Japanese points of resistance, so he assumed MacArthur would do an end run around the North Korean army. By late August, Lei reached the same conclusion as MacArthur: land at Inchon.

Lei prepared a three-page analysis and forwarded it to Mao, who in turn passed it on to Kim Il Sung. The Great Leader declined to take the advice. Kim was on the verge of beating the Americans. Mao feared the Americans would beat Kim. Despite repeated warnings from Soviet advisers and Chinese allies to pull the North Korean army back to defend the capital of Pyongyang, Kim stayed focused on crushing the Eighth Army along the Naktong.

Enemies on Two Fronts

MacArthur had to worry about his enemies to the front, the North Koreans, and his enemies to the rear, namely, the Joint Chiefs of Staff in Washington, D.C. Yes, MacArthur was paranoid, but even paranoids have enemies. In the office politics of the army, MacArthur was not exactly "one of the boys." A political general with ties to the Republican Party, MacArthur was kept far away from Washington, a strategy started by President Franklin Roosevelt and continued by Truman. Making this worse was the pecking order the army adopted after World War II. Generals marked for higher command always came from the European Theater. Hence General Omar Bradley was now chairman of the Joint Chiefs of Staff, while General "Lightning Joe" Collins rose to army Chief of Staff. These men were burdened by global responsibility, so they sought maximum gain for minimum risk. Collins questioned whether landing farther south would be more prudent. MacArthur was having none of it, as he sought maximum gain by undertaking maximum risk. He got his way with the service chiefs but still had to submit his operational plan for review before the Inchon landings got started.

Time became MacArthur's next enemy. September 15 promised a tide high enough to float the tank landing ships (LSTs) without running aground in the channel approaching Inchon. The next such tide was not for a month.

Planning was hectic. Even though the Americans had occupied South Korea for five years, no one had done a survey of Inchon harbor. Prior to the invasion, navy lieutenant Eugene F. Clark and a small band of South Koreans hunkered down on Yonghung-Do Island, just outside Inchon. There they spent the next two weeks gathering data on the tides and intelligence on enemy units based in the area.

Rear Admiral James H. Doyle, a veteran of many amphibious operations in WWII, put his hard-won knowledge to good use planning the Inchon landing. The navy had only about ten LSTs left in the Pacific. Doyle scrounged up thirty more that had been plying Japanese coastal waters as light freighters. The Japanese crews found themselves under the command of an ensign, who relayed orders with the aid of a translator. Other shortages became apparent. Doyle needed twenty-four guide ships to shepherd the fleet into Inchon. He had to make do with just ten. And then there was the possibility of mines—Doyle had only fourteen minesweepers to take care of that problem, compared with ten times that number doing the same job at Okinawa in 1945.

Doyle had many serving officers who were veterans of previous amphibious operations in World War II, so their memory became an asset. The invasion, however, was turning into a rush job, relying on leftover ships and equipment from the last war to put 70,000 men ashore. Still, even in diminished numbers, American and allied assets were handy. Four American aircraft carriers and a British flattop were ready to provide air support. Fire support would come from a quartet of American and British cruisers, while a destroyer flotilla would close in to rake the shores with their 5-inch guns.

There was not a lot of room—or a lot of time—to wield these forces. Flying Fish Channel was narrow and twisty. A single ship sinking from a mine hit would block it, trapping any other vessels forward in hostile territory. Then there was Wolmi-Do Island, which outflanked the landing beaches. It was fortified and packed with artillery. If not neutralized, the enemy on Wolmi-Do could turn the Inchon landing into another Tarawa.

The issue of available forces had to be addressed. MacArthur had only two divisions handy. The First Marine Division was reconstituted from stateside reserves and stray units, less one regiment now serving under Walker inside the Pusan Perimeter. The army's understrength Seventh Infantry Division would land in the second wave.

The plan called for massive preliminary fire to waste Wolmi-Do, allowing a single Marine battalion to be landed. Once the tide went out, the marines would be stuck on Wolmi-Do. When the tide came back in, the remaining marines would be landed to take Inchon proper.

MacArthur then made a major mistake. He assigned his chief of staff, Lieutenant General Ned Almond, to command the two-division force now christened X Corps. Almond would retain his staff position, reporting directly to MacArthur, while keeping X Corps away from Walker's command at Eighth Army. Dividing command was asking for trouble, as there should only be one commander of all ground forces, to avoid confusion. The arrangement did not quiet misgivings at the Pentagon, especially with Collins.

MacArthur had to keep the plans for Inchon secret from the enemy as well as his superiors. Preparations for the operation could not be hidden. Diversionary shelling and air strikes were launched against other possible landing sites to confuse the communists. A passing typhoon roughed up the invasion fleet in port but did not stop its departure.

Once the invasion force was under way, MacArthur dispatched a lieutenant colonel on his staff to travel back to Washington with the operational plan—about thirty-five pounds of documents. He was ordered not to hurry. Sure enough, the lowly officer arrived at the Pentagon after three days, catching flight after connecting flight. He delivered his briefing to the Chiefs, as promised before the invasion, by six hours. It was too late to call it off if the Chiefs took counsel of their fears. And they were pretty miffed by the discourtesy.

MacArthur had better be right about this, or else.

Scorched Earth

American amphibious doctrine called for lots of preparatory fire, since shells and bombs were cheaper to expend than soldiers. The marines expected the fortified North Koreans on Wolmi-Do to survive and fight back. After all, the Japanese did this in the last war.

Three days before the invasion, massive air strikes with napalm pretty much scorched Wolmi-Do. One day before the invasion, six destroyers steamed down Flying Fish Channel. Taking position just 1,300 yards offshore, they spent the next hour firing thousands of shells into hapless Wolmi-do Island, with barely any replying fire from the enemy. The destroyers suffered a few minor hits, finished their fire mission, then turned tail to ride the ebbing tide out of the harbor. One Corsair pilot who witnessed this said that "the whole island looked like it had been shaved."

On the third day, the U.S. Marines came.

Now four cruisers stood off Wolmi-Do and fired another 2,800 shells into the shot-blighted island. Three refitted LSTs poured another thousand 5-inch rockets into the scorched shore. Air strikes added to the crescendo of flame and flying metal. Navy pilots had trouble finding targets, so thorough the bombardment had been. Said one naval lieutenant: "That island was really quivering. I thought it would roll over and sink."

Holding Wolmi-Do were elements of the North Korean 226th Independent Marine Regiment, numbering some 400 troops. The massive bombardment left the survivors dazed and confused, eager to surrender to Third Battalion, Fifth Marine Regiment, as it hit the beach at 6:30 A.M.

The first objective was the island's highest point, Radio Hill. In less than thirty minutes, the American flag was tied to a scorched tree at the crest. North Koreans staggered out of their bunkers, shell-shocked, to surrender. But some defenders did not get the memo. Two companies of marines landing in the third wave had to put up with grenades tossed at them from one bunker of stubborn survivors. A Marine bulldozer turned their bunker into a tomb.

By 8 A.M., Wolmi-Do was secured. The 136 captured North Koreans were forced to strip in order to abate the risk of hidden weapons. Another 108 North Koreans were killed in action. Marine losses stood at 17 wounded. That was the good news.

The bad news was that the defenders were now alerted to the presence of the Americans. Until the tide came back in that evening, Lieutenant Colonel Robert Taplett hoped the North Koreans did not organize a counterattack against his battalion. They could still reinforce existing units in Inchon.

Fortunately, nothing happened.

Night Landing

At 5:30 P.M., as night was falling, the first wave of landing craft filled with marines nosed the seawall at Inchon. No one caught a bullet going up the scaling ladders to reach the higher "shore." As the marines advanced inland, gunfire picked up from various bunkers and strongpoints. That did not stop the marines from gaining the next two immediate objectives: "Cemetery Hill," which was Inchon's highest point, and the Asahi Brewery, the largest building in the vicinity.

Defending Inchon were about 2,200 men, split between the remains of the 226th Marine Regiment and the 918th (Coast) Artillery Regiment. They opened fire on the incoming eight LSTs laden with ammo and fuel. These ships were supposed to act as a forward supply base for the marines, as they would be beached by the ebbing tide. The vessels returned fire with their 40mm antiaircraft guns, while marines and sailors frantically put out small fires amid the combustibles. (After the landing, marines would offload fuel drums pierced with bullet holes. Good thing the bad guys weren't firing tracers.)

North Korean strongpoints were annoying, drawing blood but not offering a coordinated defense. Inchon was no Peleliu for the First Marine Division. It was more like a bloody drill. Losses totaled 20 dead, 174 wounded, and 1 missing in action. North Korean losses were estimated at 1,350 killed, wounded, or captured out of the 2,000 defending Inchon. By sunrise the next day, 18,000 Americans were onshore. A regiment of South Korean marines would do the scut work of securing Inchon while the First Marine Division and the army's Seventh Division undertook the twenty-five-mile drive to Seoul. They would be facing another 44,000 men within the vicinity of Seoul, principally the Eighteenth Rifle Division and some assorted regiments.

Walking on Water

There was no reason for North Korea to have lost the Battle of Inchon. Some contact mines were deployed, but they were easily spotted and destroyed, or beached by low tide. Simply sowing the waters of Flying Fish Channel with magnetic mines would have forced the navy to conduct sweeping operations, giving the North Koreans time to shift troops to Inchon. Perhaps mining would have forestalled the landing entirely, as it later did at Wonsan. All of this falls into the realm of "what if." The North Koreans saw Inchon for what it was: a lousy place to land. They based their defense on this expectation.

The Eighth Army broke out of the Pusan Perimeter, linking up with X Corps by the end of September. Things went wrong after that. X Corps was ordered to march back to Inchon to reembark for another landing at Wonsan, on Korea's east coast. That movement hogged the only road between Seoul and Inchon, denying the Eighth Army a second supply line to maintain its drive against the fleeing remnants of the North Korean army. Walker could not maintain contact as a result. Nor could he command X Corps to make sure its operations complemented those of Eighth Army. Likewise, Almond's command of X Corps rubbed the marines raw, as he bypassed First Marines headquarters to order regiments and battalions directly. Major General O. P. Smith ordered all Marine commanders to clear with him any orders coming from Almond.

The Marine landing at Wonsan never happened. The North Koreans finally wised up and mined the harbor. Advancing South Korean units liberated the port from the land side, reinforced by comedian Bob Hope's USO show.

For the Marine Corps, Inchon became the last amphibious landing made under fire. No opposed landing has taken place since, as of the writing of this chapter in 2013. With the amalgamation of the Navy and War departments into a new Department of Defense, Truman saw the Marine Corps as redundant with the army and came closer to doing away with the Corps than the Japanese had. Inchon validated the Corps' central mission of amphibious warfare, thus making its budget and its mission untouchable for several generations. Inchon literally saved the Corps from oblivion.

MacArthur's gamble at Inchon yielded a big payoff but also created larger hazards. His reputation was now untouchable. No one back in Washington would dare challenge MacArthur, nor would any subordinate question him should he make a mistake—both would prove dangerous later in the war.

As American units raced north, the Korean Peninsula widened, forcing units to cover greater frontages. MacArthur ignored warnings of an impending Chinese intervention and suffered a surprise attack in the snows of November. The attacks shattered MacArthur's reputation for infallability as the liberation of North Korea turned into a bitter retreat by U.S. forces back to the 38th Parallel. From there, the Korean War became a long and bloody stalemate.

Perhaps Inchon was a warning MacArthur failed to read after breaking open a fortune cookie: "Be careful what you wish for. You just might get it."

COLD WAR BURNING

Kennedy Quarantines Cuba, October 1962

BY DOUGLAS NILES

There are risks and costs to a program of action. But they are far less than the long-range risks and costs of comfortable inaction.

—President John F. Kennedy, 1917–1963

The Cold War nuclear face-off at the end of the 1950s and the beginning of the 1960s is popularly viewed as a delicate balance between two superpowers, each with the capacity to launch a massive nuclear strike at a moment's notice, sending enough thermonuclear warheads around the world on intercontinental ballistic missiles (ICBMs) to wipe out the other side many times over.

As John F. Kennedy was sworn in as the United States president in January 1961, he did in fact have forces at his disposal that were very nearly capable of attaining this horrific holocaust of destruction. The Titan and Atlas systems were well established, with nearly two hundred of them available. The revolutionary Minuteman missile system was coming on line, representing a major increase in the potential speed with which a launch could be ordered and released. These weapons could be concealed in hardened silos and were powered by solid fuel-burning engines; they could be fueled and armed and then left at the ready for an extended period of time, ready to launch at the proverbial push of a button.

The United States Air Force Strategic Air Command, under the leadership of the volatile veteran bomber General Curtis LeMay, had a fleet of B-52 bombers stationed around the world; those planes, too, could be launched against the communist enemy at little more than a moment's notice. Also recently introduced was the nuclear-powered submarine, newly armed with Polaris nuclear-tipped missiles. Without the need to surface for air or fuel, these incredible ships introduced a whole new element to sea power, since they were capable of remaining submerged and essentially invulnerable for as long as a half year at a time.

Some of the details of these weapon systems were classified, but the basic capabilities were known to the public. The "Red Menace" remained a popular bogeyman in the American consciousness, and the military and industrial elements of the United States were only too willing to exploit those fears for the funding that Congress was happy to allocate. Everyone wanted to make sure that the United States didn't fall behind in the nuclear race.

The Soviet Union boasted about its own massive program of nuclear weapons—Chairman Nikita Khrushchev let everyone know that his nation was churning out nuclear missiles "like sausages"—and there seemed no reason not to believe that this was the case. The Soviets, after all, had shocked the Americans by exploding an atomic bomb (with plans stolen from the United States' Manhattan Project) before the end of the 1940s, and they had exploded a thermonuclear hydrogen bomb not long after the Americans had developed that new, immensely destructive technology. Later in the 1950s, the Soviets had stunned the Americans, and the world, by launching *Sputnik*, the first man-made satellite to be placed in orbit around the earth. Why shouldn't the United States assume that the Soviets' nuclear weapon delivery systems were every bit the equals of its own?

Indeed, the American government itself was not averse to releasing frightening reports about the Soviet capability—from LeMay's perspective, for example, such data made it a lot easier to secure funding for new aircraft and even more advanced weapons systems. Within the Strategic Air Command, and the U.S. Air Force in general, there was a sense that the army and navy were growing obsolete and that future national security rested squarely on the shoulders of our bomber pilots and missile technicians.

The Reality

The truth, however, was far from the perception. In fact, the Soviets lagged very far behind the Americans both in number of missiles and in their reliability and durability. In the early 1960s the Soviets did in fact have some ICBMs, but there were only a few of them, and they were much more primitive than their U.S. counterparts. For one thing, all the Soviet rockets burned unstable liquid fuel. They could not be fueled and left to wait for a launch command, because the corrosive liquid would destroy the rocket engine. Instead they needed to be fueled—a process that took several hours—immediately before they were launched. Also, they could not be stored in silos; they were all on the surface of the ground, and thus vulnerable to destruction by any American bomb exploding within several miles of the missile base.

But not every front of the Cold War involved nuclear weapons. Just ninety miles south of the state of Florida, a communist revolution had overthrown the dictator Fulgencio "Juan" Batista. He had been forced to flee Cuba as the famous rebel Fidel Castro, accompanied by his legendary compadre Che Guevara, had swaggered into Havana on January 1, 1959. Before long, Castro was nationalizing many industries and confiscating the property of American corporations. One of the last acts of the Eisenhower presidency, only a few weeks before JFK was inaugurated, was to break ties with Cuba, as that new government was increasingly moving toward the communist model.

Khrushchev and Castro were naturally driven together by their antipathy for, and fear of, American military power. And the Soviet premier was only too aware of his own country's weakness in the face of American nuclear superiority. As a result, Khrushchev came up with a radical idea: he would use the territory of his new ally, just off the American coast, as a base for some of his medium-range and intermediate-range ballistic missiles (MRBM and IRBM).

He called his plan Operation Anadyr, and it was implemented beginning in the early summer of 1962. In the Soviet tradition it was a complicated combined-arms operation, involving naval units to transfer the missiles and troops, army units to protect the missile sites in Cuba, and troops of the Strategic Rocket Forces to actually install and be prepared to use the missiles.

By late that summer, the Americans were hearing rumors of a Soviet military buildup on Cuba. U. S. diplomats challenged their Soviet counterparts and were assured that all installations in Cuba were designed for defensive weapons systems only. Several months passed with no detailed intelligence reports, since Kennedy was reluctant to trigger a crisis by authorizing aerial recon flights. One of the CIA's photo reconnaissance planes, a high-flying U2, had been shot down over Russia at the end of the Eisenhower presidency, triggering a significant crisis in U.S.-Soviet relations. That shootdown had also demonstrated the surprising effectiveness of the

Soviet SAM (surface-to-air missile) 2, proving that there was a real element of risk to any further flights. Finally, in early October, the suspicions had grown to the point where Kennedy did authorize the flights. Unfortunately, the weather closed in for several weeks, and it wasn't until the middle of the month that the Americans could finally get some pictures.

These pictures were, to put it mildly, alarming. They clearly showed a network of bases under construction. Each base was surrounded by SAM sites, for air defense, but the sites themselves were obviously intended for strategic, nuclear-capable missiles. The president immediately set about making a plan, even while sticking to his normal routine and keeping the developing crisis a secret from the American press and public. The group of his closest advisers would come to be known as the Ex Comm, for the Executive Committee of the National Security Council, and routinely included the president's brother Robert (the U.S. attorney general), Defense Secretary Robert McNamara, Secretary of State Dean Rusk, and General Maxwell Taylor, chairman of the Joint Chiefs of Staff. Over the course of several days, from October 16 through about the 21st, they hammered out a strategy for confronting the Russians.

Several options were on the table. In the beginning, it seemed likely that the president would order a surprise air strike, taking out the bases with aerial bombs and missiles. However, this would represent a clear act of war, and JFK remained, throughout the crisis, committed to the idea of backing away from the crisis with resolve, but without triggering a conflict that could very easily escalate to nuclear war. Another plan called for an invasion of Cuba, and in fact troops and naval transport were ordered to move into position so that such an assault could be launched with very little notice.

It was only very gradually that a more measured response, essentially a naval blockade of Cuba, began to come to the fore as the most viable option. Kennedy would carefully avoid using the word *blockade*—partly because it invoked memories of the Soviets' blockade of Berlin in 1948, but partly because a blockade was also widely recognized as an act of war. Instead he would term it a "quarantine" and specify that only Soviet vessels containing offensive weapons would be prevented from sailing through to Cuba.

On October 22, President Kennedy made a national TV broadcast that was watched, it is estimated, by more than half the U.S. population. In it he outlined the crisis in stark and frightening terms. "Within the past week, unmistakable evidence has established the fact that a series of offensive missile sites is now in preparation [on Cuba]. The purpose of these bases can be none other than to provide a nuclear strike capability against the Western Hemisphere."

He went on to list some of the potential targets of this missiles, noting that Mexico City and parts of South America, as well as the United States, were threatened. He boldly listed several statements from Soviet officials, noting that each statement was in fact false, and he had the photographs to prove it. He concluded with the message that the United States was opposed to war, but it would not be intimidated, and that the Soviets must remove the missiles or else the Americans would take further actions.

Khrushchev Off Balance

Khrushchev had been given the text of JFK's speech before the president went on the air. The premier was stunned by the development; he had been counting on presenting the world with a fait accompli when the missiles were ready to become operational. However, they were still several days away from that point, and many crucial components, including all of the powerful warheads for the longer-range IRBMs, were still at sea, on ships making their way to Cuban ports.

The commander in chief of the U.S. Navy's Atlantic Command, Admiral Robert Dennison, wasted no time in putting the president's order into effect. At the same time, he was gathering transports and coordinating with the air force, in case a more violent response became necessary. The United States had in place Operation Plans: OPLAN 312 for air attacks and OPLANs 314 and 316, which called for various levels of amphibious assaults.

The Soviet surface ships were fairly easy to spot, and the United States and her allies, including British air units based in the Bahamas, began to observe the Soviet Union's cargo ships as they at first continued steadily onward toward Cuba. By October 24 a few Soviet ships had been stopped and boarded, and were allowed to continue on when they were found not to be carrying contraband. Other Soviet ships stopped or turned around.

A more significant threat, one that is little known from this crisis, lay under the surface of the ocean. The Soviets at this point did not have nuclear-powered submarines in their fleet, but they had some modern diesel-electric boats that, in Operation Anadyr, proved to have enough range to make the long voyage from arctic waters all the way down to the Caribbean Sea. These were *Foxtrot*-class submarines, and four of them were shadowing Russian freighters as those cargo ships approached the quarantine line.

The U.S. Navy had tracked several of these submarines, and as the quarantine was implemented they began to drop warning depth charges in an effort to drive these subs to the surface. What no one on the American side realized was that each of the Soviet subs had one torpedo that was armed with a 10-kiloton atomic bomb, a weapon with about half the yield of the bombs that had leveled Hiroshima and Nagasaki. In the darkness and tension of undersea operations, as these vessels were being harassed and pursued by the American navy, the discretion to use each of those nuclear weapons was left to the captain of the boat.

By this time, life aboard the *Foxtrots* had become an ordeal even for the hardy Soviet sailors. Fresh water was scarce, and the carbon dioxide levels were building up so much that the judgment of officers and men alike became compromised. As temperatures climbed aboard one of these subs, B-59, her captain grew increasingly agitated about the American depth charges rattling his undersea world. He ordered the nuclear torpedo loaded into a firing tube but was persuaded to rescind the order by, of all people, his political commissar (the Communist Party official who was a member of every Soviet ship's officer corps). Instead, B-59 surfaced and the immediate crisis was averted.

A few days later a secret deal was made, wherein the Americans agreed to give up some of their own MRBs based in Turkey—missiles that were obsolete and had already been scheduled for withdrawal—while Khrushchev agreed to pull his missiles from Cuba. Operation Anadyr was over, and the Cold War, for another few decades, settled back into its mostly stable chill.

WHEN BAD GUY FIGHTS BAD GUY

Operation Morvarid, November 29, 1980

BY WILLIAM TERDOSLAVICH

*The Navy has both a tradition and a future—
and we look with pride and confidence in both directions.*

—Admiral George Anderson, 1906–1992

Decisive naval battle.

The phrase has a nice ring to it, conjuring up images of huge fleets fighting each other in the middle of an ocean, winner take all.

In real life, this term can describe events more minor than you'd imagine.

Operation Morvarid was the decisive naval battle at the opening of the Iran-Iraq War. The clash pitted two small navies to see who would control the Persian Gulf, and with it the means to export oil to finance a war effort. And it would not leave the world unaffected. Forty percent of the global oil supply originates in the nations ringing the Gulf. Any nation controlling these waters has its hand on the global economy's windpipe—just one squeeze and the world's commerce will be choked. A local fight in the Persian Gulf would definitely have consequences if it got out of hand.

The eight-year-long Iran-Iraq War was poorly covered, if at all, as both nations barred outside media. Iran and Iraq had skirmished before. Iraq had fought a war against its Kurdish minority, whose rebellion had been bankrolled by Iran during Shah Reza Pahlavi's reign. A second small war occurred in 1975 over the Shatt-al-Arab waterway, Iraq's only outlet to the Persian Gulf. Iranian forces had no trouble smashing the Iraqi challenge, which ended with the Treaty of Algiers, signed that same year. That agreement drew the border between the two nations right down the Shatt-al-Arab, leaving Iraq's only port of Um Qasr too close to Iran for comfort.

In late September 1980, Iraqi dictator Saddam Hussein committed his army to take the province of Khuzestan from Iran. The strategy looked sound. Iran was consumed by domestic chaos, as the Iranian Revolution that ousted the Shah was still up for grabs between secular Iranians and the radical Shiite clergy, led by Ayatollah Khomeini. The country's internal problems might leave it incapable of defending against an Iraqi attack. Capturing Khuzestan would deprive Iran of its oil, add some territory to lengthen Iraq's shore, and buffer the Shatt-al-Arab from Iranian interference. Twelve Iraqi divisions attacked and got bogged down by the stalwart defense of two Iranian divisions.

Oil and Water Don't Mix

To pay for the war, Iran and Iraq relied on oil exports. Iranian oil from Khuzestan was sent via pipeline to a special transfer facility on Kharg Island, several hundred miles south, on the Iranian coast.

Iraq relied on two offshore oil platforms to do the same. Both sides used a combination of aircraft and patrol boats to protect their oil infrastructure.

Geography worked against Iraq. Its short coastline argued against the need for a navy, so the Iraqi fleet would be a tiny one: one frigate, a dozen patrol boats mounting anti-ship missiles, five mine warfare vessels, seventeen landing craft, and no maritime patrol or strike aircraft. Iran had a coastline that stretched about five hundred miles along the Persian Gulf, punctuated by several ports. The 20,000 men of the Iranian navy could put to sea with three destroyers, four frigates, four corvettes, nine missile patrol boats, seven other patrol boats, five mine warfare vessels, fourteen hovercraft, and four landing craft, all guided by six P3F Orion naval recon planes.

The air forces of both nations would play a large role in the struggle to control the Gulf. Under the Shah, Iran was well equipped with F-4 Phantoms, F-5 Tigersharks, and F-14 Tomcats. With U.S. support cut off, the Iranian air force faded to one-tenth of its size, as 90 percent of the planes had to serve as hangar queens to provide spare parts that kept a few aircraft flying. Iraq had a Soviet-made air force based on the MiG-21 and MiG-23 fighters, but they proved to be lacking when flown against Iranian fighters or warships.

Iraq had to use its navy and air force to protect the Khor-al-amaya and Mina-al-Bakr offshore oil platforms. These were not dinky little facilities. Khor-al-amaya measures almost a mile in length, providing four docking points for supertankers to load crude oil straight from an offshore pipeline. Mina-al-Bakr is a secondary platform to handle any extra tankers. Both are located roughly fifty miles offshore, southeast from Iraq's Fao Peninsula.

So long as Iraq possessed these two platforms, it could safeguard the approaches to its narrow shore, allowing its small navy to operate. Radar sets on the platforms could monitor maritime traffic and warn of incoming Iranian air strikes. And oil could be exported for cash, of course. If Iran could eliminate the platforms, it could prevent Iraq from exporting much of its oil and bottle up the minuscule Iraqi fleet, leaving Iran unchallenged in the Persian Gulf.

Iran opted to raid the two Iraqi platforms on October 28, using three French-made *Kaman*-class fast-attack craft: *Joshan, Gordouneh,* and *Paykan*. Each vessel was armed with a 76mm auto cannon and four anti-ship missiles. One each was tasked with firing on one of the Iraqi-held platforms, while a third packed man-portable SA-7 anti-aircraft missiles, similar to the American Stinger missile, to provide cover against Iraqi aircraft.

Iraqi radar picked up the three Iranian patrol boats as they made their way to the northern Gulf. Russian-made Iraqi OSA-class patrol boats fired on the Iranians with Soviet SS-N-2 anti-ship missiles. The Iranian boats fired their chaff dispensers, filling the air with thin metal strips to throw off the incoming radar-guided missiles, thus avoiding harm. The Iraqi air force dispatched several aircraft to sink the Iranians, but SA-7 fire from the *Paykan* shot down one jet.

Two days later, the strike was repeated against the two oil platforms, neither of which was taken. The attack provoked another sortie by the Iraqi air force, which lost yet another jet to SA-7 fire from the *Paykan*.

Trying to nix the Iranian threat for good, the Iraqis launched an air strike on the Iranian port of Bushehr, where the patrol boats were based. No hits were scored, but the Iranian air force shot down five Iraqi aircraft.

To shut down any Iraqi naval challenge, Iran now planned

to destroy the two offshore oil terminals. Operation Morvarid ("Pearl") would again rely on the *Paykan* and *Joshan,* only now the two boats would support a heliborne commando raid. The Iranian air force would provide top cover for the operation.

On November 29, the Iranians made their move.

Pearls Before Swine

Radar units on the Khor-al-amaya and Mina-al-Bakr platforms did not detect the inbound Iranian CH-47 Chinook helicopters. Commandos quickly fanned out after the big choppers put down on the landing pads. They had surprise on their side, killing all who resisted and capturing all who surrendered. With the defense neutralized, the Iranians went to work packing explosives into the radar units and oil-pumping machinery. The resulting explosions put both platforms out of action as the Chinooks raced back to Iran.

Bell 212 and AH-1 attack helicopters provided immediate escort for the returning Chinooks while the Iranian air force pasted every nearby Iraqi air base. The preemptive attacks were not thorough enough. Two Iraqi jets did make it off the runways and flew out to Mina-al-Bakr but were shot down by Iranian commandos wielding shoulder-fired SAMs.

As the *Joshan* and *Paykan* returned to Bushehr, they were caught in the open by a squadron of missile-firing Iraqi patrol boats. An Iraqi SS-N-2 exploded near the *Paykan,* causing damage. Distress calls brought the wrath of the Iranian air force down on the Iraqi OSA IIs and IIIs. A pair of Iranian F-4 Phantoms managed to sink one of the patrol boats. This action sucked in the Iraqi air force, responding with a flight of MiG-23s. No planes were shot down, but the MiGs managed to draw off the F-4s.

The Iraqi patrol boats renewed the attack, launching another volley of SS-N-2s at the *Paykan*. The Iranian patrol boat managed to dodge the missiles. Another flight of Iraqi MiGs showed up, setting up bomb runs on the *Paykan*. SAM fire from the gunboat downed a MiG. The *Paykan* then fired its last Harpoon anti-ship missile, taking out another Iraqi OSA.

The half-stricken *Paykan* was becoming a magnet for Iraqi bombs and missiles. Yet another MiG flight spotted the Iranian vessel. Again the *Paykan* returned fire with a shoulder-fired SA-7, taking out the MiG. Two Iraqi helicopters then showed up and opened fire, scoring some hits on the *Paykan*. The ship fired back, downing a helicopter. The F-4s returned overhead, shooting down two more Iraqi MiG-23s. Finally, another squadron of Iraqi patrol boats made it to the scene of the fight, firing four SS-N-2 anti-ship missiles. Two of them slammed into the *Paykan,* finally finishing it off.

This did not escape payback, as a pair of F-4s out of Bushehr now arrived overhead, lining up on eight Iraqi patrol boats that had just fought the *Paykan*. It was no contest, as all eight boats were sunk by gun, bomb, or missile fire. The Iraqis reacted by sending a pair of MiG-23s to the fight to shoot down both Phantoms, but they suffered the loss of one of the MiGs.

Four more Iraqi MiG-23s appeared, targeting the *Joshan*. Shoulder-fired SA-7s took down two of the attacking aircraft. A lone Iranian F-14, showing up late for this fight, bagged a third MiG.

By sundown, Iraq had lost about 80 percent of its tiny navy and about ten aircraft, in exchange for downing three Iranian F-4s and sinking the plucky *Paykan*. But the loss of the oil terminals told. Oil exports plunged from 3.25 million barrels a day to just 550,000. Making things worse, Iran declared a maritime exclusion zone that covered half the Gulf, pinching off any Iraqi egress from Um Qasr.

A Crude Outcome

Operation Morvarid was a largely improvised battle, as there was no real plan beyond the Iranian attack on the Iraqi oil platforms. The Iraqis and Iranians basically reacted to each other's attacks, committing planes and vessels in dribs and drabs. To the outside observer, it seemed more like a brawl, with few assets to use and poor command control to coordinate action. Nowhere did the planes and boats fight as part of a larger unit. But all of that is unimportant. The loss of the Iraqi oil terminals really hurt war income. Iran's declared exclusion zone affected Iraq but carefully left other Gulf states unaffected and unprovoked.

Throughout the 1980s, Iraq tried to win back control of the Gulf by flying anti-tanker strikes using Mirage F-1 or Super Étendard fighter planes flown by foreign pilots. Exocet missiles hit many tankers, but none was sunk.

Iraq also tried to ship oil out via Kuwait, provoking Iranian missile strikes on Kuwaiti facilities. These attacks prompted Kuwait to ask for U.S. protection in 1986, with the U.S. Navy escorting Kuwaiti tankers flying the Stars and Stripes. The United States committed more than twenty warships to the Persian Gulf, including a carrier battle group. Throughout 1987–88, the U.S. Navy and Iran fought five times, with the Americans winning every one of the small-scale actions. The Iranian navy was put out of action, leaving the Persian Gulf uncontrolled by any nation, but well policed by the U.S. Navy.

All of this was not without loss or tragedy. An Iraqi Exocet was fired on the destroyer *Stark,* killing 37 sailors. The frigate *Samuel*

B. Roberts hit an Iranian mine, nearly causing the loss of the ship. The cruiser *Vincennes* accidentally downed an IranAir jetliner while fighting Iranian speedboats.

Iran and Iraq ended the fighting in 1988, leaving neither nation in control of the Persian Gulf. Their borders remained unchanged, and it took more than a million fresh graves to make it so.

BOOKS BY BILL FAWCETT

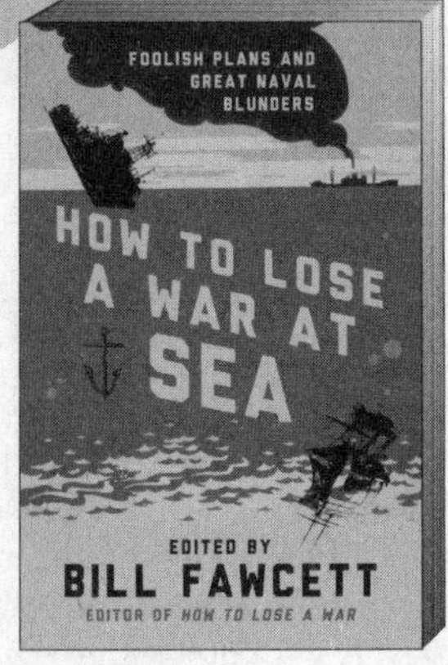

HOW TO LOSE A WAR AT SEA

Foolish Plans and Great Naval Blunders

Available in Paperback and eBook

This engrossing and fact-filled compendium offers even more great military disasters and ill-advised battle plans, this time on the high seas.

DOOMED TO REPEAT

The Lessons of History We've Failed to Learn

Available in Paperback and eBook

This collection sheds light on the historical lessons we've failed to learn and the failures this has doomed us to repeat over and over again.

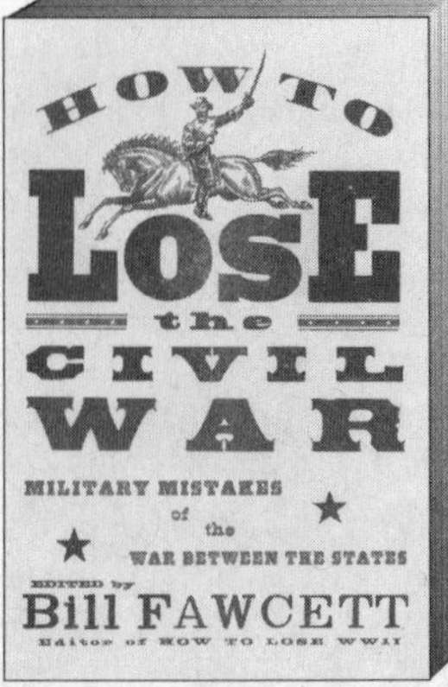

HOW TO LOSE THE CIVIL WAR

Military Mistakes of the War Between the States

Available in Paperback and eBook

Chronicles the thrilling history of the conflict between the Union and the Confederacy, with its high stakes, colorful characters, and the many disastrous decisions made by both sides.

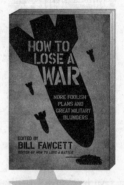

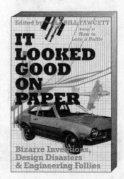